REFORMING THE
PRESIDENTIAL
NOMINATION
PROCESS

Steven S. Smith
Melanie J. Springer

editors

BROOKINGS INSTITUTION PRESS
Washington, D.C.

Copyright © 2009
THE BROOKINGS INSTITUTION
1775 Massachusetts Avenue, N.W.
Washington, D.C. 20036
www.brookings.edu

Library of Congress Cataloging-in-Publication data
Reforming the Presidential nomination process / Steven S. Smith and Melanie J. Springer, editors.
    p.   cm.
Includes bibliographical references and index.
Summary: "Looks at the presidential nomination process—the ways in which it is broken and how it might be fixed. Addresses the selection process: the importance—and perceived unfairness—of the earliest primaries, media coverage and public endorsements, 'superdelegates.' Evaluates public perceptions of the current process as well as possible reforms"—Provided by publisher.
    ISBN 978-0-8157-0288-7 (cloth : alk. paper) — ISBN 978-0-8157-0289-4 (pbk. : alk. paper)
1. Presidents—United States—Nomination. 2. Nominations for office—United States.
3. Primaries—United States. I. Smith, Steven S., 1953– II. Springer, Melanie J.
JK521.R44 2009
324.273'015—dc22   2009002997

9 8 7 6 5 4 3 2 1

The paper used in this publication meets minimum requirements of the American National Standard for Information Sciences—Permanence of Paper for Printed Library Materials: ANSI Z39.48-1992.

Typeset in Minion

Composition by Peter Lindeman
Arlington, Virginia

Printed by R. R. Donnelley
Harrisonburg, Virginia

Contents

Preface

Nominating candidates for president is one of the most important features of American governance. With the exception of campaign finance law, which is largely a dead letter, no national law governs the presidential nomination process. Rather, most of the important details of the presidential nomination process are set by national party rules and state laws. In the absence of an incumbent president or vice president seeking a presidential nomination in either party, the 2008 nomination contests tested that process. This book is about what happened in 2008 and what should happen to improve the process in the future.

Going into the 2008 primary and caucus season, we thought that 2008 would be consequential on many dimensions. Front-loading had been an issue for years, but states moved to even earlier positions on the electoral calendar—unprecedentedly, the first events were held in early January. An open contest in both parties meant that more money than ever would be raised and spent on the nomination phase of electing a president. And, Senators Hillary Clinton and Barack Obama, the first female and African American candidates who had a good chance of winning a major party's nomination, were seeking the Democratic nomination, promising an interesting contest of factional and identity politics.

But we never imagined that events would unfold as they did. With so many prominent Republicans contesting the early primaries, some observers thought the Republican nomination contest could stretch into the spring, but Senator John McCain, with the help of winner-take-all rules for delegate selection in many states, solidified his grip on the nomination in the first five weeks of primaries and caucuses. The Democrats, who had just two candidates with competitive levels of support at the start of the nomination season, appeared likely to settle their contest on Super Tuesday, February 5, just a month into the process; but, as it turned out, they did not settle their contest until June—six months after the Iowa caucuses, when Clinton retired from the campaign and Obama became the presumptive winner.

The drawn-out Democratic contest in 2008 generated unfavorable reviews of nearly every aspect of the nomination process. Criticism was directed at the early dates of the first primaries and caucuses, the scheduling of so many primaries and caucuses on Super Tuesday, the length of a primary and caucus season that stretched from the first week of January to the first week of June, the long gap between the primaries and caucuses and the national party conventions (which took place later than usual, in late August and early September), the important and potentially decisive "first in the nation" elections in Iowa and New Hampshire (two small, seemingly unrepresentative states), the eligibility of Independents to vote in party primaries, the order of candidates' names on ballots, the conflict between state laws and party rules over the timing of primaries and caucuses, the large sums of money raised and spent by the top candidates, the demise of the presidential campaign finance system, and the role of "superdelegates" in the selection of the Democratic nominee.

Serious interest in reform among the general public and journalists is seasonal, but candidates, party insiders, and other political elites have shown a willingness to consider reform in the off-season, and they seem likely to do so again. As we write this, we expect the national parties to reconstitute study commissions to consider reforming party rules and to analyze proposed statutory remedies. Congress is also expected to consider reform proposals. Most of the reform initiatives being circulated are concerned with the timing and sequence of events in the nomination process and also seek to make the system more orderly, transparent, and fair. The obstacles to effective reform are substantial. The constitutionality of congressional action is in question, the ability of the parties to limit gamesmanship by state legislatures remains a challenge, and effective reform may require coordination between the major parties, which is always problematic.

We offer this volume of scholarship as a contribution to the reform process. Each of the authors is a scholar who has contributed in important ways to our understanding of presidential nomination politics, campaigns, and elections. Here, each offers new thoughts about the nomination process and the current reform proposals.

Overview of Chapters

The essays assembled in this volume address many facets of the presidential selection process. To begin, chapter 1, "Choosing Presidential Candidates," provides a brief history of the presidential nomination process in the United States. Because controversy surrounding the presidential nomination process is not specific to 2008, we seek to add some historical context to the current experience. Although the single most important change to the primary process was the relegation of most state party leaders to the sidelines and the rise of national nomination campaigns, there were many other important, more incremental, changes throughout the twentieth century that helped create the selection system we have today. These changes include alterations to the rules governing who is eligible to participate in caucuses and primaries, how votes are translated into delegates, the creation of superdelegates in the Democrats' process, the elongation of the process, the movement of more states' primaries and caucuses to earlier positions on the electoral calendar, and radical changes in candidates' financing strategies. After reviewing this extensive institutional history, we conclude with some reflections about the particulars of the 2008 experience and offer an introduction to the current reform proposals that are discussed in greater detail in later chapters.

We observe in chapter 1 that there is no strong consensus about the key values to be reflected in the nomination process. There is good reason for this: The features of a process that are valued by the parties, candidates, and voters are not compatible in many key respects. Advocates for a process that allows lesser-known and less well-funded candidates to earn attention favor a slow starting process that grants a special role to a few small states, such as Iowa and New Hampshire, to initiate the process. Some value a longer process that winnows the candidates gradually, allowing voters at each stage to see the candidates and express preferences about the remaining choices, and tests each candidate's ability to organize effectively over a multistage process. In contrast, strong advocates of a convention that is representative of the mix of preferences in a party must worry that the gradual elimination of candidates would limit the choices of states that hold late primaries or caucuses. Furthermore, many partisans prefer a process that quickly produces a decisive winner who can start a general election campaign at an early date. They might prefer a winner-take-all system, even if it produces a convention stacked with delegates who are unrepresentative of the party as a whole. Choosing a candidate who will be effective in the general election might not be easy to do early in the calendar year and could require that some partisans, such as party

leaders, be given greater influence over the choice. Caucus advocates emphasize the value of neighbors gathering to deliberate over candidates and issues;
primary advocates emphasize the importance of giving all citizens a meaningful opportunity to participate.

Given the complex dynamics of nomination campaigns and the competing values at stake in any reform, we conclude that it is not likely that the "fix"
to front-loading will be a permanent solution with fully predictable and stable externalities. Changes in technology, fundraising, the media, party coalitions, and other factors will eventually yield unforeseen consequences to any
set of rules. Support for particular proposals will often be temporary as people's preferences for process evolves with their strategic interests in nomination politics. Thus we prefer approaches that allow adjustments without high
obstacles to future reforms, and recommend a multidimensional response to
the current circumstances that calls for the national parties to continue to take
the lead in reform.

Chapters 2 through 6 report studies on nomination politics. In chapter 2,
"Rules and the Ideological Character of Primary Electorates," Gerald Wright
evaluates the seeming unrepresentativeness of early primary and caucus
states and the effect that the order of nomination events may have on electoral outcomes. Clearly, there are many dimensions on which specific candidates would fare better under some rules than others, or in some places
rather than others. Thus the chapter is concerned with the policy implications of possible biases in primary rules. Wright seeks to discover whether
fundamental decisions about the sequencing and form of the state primaries and caucuses affect who turns out to vote, and specifically whether differences in the rules favor more or less ideologically extreme candidates. By
looking at the primary process from an issue perspective, Wright focuses on
how the rules (sequencing and factors that influence the costs of participation) influence the ideological profiles of those who participate in the delegate selection process. Interestingly, findings suggest that the impact of
sequencing, with Iowa and New Hampshire going early, presents a small ideological advantage for non-moderate candidates among caucus/primary participants, but there are no significant differences in the early states' partisan
ideological profiles. While one cannot claim that Iowa and New Hampshire,
or even Nevada and South Carolina, are typical of other states—they are
individually distinct in lots of ways—on the central dimension of ideology,
the rank and file of the early states are not distinguishable from their co-
partisans in the country at large.

In chapter 3, "Voter Participation: Records Galore This Time, but What about Next Time?" Thomas Patterson examines the link between presidential nomination processes and the record levels of voter turnout witnessed during the 2008 primaries and caucuses. When compared with other recent elections, voter participation in 2008 was extraordinarily high. About 55 million Americans voted in the 2008 nominating elections, easily eclipsing the 31 million who voted in 2000, the last time both major parties had contested races. Of course, as Patterson explains, the 2008 nominating contests included the candidacies of the first woman and the first African American with a real chance to become the nominee. In addition, in 2008 the contest went on long after Super Tuesday, so residents of states with later primaries and caucuses were highly motivated to vote; and for the first time since 1952 neither the incumbent president nor the vice president was a candidate. Because there were so many candidates in the race, there was also a large degree of uncertainty about the outcome. With these factors in mind, Patterson presents an interesting comparison of participation rates and electoral rules during the unique and historic 2008 contests and previous presidential nomination elections. After making these comparisons, he contends that, despite the unique aspects of the 2008 elections, increased participation in this election cycle will contribute to higher voter turnout in the future.

In chapter 4, "Media, Endorsements, and the 2008 Primaries," Kathleen Hall Jamieson and Bruce Hardy examine the impact of media use and knowledge of candidate endorsements in the 2008 primaries by analyzing data from the 2008 National Annenberg Election Study (NAES). In particular, they assess the signaling effect of well-publicized endorsements when voters have varying amounts of knowledge about policy differences among candidates. Jamieson and Hardy contend that media endorsements should matter most in these sorts of low-information environments—namely, when only a few issues divide the major contenders, as in primary elections. Since an endorsement can matter only if voters know about it, endorsers routinely communicate directly with those affiliated with them; however, the mass media are a central vehicle for communicating to those outside the immediate fold. Therefore the 2008 primaries provided a clear demonstration of the media's capacity to magnify knowledge of endorsements. Jamieson and Hardy show that in 2008 endorsements made by prominent national newspapers and prominent liberal and conservative groups and individuals affected perceptions of the candidates among those who identified with the endorsers, and among those who dissociated themselves from them. They also demonstrate that endorsements have the capacity to affect an individual's ideological placement of the candidates and her assessment of traits such as experience and judgment.

In chapter 5, "Superdelegates: Reforming the Reforms Revisited," William Mayer explores the rationale for, and the role played by, superdelegates in the presidential nomination process. Although many of the rules governing the selection method go unnoticed, every so often it becomes apparent that one of these rules could have a critical impact on who wins a party's presidential nomination—and that not everyone approves of the rule. In 2008 it was the superdelegates' turn in the spotlight. Yet, as Mayer explains, the story of superdelegates really began, like most of the distinctive features of the contemporary presidential nomination process, with the Democratic Party's reforms in the late 1960s and early 1970s. The automatic, or ex-officio, selection of these delegates was added to the Democratic Party's national rules in 1982 in an effort to make sure that more party leaders and elected officials served as national convention delegates. That is to say, these individuals become delegates to the Democratic national convention not by winning the slots in primaries and caucuses, but because they held leadership positions in government or in the formal party organization. Although there was some concern that superdelegates might play a disproportionate role in determining the Democratic presidential nominee in 2008, and they accounted for about 20 percent of the total votes at the 2008 Democratic national convention, Mayer demonstrates that superdelegates have had less impact on Democratic presidential nominations than their proponents had hoped or their opponents had feared. Although there is evidence that superdelegates gave a valuable assist to Walter Mondale in 1984, the next six Democratic contests would have played out almost exactly as they did even if there had been no superdelegates. All of this helps explain, of course, why so many Americans were, at least until the 2008 elections, entirely unaware that they even existed.

In chapter 6, "Public Opinion and Systems for Nominating Presidential Candidates," Melanie Springer and James Gibson report the findings of a recent national survey measuring the views of the American people toward the methods by which the political parties nominate candidates for president. They systematically evaluate the preferences of the American public with respect to the presidential primary system and assess public opinion on current reform proposals. Previous work has suggested that reforming the primary process is not something Americans care about, but Springer and Gibson demonstrate that the issue is actually quite salient to the masses, and that the public has real, informed opinions about the process. Even if individuals do not appreciate every intricacy of the state-by-state selection system, the public has clear preferences about the goals and intentions of the process itself. In gauging public opinion about this partisan process, the authors find important differences between partisan groups, as well as differences in the strength of partisanship. This work convincingly identifies the links between the public's ideological preferences about structures of government, representation, and the presidential nomination system, and reaffirms the importance of incorporating the American public systematically into current reform discussions.

Chapters 7 and 8, in addition to chapter 1, offer suggestions for reform. In chapter 7, "Picking Presidential Nominees: Time for a New Regime," Larry Sabato reviews many of the drawbacks of the current presidential nomination system, and in particular, the negative consequences of front-loading. He contends that most of the difficulties with the current system are rooted in the fact that the Constitution gives no guidance and sets no rules for the nominating process. Specifically, he argues that the omission of modern politics in the Constitution and its amendments poses difficulties for regulating the structure of presidential selection, the manner of congressional elections, electioneering law, and campaign finance reform, none of which can be effectively addressed without the inclusion of thoughtful provisions in a new twenty-first-century Constitution. Considering the circumstances in which the Founders designed the original version of the system—a pre-party, pre-popular-democracy age—he sees a need for constitutional reform via the enactment of the Regional Lottery Plan. This regional, staggered lottery system would be carried out over four months, be designed to avoid the negative effects of front-loading, and ultimately shorten and focus the election campaign. Under this plan, Sabato says that all regions and states would have an opportunity to substantially influence the selection of presidential nominees, and that civic participation would benefit from a rational, conveniently arranged schedule.

In chapter 8, "Is This Any Way to Pick a President? Lessons from 2008," Thomas Mann weighs the political values at stake in reforming the nomination process. With the 2008 experience in mind, he addresses the topics motivating current reform discussions, including front-loading, campaign finance, and party interests. Specifically, Mann reflects on the calls for reform that began just months after Senator Barack Obama became the presumptive Democratic presidential nominee and Senator John McCain effectively wrapped up the contest to be the Republican Party's standard-bearer. For some perspective, the author reminds readers that the litany of complaints that occurred in 2008 is not new. In fact, he argues that current criticism merely reinforces and supplements the critiques of the presidential nominating process that have been leveled after every election since the advent of the modern selection system in 1972. While it is clear that the institutional context of presidential nominations—party rules governing the selection of delegates, the scheduling of primaries and caucuses, and campaign finance law—importantly shape the dynamics and outcomes of each party's contests, 2008's extraordinary nomination season reminded us that these processes do not operate in a vacuum. Both the political environment that defines each party's strategic situation and the field of candidates determine how the rules of the game play out. Further, despite its complexities, in 2008 the selection process was able to produce satisfactory results with respect to candidate selection, party unity, and public participation. It facilitated the emergence of unconventional candidates and a surge of public interest and participation, accommodated and fairly resolved an unprecedented level of competition for each party's nomination, and produced candidates broadly acceptable to their parties and qualified to serve in the White House, all without allowing money to damage the process or distort the outcome. This is no small accomplishment.

In the final chapter, "Presidential Nomination Reform: Legal Restraints and Procedural Possibilities," Daniel Lowenstein examines the processes by which reforms of the presidential nomination process may be adopted, and the legal constraints to which they may be subjected. Specifically, the chapter reviews the legal question of whether Congress may, under the Constitution, control when nominating events take place in the states. Although the politics and law of presidential nomination reform are complicated by the multiple entities that play a direct and major part in determining the nomination process, Lowenstein concludes, as the majority of scholars have done, that congressional action probably would be constitutional; yet he contends that, if Congress finds it necessary to intervene, it ought to consider facilitating solutions devised by the national parties rather than imposing its own solutions. Lowenstein adds that while Congress could seek to regulate other aspects of the presidential nominating process besides the timing of nominating events, experience shows that Congress is not easily induced to intervene in the presidential nomination process. Further, he contends that there is little reason to believe Congress is capable of coming up with a particularly beneficial system, and any system it imposed on the nation would have unpredictable consequences that would be difficult to remedy. While this could change, the chapter demonstrates that for the foreseeable future, if Congress intervenes at all—which according to Lowenstein is by no means certain, or even probable—it would be on the subject of timing.

REFORMING THE
PRESIDENTIAL
NOMINATION
PROCESS

STEVEN S. SMITH *and* MELANIE J. SPRINGER

1 | *Choosing Presidential Candidates*

Choosing presidential candidates is the most bewildering process in the American electoral system, if we dare call it a system. Only since the early 1970s, nearly two centuries into the history of the republic, have the two major parties employed rules governing the state delegate selection processes in much detail—and the two parties adopted quite different rules. Since the early 1970s, many, but not all, state legislatures have stepped in to establish by state law the timing of primaries and caucuses, eligibility to vote in primaries, the placement of candidates' names on ballots, and the process by which delegates are named by candidates. No two states have identical processes. No federal law governs the process of selecting delegates to the parties' national conventions, at which the presidential candidates are officially nominated.

In all of the recent presidential election cycles, the nomination process has generated controversy. Almost without exception, the controversy has been in the Democratic Party, which took the lead in reforming its nomination process in the 1970s. The 2008 nomination process proved to be the most contentious since 1968. Complaints were voiced about nearly every major feature of the process—the early dates of the first primaries and caucuses, the special role of Iowa and New Hampshire, the front-loading of so many state primaries and caucuses in the delegate selection season, the conflict between state laws and party rules over the timing of primaries, the large sums of money raised and spent by the top candidates, the role of "superdelegates"—party and public officials—in the selection of the Democratic nominee, and the long gap between the state primaries and caucuses and the national party conventions. Once again, calls for reform were heard from many quarters.

1

Over the past few decades, primaries have substituted for the traditional caucuses and conventions as the most important means for selecting delegates to the national conventions. As this happened, very different visions of fairness, party prerogatives, and public interest in the presidential nomination process emerged. Some observers insist that the somewhat chaotic, changing process is a good test for people seeking the presidency. The process tests candidates' strategic acumen, mental toughness, and physical stamina. Others argue that the national parties lack necessary control over the process by which they choose their own presidential nominees. They say that the national parties must more effectively address problems such as the timing of primaries and caucuses and, for the Democrats, the potentially decisive role of superdelegates. Another view is that the national parties have been unable to check the decisions of state legislatures and that state parties have produced a front-loaded, excessively long process with a mix of rules. Accordingly, some contend that federal legislation is necessary to protect the public interest. In fact, members of Congress have proposed a variety of plans to create more order in the nomination process.

In this chapter we provide a guide to the recent history of the presidential nomination process, the lessons of the 2008 experience, and an introduction to current proposals for reform. The most important story of the second half of the twentieth century is the relegation of most state party leaders to the sidelines of the nomination process and the rise of national nomination campaigns that focus on the mass public. The subplots are numerous and important. They include the alteration of rules governing who is eligible to participate in caucuses and primaries, changes in how votes are translated into delegates, the addition of superdelegates to the Democrats' process, the elongation of the process, the movement of more states' primaries and caucuses to the early stages of the schedule, and radical changes in the cost and financing strategies of candidates.

A Brief History of Modern Nomination Processes

Before 1972, delegates to the national party conventions were selected through a wide variety of mechanisms. In the early twentieth century, when a few states began to use primaries, the two most common mechanisms were election at state or district conventions and "delegate primaries" in which delegates' names, but usually not presidential candidates' names, were on the ballot. Far less frequently, state parties authorized their central committees to name delegates. All three mechanisms tended to be dominated by party leaders, who controlled the selection of delegates and often handpicked their cronies. All methods were often combined with the practice of making many party leaders ex-officio and voting members of the delegation. This process generated insider nomination campaigns that drew on candidates' personal relations with party leaders and usually involved building coalitions among party activists; it seldom involved appeals to the broad public in a meaningful way. Nominees tended to be the favorite candidates of long-term party insiders. So-called regulars, long-term activists in party organizations, dominated the process.[1]

After the mid-twentieth century, nomination campaigns were national in scope and the outcomes of the national conventions were not in doubt. As political scientist Byron Shafer argues persuasively, several forces contributed to the emergence of more truly national campaigns for the nomination, which increased the probability that national momentum would generate a clear winner among delegates on the first ballot at the convention. First among those forces was the decline of local parties. This occurred as states implemented primaries for nominating candidates for state and local offices and patronage nearly disappeared as a means of appointing state and local employees. In fact, between 1968 and 1992, the number of states using a primary election for delegate selection increased from fifteen to forty for the Democrats and from fifteen to thirty-nine for the Republicans. State parties that continued to use caucus-convention systems opened them to broader participation. No longer were local political bosses the key to winning delegates in most states; power was more diffused.

The second force in changing the nature of nomination campaigns was the emergence of the national television networks, which spread the news about the candidates and delegate selection in the states and substituted for more local and partisan sources of information. This invariably created the possibility of nationwide shifts in sentiment about the candidates. Third, technology and money combined to enable truly national campaigns that exploited the weakened state parties and national media to build nationwide support, which contributed to building momentum from state to state for winning candidates. In fact, 1952 was the last year that either party's convention outcome was in serious doubt before the convention began (although some doubt existed for the Republican convention of 1976 and the Democratic convention of 1980).[2]

As much as the informal features of nomination campaigns were changing in the mid-1950s, the formal mechanics of delegate selection changed little. As we show in table 1-1, during the 1908–68 period only a minority of states

Table 1-1. *Mechanisms for Delegate Selection in the States, the District of Columbia, and the Territories, Selected Years*
Percent

Year	Party committee	Party caucus/ convention	Delegate/ loophole primary[a]	Participatory caucus/ convention	Candidate primary
Democrats					
1936	8	31	31	15	14
1968	13	24	19	21	23
1972	2	2	14	36	46
1984	0	0	0	37	63
2008[a]	0	0	0	30	70
Republicans					
1936	4	31	32	20	14
1968	5	24	23	28	20
1972	3	16	20	24	37
1984	4	1	8	32	54
2008[a]	0	0	4	34	62

Source: Shafer, *Bifurcated Politics*, 86–87; authors' calculations.

a. The Democrats sometimes called the district-level primary at which delegates were selected a "loophole" primary. These are candidate primaries in this classification. The term generally applies to primaries in which separate votes are cast for delegates and, in a merely preferential way, for candidates.

b. Excludes mixed caucus/primary systems in 2008: three Democrat and five Republican.

used "participatory conventions" or "candidate primaries." Participatory conventions involved local caucuses at which anyone willing to associate with the party could participate, followed by district and state conventions at which national convention delegates were selected. In candidate primaries, the names of presidential candidates were on the ballot to allow voters to directly express their preferences for the candidates. The majority of states, however, used processes dominated by party regulars through 1968.

The Democrats

The precipitating event for a revolution in formal delegate selection mechanisms was the 1968 Democratic convention. That event, which nominated the incumbent vice president, Hubert Humphrey, for the presidency, occurred in the midst of intensifying anti–Vietnam War sentiment in the party, in the aftermath of the April assassination of the Reverend Martin Luther King Jr.

and the June assassination of Senator Bobby Kennedy, and during clashes between protesters and Mayor Richard Daley's Chicago police. Humphrey won the nomination without participating in any primaries and instead pursued the traditional campaign of working with party leaders and activists to win delegates through state party committees and conventions. Dissatisfaction with this outcome prompted liberals—mainly supporters of Eugene McCarthy and Bobby Kennedy—to call for reform of the nomination process. The convention authorized the creation of the Commission on Party Structure and Delegate Selection, known as the McGovern-Fraser Commission for its chairmen, Senator George McGovern and Representative Donald Fraser. The commission proposed reforms that were adopted by the Democratic National Committee for the 1972 nomination season.

The McGovern-Fraser Commission produced several key rules intended to broaden participation in the candidate selection process and to produce delegates who reflected the sentiments of partisans.

—State parties were required to develop written rules to govern delegate selection so that party leaders could not manipulate the basic selection process on an ad hoc basis.

—Ex-officio delegates were banned in order to limit the automatic selection of party insiders as delegates; only 10 percent of delegates could be appointed by the state party committee.

—The selection of delegates before the calendar year of the election was banned in order to undermine the control of delegations by party leaders; local parties were required to advertise delegate selection events in advance.

—The unit rule—giving the winning candidate all of the delegates from a caucus or convention—was banned to give minority factions "fair representation" in delegations. A new rule was adopted that required that blacks, women, and young people be represented "in reasonable relation to their presence in the population of the state" on all delegate slates.

—A state that failed to follow the guidelines risked that its delegation would not be credentialed at the convention.

A process in which candidates received delegates in proportion to the vote in a primary election was a sure way to comply with the new Democratic rules. Democratic reformers in many states requested state legislation for a publicly run primary, and many state legislatures responded. Thus the immediate effect of these new party rules was the adoption of candidate primaries in a number of states, doubling the number of primary voters between 1968 and 1972 and eliminating the old processes that were often manipulated by state party leaders.

The 1972 Democratic presidential nominee, George McGovern, won only one state in the general election, a loss that some regulars, as well as top labor leaders, blamed on a nomination process that allowed extremists to take over. A commission headed by future senator Barbara Mikulski, then a Baltimore city council member, adopted a new rule that allowed up to 25 percent of a state's delegation to be made up of delegates chosen by the state party (now called "superdelegates"). These delegates, it was assumed, would be party regulars who were more concerned about party interests than about candidate or factional interests. Another new rule required primary ballots to list each delegate's preferred candidate, firming up the requirement that candidates' delegate shares be proportional to their caucus or primary percentages (for candidates receiving at least 10 percent of the vote). The new rules also abolished the implied quotas for race, gender, and age and substituted an obligation to ensure broad participation.

The rapid shift to primaries, particularly in most of the big states, surprised Democratic reformers and even disappointed some. Fraser, for example, advocated participatory caucuses that involved hours of discussion of the candidates and issues and gave the more highly motivated partisans more influence over outcomes. In fact, the McGovern-Fraser Commission heard arguments for a national primary, but rejected the idea because reformers preferred a system that allowed less-well-known candidates to build support in individual states. Incidentally, Fraser's home state of Minnesota was one of the states that continued to use a caucus-convention system.

Despite these changes, dissatisfaction with the nomination process continued. The performance of the Carter administration, the contest between President Jimmy Carter and Senator Ted Kennedy for the 1980 nomination, and the defeat of Carter by Ronald Reagan in 1980 left many Democrats frustrated with their party's nomination process and generated a bitter rules fight after the 1980 convention. Some Democrats, viewed as counter-reformers in some circles, wanted a stronger role for the party's leaders and public officials to improve the odds that the party's most effective candidate for the general election would be nominated. Others wanted a process that would produce a winner earlier so as to minimize intraparty conflict. A new commission, known as the Hunt Commission for its chair, Governor James Hunt Jr. of North Carolina, moved to allow states to create winner-take-all processes, but only for districts within states, and to mandate the election of unpledged party leaders and elected officials, who were soon called superdelegates. For the 1984 convention, about 14 percent of all Democratic delegates would be superdelegates, including about three-fifths of the Democrats in Congress, and an additional 8 percent would be pledged party leaders and public officials. Both the winner-take-all districts in a few states and the superdelegates were important to the nomination of former vice president Walter Mondale, but the protracted contest between Mondale and Senator Gary Hart showed that the proportionality rule, dating to the early 1970s, could prevent early resolution of the nomination by giving a losing but competitive candidate a large share of the delegates.

Democratic reforms in 1988 banned winner-take-all districts for both caucus-convention and primary systems, established a 15 percent threshold for winning delegates in a caucus, convention, or primary, and added more superdelegates. In subsequent election cycles, the number of superdelegates continued to grow incrementally. In 2008, superdelegates constituted over 18 percent of all delegates (before the Florida and Michigan delegations were penalized for violating a scheduling rule). The superdelegates proved inconsequential and noncontroversial between 1988 and 2004 because delegates pledged through caucus-convention and primary systems determined the Democratic outcome in all contests. In 2008 superdelegates became very controversial when it seemed that Senator Hillary Clinton and Senator Barack Obama, neither of whom had won a majority of convention delegates with just the pledged delegates from the caucuses and primaries, would need to appeal to superdelegates to gain a convention majority. With such closely matched candidates, the propriety of party leaders and public officials deciding the outcome was very controversial.

The Democrats' rules governing the basic delegate selection mechanisms did not change in any major way between 1988 and 2008, but a new issue arose. Beginning in the late 1980s, attention in both parties shifted to the timing of the early caucuses and primaries.[3] "Front-loading"—more states moving their caucuses and primaries earlier in the calendar—and the special place granted to the Iowa caucuses and New Hampshire primary were the dominant concerns. By the 1980s, it was obvious that early events received far more candidate and media attention and caused many candidates to drop out once their popularity and fundraising ability proved inadequate to continue. As a result, front-loading became the preeminent concern once California moved its primary up to early March for the 2000 nomination cycle.

There was some irony in the concern about front-loading. In the 1970s and early 1980s, some partisans considered an early start and early identification of a winner to be an advantage for the party. It ended intraparty conflict early in the presidential election year and gave the nominee more time to focus on the general election campaign. Starting in 1980, the Democrats had a rule that set a "window" for primaries and caucuses—roughly from early March to early June—that was thought to provide appropriate balance between getting a nominee identified promptly and giving many states a role in the process. But increasingly, with more states moving their events forward on the calendar and the outcome known earlier in the process, party leaders and voters in states with late events felt disenfranchised. While serious examination of this problem began in both parties during the late 1990s, in 2004 the Democrats extended the window by a month by allowing states to hold an event in early February. They did so after the Republicans moved their first events to February in 2000 and benefited from the earlier surge in media coverage of their candidates. In 2004, this led Democrats in eighteen states to move their caucuses or primaries into February, which led the elections in Iowa and New Hampshire to be moved into January. Republicans also moved their caucuses and primaries earlier in a majority of those twenty states.

Then, before the 2008 nomination season began, the Democrats adopted a rule that banned caucuses or primaries before February 5, 2008, exempting Iowa and New Hampshire as well as two others (the Nevada caucuses and the South Carolina primary) to create some additional diversity in the early primary electorates. The new rule also created an automatic penalty—a loss of 50 percent of a state's delegates—for violating the timing rule and permitted the Democratic National Committee to increase the penalty. In 2008, the state legislatures in Michigan and Florida scheduled their states' party primaries before February 5 in violation of the rule. The Democratic National Committee penalized both states with the loss of all of their delegates, but when the penalty was appealed to the party's Rules and Bylaws Committee it was reduced to a loss of 50 percent of the votes (their delegates were given one-half vote each). Ultimately, the penalty was eliminated altogether at the convention when it was clear that delegates from those states would not affect the outcome for the nominee, Senator Barack Obama.

The Republicans

Between the early 1970s and the late 1990s, the Republicans' delegate selection processes evolved in tandem with reforms in the Democratic Party. Partly because many reform-minded Republicans also favored primaries and partly because state legislators wanted symmetry in the processes used by the two parties, most state legislatures that enacted presidential primaries for the Democrats in the 1970s did so for the Republicans at the same time. Consequently, between 1968 and 1976, the percentage of delegates selected through primary elections increased from about 40 percent to about 70 percent in both parties. The Republicans, like the Democrats, also moved to processes that encouraged broader participation in those states that had closed party committee or caucus systems. The nationalization of candidate campaigns, movement to less politically seasoned delegates, and front-loading have also been similar for the two parties.

There are also important differences between the parties. Republican national party rules do not impose as many restrictions on state delegate selection processes as the Democrats' post-1968 rules. Republicans never banned winner-take-all systems that facilitated the accumulation of delegates by early front-runners for the nomination; they never adopted a proportionality rule; they never adopted quotas for demographic groups; they never reserved seats for members of Congress; and they never imposed a national threshold for acquiring delegates in caucuses or primaries. The only automatic delegates are each state's two members of the Republican National Committee and each state or territorial party chair (they are sometimes called superdelegates after the practice in the Democratic Party).

The differences in the parties' processes were reflected in the speed with which Senator John McCain accumulated delegates in 2008. Figure 1-1 shows the percentage of delegates won by McCain and Obama on the day of each caucus or primary. At first, because of the winner-take-all rules for Republicans in many states, McCain won large shares of the delegates in the early contests. He won even higher shares after his opponents began to drop out of the race. In contrast, Obama won a share of delegates roughly proportionate to his votes (in his contest with Clinton) throughout the nomination season, with only a few exceptions due to special rules in a handful of states.

Over the past few decades, Republicans have been spared the bitter battles over delegate selection procedures that engulfed the Democrats and their candidates from time to time. Nevertheless, issues have arisen. In the 1980s, for example, social conservatives sought rules to force states to select delegates to the national convention at the local level—where social conservatives' strength would be greatest. Delegates who were elected to congressional district and state conventions, they believed, tended to be older, more prominent, regular Republicans who did not give social issues sufficient priority. Their efforts failed, although social conservatives successfully organized to get delegates elected to state and national conventions.

Republican Caucus-Convention Systems

While Republicans followed the Democrats in the move to primaries, Republicans took the lead in considering national rules to address front-loading. In 1996, many states moved their primaries and caucuses into March from later dates, which created an early and compact schedule that many party leaders

Figure 1-1. *McCain and Obama Vote and Delegate Shares, by Event Day, 2008*

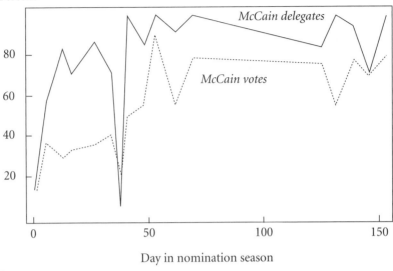

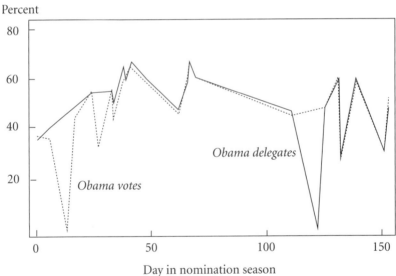

agreed was detrimental to the process. Republican leaders expressed concerns about (1) the difficulty of lesser-known candidates becoming competitive when there was such a premium placed on having money and support in the first events, and (2) the challenges candidates faced in campaigning in so many states in such a short period. They preferred a process stretched over several months that allowed candidates to gain support in a few early contests and gradually attract support and attention. Many in the party opposed placing mandates on state parties to limit front-loading. Instead, the party adopted an incentive system that gave states more delegates the later they held their primaries or caucuses. For 2000, under the adopted plan, states that held their events between March 15 and April 14 received 5 percent more delegates, states with events between April 15 and May 14 received 7.5 percent more delegates, and later states received 10 percent more delegates. The Republicans also for the first time established that no delegate selection event should take place before the first Tuesday in February, although no penalties were created for violating the rule.

The new incentives proved inadequate. California moved its 2000 primary to the first Tuesday of March. With New York and the New England states already scheduled for that day, the California move meant that about 40 percent of Republican delegates—and even more for Democrats—would be selected on that day. Later states risked that the nomination would be determined before they voted, so other states began to consider earlier dates in order to get more candidate and media attention. These considerations completely overwhelmed the small incentives the Republicans had established. A few more delegates at the convention did a state little good if the nomination outcome was determined before it voted.

In response to the increased front-loading that year, the 2000 Republican reform commission recommended a plan that would have the smallest states hold their events first and on a certain date, and then move through three more tiers of states in increasing size over a period of a few months. The plan was intended to encourage retail campaigning in the early smaller states while still leaving most delegates to be selected later in the process. The Republican Rules Committee approved the plan, but the idea was dropped at the request of George W. Bush's campaign. Many states did not like their place in the scheme, and the Bush campaign did not want a fight over the matter. No similar plans have been given serious consideration since then.

Republicans' frustration with front-loading continued during the 2004 cycle and led to the adoption of a window for 2008 caucuses and primaries similar to the Democrats' rule. Giving up on the positive incentives for event timing, the Republicans adopted a penalty that would take away delegates if a state or state party selected delegates too early. Under the rule, a state loses 50 percent of its delegates if the delegates are selected before the opening date for the window, set for the first Tuesday in February. Florida, Michigan, New

Hampshire, South Carolina, and Wyoming violated the rule and lost half of their delegates to the 2008 convention. Iowa also held its precinct caucuses early, but it did not violate the party rule because it did not actually select delegates to the national convention in its precinct caucuses. In contrast to the Democratic experience in 2008, it was clear that the lost Republican delegates would not figure in a significant way in the nomination outcome, so little media attention was given to the penalties in the Republican Party.

With such similar concerns about front-loading and compactness in the two parties, discussions between the two parties began in 2007 to coordinate on a schedule for the 2012 cycle. At this writing, no agreement has been reached on how the parties will proceed.

The Unpredicted 2008 Nomination Season

By 2008, critics of the delegate selection process focused on two of its acquired features: (1) front-loading and compactness, and (2) superdelegates. In 1976, hardly a generation earlier, no state held a delegate selection event until mid-February. Only Iowa, New Hampshire, and Massachusetts held events in February, and it took until mid-May for 55 percent of all delegates to be selected in either party. In 2008, with so many states, particularly large states, moving their primaries to February 5, about 60 percent of delegates were decided by the end of that day. For the Republicans, for whom many primaries were winner-take-all, 55 percent were determined by February 5, excluding the nonpledged members of the Republican National Committee and half of the five delegations that lost 50 percent of their delegates by going before February 5.

The front-loaded 2008 process led most observers, and probably most campaign strategists, to predict that the presidential nominees would be identified by mid-February. After all, in the previous few cycles a front-runner emerged quickly, and 2008 had an even more front-loaded schedule. It turned out that way for the Republicans, for whom Senator John McCain was the clear expected winner after doing well on Super Tuesday and in the February 12 primaries in the District of Columbia, Maryland, and Virginia a week later. Mayor Rudy Giuliani, who chose not to compete actively in Iowa, New Hampshire, and South Carolina, waited for Florida, but fell too far behind in the polls after McCain's early wins. Mitt Romney contended ferociously with McCain but his withdrawal after Super Tuesday gave McCain a large lead. Governor Mike Huckabee stayed in the race, appealing to social conservatives, but fell farther behind as McCain continued to accumulate delegates with the help of winner-take-all systems.

The front-loaded process did not turn out as predicted for the Democrats, for whom the contest between Senators Clinton and Obama extended until June. Clinton trailed Obama in the media's informal delegate counts by about 200 delegates at the end of May, with three primaries yet to be held. Because of the closeness of the contest, superdelegates were important for the first time since 1984. As a consequence, the role of superdelegates proved controversial because, in the view of many Obama supporters, superdelegates were not elected through primary or caucus voting and lacked the legitimacy to determine the outcome. In the end, a majority of the late-deciding superdelegates committed to Obama, with some of them arguing that they had an obligation to support the candidate that led among delegates pledged through caucuses and primaries, and Obama won the nomination.

After the dust settled, Democrats also wondered about the proportionality rule that gives candidates who receive at least 15 percent of the vote a proportionate share of state or district delegates. The rule, combined with the nearly even support for Clinton and Obama and their dedicated supporters in different segments of the party, seemed to lengthen the Democratic nomination contest. In contrast, the winner-take-all rule used in many states on the Republican side allowed McCain to accumulate delegates quickly with a series of plurality wins. McCain's wins led Governor Mitt Romney to drop out of the contest after Super Tuesday and seemed to reduce support for other contenders. By becoming the nominee apparent so early, McCain was able to start a general election campaign earlier than Obama and avoid the additional months of criticism from within his own party.

The Democrats' 2008 nomination contest ended with considerable interest in addressing front-loading and compactness with new party rules. Great frustration with the function and potential decisiveness of superdelegates also left many Democrats demanding their removal all together. More interest than usual was also given to the possibility of a coordinated approach between the two parties in addressing the schedule of caucuses and primaries. Several members of Congress introduced legislation to provide for a national scheme.

Proposals for Reform, circa 2009

The essays in this volume address many of the implications of the current system and the major proposals for reform. Here we outline the central ideas of the most important proposals.

Complaints about the current process come from many sources and with a mix of motivations. It is useful to realize that many of the concerns about the current process have generated somewhat incompatible proposals, often flowing from competing values about democratic processes and the substantial remaining differences in the way state delegate selection processes are structured. Consider the following dualities. For example, some insist that the process remains too closed in many states where participation in caucuses and primaries is limited; and yet others argue that party outsiders—independents and supporters of the other party—are influencing the choice of a nominee that should be left to partisans. Some complain that the process is too long and tests the patience of the electorate, while others observe that the process is so compact that the winner is usually identified so early that a large part of the electorate is disenfranchised.

Proposals for reform have accumulated and are again being given serious consideration. Reform commissions were authorized by the 2008 conventions, this time with the Republicans, as the Democrats had done in the past, allowing rules to be changed between conventions. We highlight the main variants.

Stiffen Current Rules

One school of thought is that the somewhat chaotic process of allowing states and state parties to control the process is desirable or, at worst, a necessary evil. It lets candidates start early in small states where face-to-face campaigning is possible; it winnows the candidates gradually; and it tests their stamina, strategic skills, and fundraising appeal. All that is needed, according to this view, is some tough-minded action by the two national parties to enforce their nomination season windows to reduce front-loading. The parties have been too timid so far, and the draw of candidate and media attention has overwhelmed party incentives. To stiffen penalties for holding a caucus or primary before the parties' start dates, the parties could increase the automatic loss of pledged delegates and superdelegates from 50 to 75 or 100 percent, cut the allocation of delegates in the next nomination cycle, or reduce state representation on the national committees. To foster compliance with the rules, the parties could allocate a large bonus of delegates—say, up to 50 percent—to states that hold caucuses or primaries late in the nomination season.

Tightening rules and increasing penalties for violations of timing and other rules is controversial. One issue is fairness. Often the timing of a state's primaries for both parties is determined by a governor and a state legislature in control of one party. That was the situation for Florida Democrats in 2008, whose primary date was determined by a Republican state legislature and governor. Another issue is the effect of the penalty on the popularity of the party in the affected state. In 2008, Democrats worried openly and repeatedly that the penalty imposed by the Democratic National Committee on Florida and Michigan would hurt the party's chances in the fall election. Finally, it is not clear that it is possible to structure incentives any more strongly than the Democrats did for 2008, when Florida and Michigan risked losing all of their delegates if they held their primaries before the February 5 start date.

Winner-Take-All Systems

Some Democrats envy the way the winner-take-all system used by Republicans encourages the early identification of a winner. A variety of proposals to loosen Democrats' proportionality rule have been suggested, although seldom by senior Democrats. They range from eliminating the rule, to freeing state parties to choose their own system, to allowing only a part of a state's delegation to be determined on a winner-take-all basis. None of these proposals appears to be popular with a majority of Democrats, who seem to give greater weight than Republicans to the representativeness of delegations and the convention than to the decisiveness of the caucus and primary contests. As a result, senior Democrats have not dared advocate this "antidemocratic" reform.[4]

Structured Sequencing Plans

Several proposals involve a more radical structuring of the schedule to (1) group states (by region or size) and (2) sequence caucuses and primaries over a specified schedule by group. Some reformers allow Iowa and New Hampshire, or other states, to get an early start in order to allow the process to begin with retail politics in small states. All are intended to address front-loading and compactness.

Regional primaries are the most widely discussed proposals. Each scheme groups states into a set of regions (usually four to eight), has the states in each region vote on the same day, schedules the voting dates two to four weeks apart, and, randomly or on a rotating basis, changes the order of regions every four years. First proposed by Senator Robert Packwood in 1972, the plan was advocated by Vice President Walter Mondale in the 1980s and the National Association of Secretaries of State (NASS) in the late 1990s. The NASS would allow Iowa and New Hampshire to hold the first caucus and first primary. Another variant is a time-zone primary, with each region being defined by the states in each of the four continental time zones. (The Regional Lottery Plan, with the order of region voting determined by lot, is described in chapter 7.)[5]

Proponents argue that, with a structured sequence of geographically concentrated caucuses and primaries, candidates could focus on one region at a time, allowing them to center their resources on regional media markets and limit their travel time. Caucuses and primaries would be distributed over time and so would not be as front-loaded as they have become. Furthermore, it is noted, regions are diverse enough to keep the campaigns from becoming too parochial. Yet critics observe that however diverse most regions might be there is no way to guarantee that some candidates would not be greatly advantaged by the order in which the regions voted. Moreover, the regional schemes do not eliminate the risk that the effective winners will not be determined before the electorates in the last one or two regions have an opportunity to vote.

Graduated Plans

Reformers have offered solutions to the limitations of the regional primary plans, two of which have become known as the Delaware Plan and the California Plan. The Delaware Plan, advocated by a Delaware state Republican chairman, creates four groups of states arranged from the smallest to the largest states and has state caucuses and primaries in each group vote on the same date or period, with the groups voting in ascending order of population, the largest states last, in successive months. The plan was endorsed by the Rules Committee of the Republican National Committee in 2000, but was unceremoniously dropped when the leaders of the party and George W. Bush's campaign team realized that it would be controversial on the floor of the convention and distract attention from the presidential candidacy and campaign at hand.

The *Delaware Plan* has attracted significant attention in both parties. Iowa and New Hampshire are given no exemption in the plan, but, the plan's advocates observe, retail politics and easy candidate entry is preserved, at least to some extent, by having the smallest states' caucuses and primaries first. If the largest quarter of the states with about half of all delegates go last, the nomination is less likely to be settled as early as it is under current arrangements. Detractors note that the campaign efficiencies of the regional schemes are lost with the Delaware Plan. They also observe that the small states are not representative of the nation as a whole, being less urban and less diverse than larger states, and yet might winnow candidates in a way that would not happen if some larger states went early.[6]

The *California Plan*, so called because of its endorsement by the California Democratic Party, is also known as the American Plan and the Graduated

Random Presidential Primary System, and is closely associated with California Democratic activist Thomas Gangale. It was designed to deal with a claimed weakness of the Delaware Plan—that large states are always last—but is by far the most complicated of the reform proposals. Under the plan, caucuses and primaries take place over ten two-week periods. Randomly selected states with no more than eight congressional districts vote in the first period. In each successive voting period, the number of districts is increased by eight and states are randomly placed in a group. Thus New York would vote no earlier than the fourth round. If left at that, larger states have too many electoral votes to go early, so the plan makes an adjustment to the order: Group 7 is placed before Group 4, Group 8 is placed before Group 5, and Group 9 is placed before Group 6. Groups are determined well in advance of the twenty-week caucus/primary season by a central authority, either the national parties or a federal agency.[7]

The California Plan attracted some support from the Democrats' 2005 reform committee. The plan allows larger states, randomly selected, to vote in the middle of the schedule and so corrects the key problem associated with the Delaware Plan while eliminating front-loading. It allows retail politics in the smaller states in the early rounds. It favors no specific states by virtue of its random selection of states into groups. Although the schedule is somewhat complicated, it would be fixed in advance and surely would be no more complicated than the current schedule.

A National Primary

Even the California Plan might impose an "ordering effect" on the outcome. Random or not, the order of state voting in any year could advantage some candidates and disadvantage others by granting more influence over the outcome to early states than to later states. Moreover, it is nearly inevitable that many contests would be settled before all states have their caucuses or primaries. This leads some observers, although a remarkably small number in recent years, to favor a national primary election to determine each major party's presidential nominee. Advocates argue that only by having a simultaneous vote on a nationwide basis, with the outcome determined by popular vote, can each voter in a party's nomination process have equal influence over the outcome, and bias due to the ordering of caucuses and primaries would be avoided.

A national primary surely would alter the process in fundamental ways. Opponents usually note two consequences. First, candidates would be forced to build national campaigns from the start, rather than having the ability to focus on Iowa, New Hampshire, and other relatively small states to build support and attract free publicity from the national media. Less well-known and well-financed candidates would be greatly disadvantaged by a national primary. Second, the voting public in states that do not have early events now would lose the benefit from the elongated process that gives voters time to learn about the candidates.

The national primary has not been given serious consideration by either party since the early 1970s, when Democratic reforms spurred the primary movement. Instead, reformers who advocate the structured sequencing plans seek to preserve sequencing that allows retail politics in early contests, spreads delegate selection events over a three- or four-month period, and allows lesser-known candidates to build support over the many weeks of the process. Of course, all structured sequencing plans create the possibility that outcomes will be determined before some states have an opportunity to participate, with the corresponding disenfranchisement and potential bias that may result.[8]

Reform in Perspective

As the 2008 caucus and primary season began, party leaders showed great frustration with their inability to keep states from moving their caucuses and primaries earlier in the year. Yet the 2008 Democratic contest cast doubt on the thesis that front-loading is sufficient to produce early winners, although early events knocked out most Democratic candidates and the Republican process yielded the predicted early outcome. An old issue, the role of superdelegates, resurfaced, and a seemingly settled issue, proportionality in delegate selection, generated new discussion. On the Democratic side, the 2008 experience seemed to increase the salience of, and even scramble long-standing attitudes about, these key features of the process. In concluding this chapter, we make some observations about the proposed reforms.

Our first observation is that there is no strong consensus about the key values to be reflected in the nomination process. There is good reason for this: The features of a process that are valued by the parties, candidates, and voters are not mutually compatible in all respects. Advocates for a process that allows lesser-known and less-well-funded candidates to earn attention favor a slow starting process that grants a special role to a few small states, like Iowa and New Hampshire, to initiate it. Some place high value on a longer process that winnows the candidates gradually, allowing voters at each stage in a long sequence to see the candidates and express preferences about the remaining choices, and testing the candidates' ability to organize effectively over a multi-stage process. In contrast, strong advocates of a convention that is representative of the mix of preferences in a party must worry that the winnowing of candidates will limit the choices of states with late events. Furthermore, partisans may favor a process that produces an early decisive winner who can start a general election campaign at an early date. They might like a winner-take-all system, even if it produces a convention stacked with delegates who are unrepresentative of the party as a whole. Choosing a candidate who will be effective in the general election is harder to do early in the calendar year and might require that some partisans, such as party leaders, be given greater influence over the choice. Caucus advocates emphasize the value of neighbors gathering to deliberate over candidates and issues; primary advocates emphasize the importance of giving all citizens a meaningful opportunity to participate.

Given the complex dynamics of nomination campaigns and the competing values at stake in any reform, we conclude that it is not likely that any "fix" to front-loading will be a permanent solution with fully predictable and stable externalities. Changes in technology, fundraising, the media, party coalitions, and other factors will eventually yield unforeseen consequences to any set of rules. Support for particular proposals often will be temporary as preferences for process evolve with strategic interests in nomination politics. Consequently, we are skeptical about the long-term viability of any solution to front-loading or the other issues that have been raised. We prefer approaches that allow adjustments without raising high obstacles to future reforms, and recommend a multidimensional approach to revising the current system that calls for the national parties to continue to take the lead in reform.

We believe that the national parties are best equipped to reform the nomination process, for both practical and legal reasons. First, only the national parties have any hope of reforming the process in a way that is effective and retains future flexibility. Many states and state parties simply do not have national party interests in mind when establishing their delegate selection rules. Many state legislatures are controlled by one party, have no interest in cooperating with both parties, and may even have an incentive to cause trouble for one of the parties. But reform through federal legislation would create a process that is difficult to adjust to future circumstances. It would inevitably lock in the role of the two major parties and disadvantage upstart parties. Moreover, new legislation would be subject to veto by the House of Representatives, the Senate (or a filibustering Senate minority), or the president. Thus only the national parties themselves can move in a way that is both comprehensive and reasonably adaptable.

Second, governmental action at either the state or federal level that dictates the national parties' rules for endorsing candidates may not be constitutional. The courts clearly give national party rules on delegate selection priority over state law. Less clear is whether there is a foundation in the U.S. Constitution for federal legislation for, say, creating a system of regional primaries, as has been proposed in many bills introduced in Congress. The Constitution is silent on the matter, although campaign finance laws have been found constitutional even in the absence of express authorization in the Constitution. Some reformers advocate a constitutional amendment to authorize federal regulation of the nomination process, but we still would not find federal intervention desirable over the long term. That would be wise only if the legislation reflected real wisdom about the long-term interests of the nation and the parties. We doubt that that wisdom exists. (Chapter 9 addresses these issues in more detail.)

We realize that depending on the national parties to reform the nomination process is problematic. Effective reform would require the two parties to coordinate, at least on scheduling matters, so that states are given compatible instructions and neither party views itself as disadvantaged by the process. Effective reform also requires coordination on enforcement mechanisms. For example, the parties might agree to apply any punishment equally and simultaneously for states that schedule events too early. Maintaining this kind of coordination would not be easy since it would be voluntary and the parties' interests would frequently diverge, as when an incumbent president is seeking reelection and controls the national chairman and committee.

Unfortunately, not all features of democratic practice can be fixed for the long haul. Tolerance of imperfection, which is hard to find in the reformist political culture of the United States, remains essential for many key features of American democracy. In this case, we believe that a party process should be left to the parties. The question, then, is how to coordinate the rules of the national parties. There is no obvious formula for doing so, but we conclude by offering two suggestions: the creation of a joint party commission on delegate selection and action on the timing of delegate selection events.

First, the parties should establish a joint commission on delegate selection, authorized by both national conventions for a ten-year period, to address the scheduling of events. The commission should have the authority to propose rules to the two national committees, which in turn should have the authority to adopt amendments to party rules on delegate selection. A long-term authorization would give the commission the opportunity to propose changes in two or three steps. The national committees would be allowed to make changes in the rules between conventions. And of course both parties would have to approve of any new rules.

Second, the commission should look for ways to make the rules of the two parties identical with respect to the timing of caucuses and primaries and similar in other aspects of delegate selection. By far the most important responsibilities of a commission would be coordinating the schedule of caucuses and primaries and creating strong incentives for states to adhere to it. Purists would argue in favor of some specific scheme, such as dropping the Democrats' exemption for Iowa, New Hampshire, and other early states from the first-event rule. We would prefer to leave the details to the commission and instead encourage the commission to address front-loading with the maintenance of stiff penalties for states that violate the scheduling rules and strong incentives in additional delegates for states that do not schedule their events at the start of the process.

Notes

1. This chapter draws from many sources on presidential nomination processes in recent decades. See Bruce A. Altschuler, "Selecting Presidential Nominees by National Primary: An Idea Whose Time Has Come?" *The Forum* 5 (2008) (www.bepress.com/ forum/vol5/iss4/art5/ [November 5, 2008]); James W. Ceaser, *Reforming the Reforms: A Critical Analysis of the Presidential Selection Process* (Cambridge, Mass.: Ballinger, 1982); William J. Crotty and John S. Jackson, *Presidential Primaries and Nominations* (Washington: CQ Press, 1985); James W. Davis, *Presidential Primaries: Road to the White House* (Westport, Conn.: Greenwood Press, 1980); Paul T. David, *Presidential Nominating Politics in 1952* (Johns Hopkins University Press, 1954); Paul T. David and James W. Ceaser, *Proportional Representation in Presidential Nominating Politics* (University Press of Virginia, 1980); Robert E. DiClerico and James W. Davis, *Choosing Our Choices: Debating the Presidential Nominating Process, Enduring Questions in American Political Life* (Lanham, Md.: Rowman & Littlefield, 2000); Scott Keeter and Cliff Zukin, *Uninformed Choice: The Failure of the New Presidential Nominating System, American Political Parties and Elections* (New York: Praeger, 1983); James I. Lengle, *Representation and Presidential Primaries: The Democratic Party in the Post-Reform Era* (Westport, Conn.: Greenwood Press, 1981); William G. Mayer, ed., *In Pursuit of the White House 2000: How We Choose Our Presidential Nominees* (New York: Chatham House, 2000); William G. Mayer and Andrew Busch, *The Front-Loading Problem in Presidential Nominations* (Washington: Brookings, 2004); Nelson W. Polsby, *Consequences of Party Reform* (Oxford University Press, 1983); Nelson W. Polsby, Aaron B. Wildavsky, and David A. Hopkins, *Presidential Elections: Strategies and Structures of American Politics*, 12th ed. (Lanham, Md.: Rowman & Littlefield, 2008); David E. Price, *Bringing Back the Parties* (Washington: CQ Press, 1984); Austin Ranney, *The Federalization of Presidential Primaries* (Washington: American Enterprise Institute, 1978); Howard L. Reiter, *Selecting the President: The Nominating Process in Transition* (Uni-

versity of Pennsylvania Press, 1985); Gary L. Rose, ed., *Controversial Issues in Presidential Selection*, 2nd ed. (State University of New York Press, 1994); Byron E. Shafer, *Quiet Revolution: The Struggle for the Democratic Party and the Shaping of Post-Reform Politics* (New York: Russell Sage Foundation, 1983); Byron E. Shafer, *Bifurcated Politics: Evolution and Reform in the National Party Convention* (Harvard University Press, 1988).

2. Shafer, *Bifurcated Politics*, pp. 6–39.

3. A summary of Democratic rules related to the timing of caucuses and primaries is available at www.democrats.org/page/s/nominating [June 1, 2008].

4. Some Democrats see instant runoff voting (IRV) as a way to provide for winner-take-all outcomes without the troubling possibility that the winners might have the support of only a small plurality of voters. With IRV, voters rank the candidates in order of preference. Winning requires a majority of votes. If no candidate receives a majority of first-place votes, then the candidate with the fewest first-place votes is eliminated and his or her second-place votes are distributed to the other candidates. This process continues until one candidate has a majority of votes among the remaining candidates. IRV is good for preventing candidates with little support from spoiling the outcome for a more popular candidate, as long as there are only two top candidates. It is not a sure solution to the spoiler problem when there are three or more very competitive candidates, as there often are in presidential primaries. To see this, consider three competitive candidates, A, B, and C, and other less popular candidates. Assume that your preference is for C first and B second and you vote that way. Further assume that at some point A, B, and C are the remaining candidates and that A has the most support and B the least, so B will be the first of the three who is eliminated. Unless most of the B votes transfer to C, which is extremely unlikely, A might then beat C. You preferred B over A so, in retrospect, you should have given B your first-place vote. That is, you should have voted strategically to get the best possible outcome for you, which was B. That is the same strategic problem you face under the current plurality rule.

5. For a description of the 2008 NASS regional plan, see http://nass.org/index.php?option=com_content&task=view&id=74&Itemid=45 [October 23, 2008].

6. Mayer and Busch, *The Front-Loading Problem in Presidential Nominations*, pp. 108–09.

7. For detail on the California plan, see Thomas Gangale, "The California Plan: A 21st Century Method for Nominating Presidential Candidates," *PS: Political Science and Politics* 37 (January 2004): 81–87; and Thomas Gangale, *From the Primaries to the Polls: How to Repair America's Broken Presidential Nomination Process* (Westport, Conn.: Praeger, 2008).

8. For an argument for a national primary, see Thomas Cronin and Robert Loevy, "The Case for a National Primary Convention Plan," *Public Opinion* 5 (December–January 1983): 50–53.

GERALD C. WRIGHT

2

Rules and the Ideological Character of Primary Electorates

Americans have a peculiar way of selecting candidates for president of the United States. Whereas the powers of the office are laid out by the U.S. Constitution, with its checks and balances and a history of Supreme Court decisions demarcating the duties and powers of the office, the selection of candidates is left to the individual whims of the states and political parties. And because the rules for candidate selection are not cemented in the Constitution, they have evolved and continue to change much more than the rules that govern the operation of most other aspects of American national government. As other chapters discuss, the presidential primary system has undergone a wholesale transformation from being the purview of a relatively tight party elite to delegation of most responsibility to citizens via the direct primary, with quite a few changes in the rules, timing, and who participates.

This relative fluidity in the rules of our primary system makes it a target for criticism and investigation because activists, those with a stake in the outcomes of the system, and scholars seeking to understand its operation, all make the fundamental assumption that rules matter. That is, rules for selecting the parties' nominees do a lot to determine who wins, both the nominations and the presidency. As a result, there is an enormous amount of interest in and media coverage of the horse-race aspects of the primary season. (Throughout this essay when I refer to the presidential primaries, I mean the caucuses as well, unless it is clear from the context that I intend to differentiate between caucuses and primaries.) Although personalities, gaffes, and the character of the candidates are the focus of both the media and probably most people during the primaries, there is an underlying struggle that receives less attention but which, in the long run, is arguably every bit as important as the individual persons who seek to be president. That battle is for the policy directions of the parties. The primaries select the individuals who will be the parties' nominees, but they also have a huge impact on what the parties come to stand for, and thereby on how the nation is governed. Some of this impact is through the party platforms written by the delegates the primary system sends to the two national conventions, but probably even more profound is the effect on governance of the policy visions and priorities of the nominated candidates. That is, presidential primaries, like most aspects of the electoral process, have profound, if not regularly appreciated, policy significance. My concern here is with the policy implications of possible biases in primary rules. Put simply, does the sequencing or form of the state primaries and caucuses affect who turns out to vote and express their preferences? In particular, do differences in these rules favor more or less ideologically extreme candidates?

There are many ways in which nomination process rules may advantage some candidates over others. In the 2008 nomination process, race was clearly a factor in the Democratic primary, as were age and education in separating supporters of Hillary Clinton and Barack Obama. However, these leading Democratic candidates took remarkably similar positions on issues. More generally, the differences between candidates, at least those differences with the most predictable policy consequences, are those that correspond to ideological differences between the parties.[1]

In primaries, it is the differences in candidates' policy positions that matter. The parties are not homogeneous, even though recent years have seen sharp ideological polarization between them. Even in the 2008 primaries there were reasonably clear distinctions between the candidates. The exit polls show that John Edwards did significantly better among Democratic moderates and conservatives than among self-proclaimed liberals (suggesting voters were responding as much to his 2004 candidacy as to his clearly liberal stances in 2008); and on the Republican side there were ideological differences, with John McCain rather generally attracting more support from moderates than from conservatives.

There is a fair degree of ideological heterogeneity among voters within each party. Figure 2-1 shows the distribution of ideological preferences of the participants in the 2008 caucuses and primaries. Respondents in the media exit polls were offered the choices "very liberal," "somewhat liberal," "moderate," "somewhat conservative," and "very conservative."[2]

The parties have unmistakable ideological centers of gravity, with Republicans more consistently holding to their "conservatism," which comports

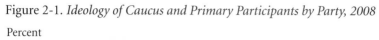

Figure 2-1. *Ideology of Caucus and Primary Participants by Party, 2008*

Percent

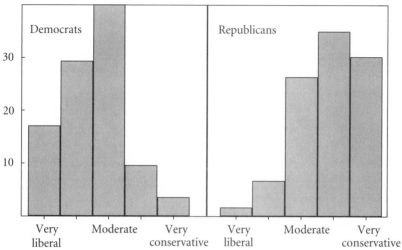

with the differences between the parties since the New Deal. Nevertheless, even in this age of polarized parties, there is ample representation of both moderates and more extreme partisans in both parties. Moderates form a plurality among Democratic primary participants but are a clear minority in the Republican Party. Still, as McCain's success in 2008 suggests, a candidate known to appeal to moderates can succeed in the Republican Party. While there is a great deal of slippage between ideological labels and whom an individual votes for, it is nevertheless true that those who are moderate and "somewhat conservative" constitute a clear majority of those who cast ballots in the Republican contests.

Looking at the primary process from an issues perspective, one avenue for change in the party system is the selection of candidates to represent the more ideological and more moderate wings of the parties. Thus I focus here on how the rules—sequencing and factors that influence the costs of participation—influence the ideological profiles of those who participate in the delegate selection process. My interest is in whether differences in the rules provide any systematic advantage to the more ideologically extreme or more moderate voices in the parties. This focus on ideology grows from a theory of party electoral behavior that connects the electoral process with governing.

Primaries as Gatekeepers

Our current setup of primaries and caucuses is the result of layers of reform over the years. These reforms have frequently, though not always, been in the name of changing the interests that "should" be represented in selecting the parties' presidential candidates. Here we run into a normative vacuum. In the case of legislative representation there is a clear normative guide that elected leaders should "stand for" the interests of their constituents, defined as those living in their legislative districts.[3] It is much less clear who should be represented in the selection of the parties' candidates for office. Because the person elected will be entrusted to act on behalf of all constituents, it is arguable that everyone should have a say. But the candidates, of course, run under party labels, so the more common view is that party primaries should represent the interests of the party rank and file.

Before the reforms of the 1970s, party officials and elected leaders had a great deal of influence through control of their state delegations. The "party" was the party-as-organization, to use Key's useful distinction.[4] The change to binding primaries was a clear shift of power to the party-in-the-electorate, although with the Democrats' provision for superdelegates it is clear that that transfer of power to the rank and file is not complete (see chapter 3).

The rules that govern the primaries are devices for regulating influence. Rules affect what it takes for a candidate to run and the conditions under which he or she will run. But, and this is what concerns us here, they also influence who participates and how much weight is given to the preferences of those who do participate.

The high level of front-loading in 2008, as well as the fiasco over Florida's and Michigan's jumping the queue in violation of the Democratic National Committee's rules, will almost certainly entail another round of rule changes, or reforms, of the process. Whatever rule changes are considered or adopted, it is wise to keep uppermost in our minds how they affect representation within the parties. That is, how have the rules affected, and how will new rules affect, which party interests are favored or disadvantaged?

Here I consider two important features of the system for their influence on whose ideological preferences are advantaged. The first is sequencing, which is a question of geographic representation. Iowa and New Hampshire have long been the first in the country on the primary calendar, and their influence seems to have grown with each presidential primary. Both states want to keep those positions. The concern is whether their early position and influence favors any ideological wing of the two parties. That is, are the caucus participants in Iowa and the primary voters in New Hampshire ideologically unrepresentative in some sense?

The second feature is how the rules that govern participation influence the ideological character of the participating electorates. In selecting delegates, the states and parties decide how inclusive they will be in extending the right of participation in the primaries. Our concern is the extent to which variations in inclusiveness influence the ideological profile of the states' primary participants.

Sequence: How Unrepresentative Are Iowa and New Hampshire?

New Hampshire initiated presidential primary seasons for decades, and Iowa moved its caucuses forward in the schedule in the early 1970s. As a result, Iowa and New Hampshire have assumed importance far out of proportion to their contributions to the delegate counts. They got their early positions for accidental reasons, having little to do with trying to have a disproportionate influence on who is selected as each party's nominee. As candidates and the media got used to the implications of the new delegate selection procedures, early wins assumed more and more importance. And with that growing sense of the importance of the early states, media attention grew and, in turn, heightened the candidates' investment of time and resources in Iowa and New Hampshire.

The importance of the early states is related to the phenomena of momentum and winnowing. Candidates who beat expectations in Iowa or New Hampshire are viewed as having or attaining momentum. They gain attention and rising expectations about their viability as candidates. They are taken more seriously by contributors, the media, and primary voters. For those who do not get a momentum bounce and who are not in or near the lead, the winnowing process wears heavily. Attention on those candidates wanes, and expectations decline. With a precipitous drop in media attention and a growing sense that the campaign is not going anywhere, contributors shift their funding to other candidates and the media and voters turn their attention to the shrinking set of still viable candidates.

Here is where the bias of the early states is likely to be significant. If the participants in the early states are indeed somehow unrepresentative of a larger set of decisionmakers whose preferences should weigh on the final nomination choice, then their participation constitutes a bias favoring some kinds of candidates over others. In particular, they may screen out candidates who might gain momentum and competitiveness with a different set of early states.

The strategic importance of the winnowing process helps to explain the troublesome process of front-loading that has characterized recent election cycles. For a long time the early contests in Iowa and New Hampshire were interesting oddities, but were not seen as having any kind of determinative effect on the eventual outcome. But once the dynamics of the primary process became evident, some states, such as California, which used to hold the strategic position of having the last big pot of delegates to be contested before the summer conventions, felt increasingly irrelevant to the process. The nominee selections were wrapped up in early spring with no role for many states with much bigger buckets of delegates. Their response was to move their primaries and caucuses forward on the calendar. And as they did, Iowa and New Hampshire vowed to keep their now "traditional" positions, and backed up those promises in state laws: They would be first in the nation, even if in the 2008 election season that meant moving their contests into 2007.

The process of front-loading, then, is an outgrowth of the perceived importance of the early primaries. If all candidates were guaranteed that they could compete throughout the primary season, even with no drop-off in funding, the early contests might not be so important. But those unable to demonstrate considerable drawing power in the early contests usually fade quickly. Thus, as ideas for another round of reforms are formulated and argued, it is important to establish whether the early states reflect ideological biases within the parties.

To do this, we need to compare the early states with the others. Are the Democrats who participate in Iowa different from those in the other states? And similarly, are the ideological preferences of the early states' Republicans in accord with those in the other states? I address this question from two perspectives: (1) the profiles of partisans in the states, and (2) caucus and primary participation in 2008. By looking at partisans, regardless of whether they participated in the primaries, we address the question of whether the political proclivities of the early states are different or unrepresentative. But because the rules combined with citizen preferences go into making up the electorates, I also focus on the attitudes of those who actually took part in the caucuses and primaries.

STATE PARTISANS. The data for the first comparison come from CBS News/*New York Times* polls conducted from 2000 through September 2007. These include almost 133,000 respondents, with over 1,600 respondents from both Iowa and New Hampshire. I am interested in the ideological preferences of those states' partisans and how representative they are of Democratic and Republican identifiers nationally. Ideology is measured by self-identification: people in these telephone surveys tell the interviewers whether they are liberals, moderates, or conservatives, which I score as –1, 0, and 1, respectively.[5]

The average by party is the measure of the ideological tenor of partisans in the states. The average of the state Democratic ideology scores is –.162, and the means across the states range from –.36 to .06. Because of the large number of respondents the measure of the state Democratic partisans' mean ideology is highly reliable (.93).[6] The Democratic means in Iowa and New Hampshire are –.15 and –.31, which are above and below the mean of the fifty states as a whole.

Average state ideology for the Republicans is clearly on the conservative side, at .49, and with a somewhat lower, but still respectable, measurement reliability of .85. The mean for Iowa's Republicans at .51 and New Hampshire's at .49 suggest that those states' electorates are little different ideologically from Republicans in the rest of the country.

The "early states" in 2008 included not just Iowa and New Hampshire, but also Nevada and South Carolina, which held their caucus and primary before the large number of states on the February 5 Super Tuesday. To more systematically compare the early states (both the traditional duo of Iowa and New Hampshire and the expanded group that includes Nevada and South Carolina), I create a pair of dummy variables to mark these definitions of early states. My interest here is electorates rather than individuals, so I do the analysis at the state level ($N = 50$ for each party). We can see whether the differences between the early states differ significantly from the rest of the country. This is done by regressing party ideology on the early state dummy variables. The results are shown in table 2-1.

The results are clear. The differences between mean state ideology of the partisans in the early states are not significantly different from those of the partisans in the rest of the states. Iowa and New Hampshire together are slightly more liberal than the rest of the state Democratic electorates, but this difference vanishes when we include Nevada and South Carolina as early states.

This does not mean, however, that all state electorate preferences or all regions are adequately represented by the early states. The American South has long been more conservative, and the first "Super Tuesday" in 1980 was instituted to provide the southern states with an early voice in the primary process. When we compare southern and non-southern state partisans' ideological preferences, we see that, indeed, the early states remain unrepresentative of southerners' stances. The southern states' Democratic electorates are significantly more conservative than their counterparts outside of the South (difference = .15, $t = 4.5$). This holds even if we control for early states, including the expanded definition that includes South Carolina.

Table 2-1. *Partisans in the Early States Are Not Ideologically Unrepresentative*

Item	State Democratic ideology		State Republican ideology	
Iowa and	−0.072		0.006	
New Hampshire	(0.91)		(0.13)	
Early four states		0.002		0.020
		(0.03)		(0.56)
Constant	−0.160	−0.163	0.494	0.493
	(10.09)**	(9.98)**	(49.09)**	(48.07)**
Number of	50	50	50	50
observations				
R^2	0.02	0.00	0.00	0.01

Source: CBS News/*New York Times* national polls, 2000–07, collected by the author from the Roper Center and Interuniversity Consortium for Political and Social Research.

Notes: Dependent variables: Self-identified liberalism-conservatism of partisan identifiers in the states.

Absolute value of *t* statistics in parentheses.

* significant at 5 percent; ** significant at 1 percent.

Southern Republicans also are more conservative than Republicans in the other states, but the differences are much more muted (difference = .04, *t* = 1.7). This also does not change with regressions that include the early state variables.

In sum, the early states are not clearly more liberal or more conservative than the rest of the states' partisan electorates. Nevertheless, it also is true that the southern Democratic electorates, even in 2008, remained less liberal in their ideological identifications than either Democrats in the early states or the rest of the Democratic electorate.

PRIMARY ELECTORATES. Interestingly, the same null pattern is not evident among actual caucus and primary participants. To address the same question I use the exit poll respondents' answers to a question about how they identify themselves on the five-point ideology scale (see figure 2-1). Higher scores indicate more conservatism. On the Democratic side, the early state participants are a bit more liberal than Democratic participants nationally (2.33 for Iowa and New Hampshire, 2.44 for the four early states, and 2.54 for the later states). The differences for Iowa and New Hampshire are statistically significant at the 10 percent level.[7] On the Republican side we see a difference. Iowa fielded the most conservative group of Republicans measured in the 2008 caucus/primary exit polls (4.32), and New Hampshire a relatively moderate group (3.63); the national mean was 3.85.[8] Comparing the early states among

Table 2-2. *Early State Caucus/Primary Participants' Ideology Compared to Those in Later States*

Item	Democratic contests		Republican contests	
Iowa and	−0.208		0.132	
New Hampshire	(1.76)+		(0.98)	
Early four states		−0.092		0.170
		(1.04)		(1.78)+
Constant	2.542	2.541	3.843	3.827
	(94.66)**	(89.68)**	(104.36)**	(103.84)**
Number of	39	39	27	27
observations				
R^2	0.08	0.03	0.04	0.11

Source: 2008 Primary and caucus exit polls conducted by Edison Media Research and Mitofsky International for major media outlets.
Notes: Absolute value of *t* statistics in parentheses.
+ significant at 10 percent; * significant at 5 percent; ** significant at 1 percent.

Republican exit poll voters, however, does not reveal much of an ideological bias among the early states' participants. The means of the early states are slightly more conservative, but when we use the four-state definition of early states, the results reach a minimal level of statistical significance (table 2-2).

As above, there are regional differences, with the more conservative southern Democratic electorates standing out from the states' electorates outside the South (difference of .17, *t* = 3.1). The Republican exit poll participants in the southern states also are more conservative than participants in the non-South, but the differences are smaller than on the Democratic side and are not statistically significant (difference of .11, *t* = 1.6).

We find, then, that the early states in the Democratic contests are more liberal, especially by the traditional definition of "early" as including only Iowa and New Hampshire. However, the South/non-South differences are clearly significant and substantial among Democratic caucus and primary participants, as they were for state partisans. This shows that the concerns of the southern wing of the party, which insisted that the initial Super Tuesday be composed of southern state primaries in 1980, remain valid in 2008. With South Carolina included in the definition of "early states," as it was in 2008, this regional difference is mitigated but not eliminated. The Democratic electorates of the southern states remain clearly more conservative than their northern counterparts.

If the southern states' Democratic preferences are not reflected in the choice of the presidential nominee, then we might well have anticipated the pattern of southern defections, particularly among whites, that were initiated in 1964 in the Johnson-Goldwater contest and have been evident in most of the succeeding presidential elections. The exceptions, of course, are the presidential elections in which the Democrats nominated southerners (Jimmy Carter and Bill Clinton). In short, we find that the early states are not unlike the other non-southern states, but that the Democratic participants in the southern states have clearly more conservative preferences.

The differences in the Republican Party are interesting too. In part because of the conservatism of Iowa's Republican caucus-goers, there is a noticeable tendency for the Republican early state participants to be more conservative than those participating in later caucuses and primaries. Unlike on the Democratic side, this slight bias is in the direction of the preferences of southern Republicans. Put together, the pattern would seem to set up, all other things being equal, the early states on the Democratic side to favor more liberal candidates who are less likely to fare well in the South, while for Republicans there is a predisposition in the early states to favor the more conservative candidates with whom southern Republicans are likely to be comfortable.

The conclusions here, unfortunately, cannot be as definitive as one might like, for at least two reasons. One reason is that exit polls were not conducted in all the states. Where the participants were not polled, we cannot provide comparable measures. Second, who votes and who does not is not set in stone but is a function of the political environment. Thus Iowa and New Hampshire get many more visits from candidates than later primary states, as well as a great deal more media coverage. If they were to receive only cursory attention from the candidates and media it is probable that a different mix of people would participate. Unfortunately, we cannot know how these states' primary electorates would change, although we can be certain that the levels of turnout would be lower. Another aspect of the political environment is who is (still) running when the state nominating contests are held. Iowa and New Hampshire usually get the full slate of candidates in both parties; the latest states have almost no contest because one candidate has achieved the status of "presumptive nominee" (as happened on the Republican side shortly after Super Tuesday 2008), or the choice set is much more restricted (as it was for the later states in the Democratic 2008 primaries). Thus differences in the political environment confound, to some extent, efforts to isolate the character of the early state electorates. The fact that we found insignificant differences in the partisans of the early states (see table 2-2) suggests that the differences we find are some combination of rules (discussed below) and of being early and the attention that comes with that.

REGULATING THE ELECTORATE: THE IDEOLOGICAL CONSEQUENCES OF THE COSTS OF VOTING. The caucuses and primaries are fundamental elements in the way we select the party nominees. As with any political decision, a key to success is in regulating who participates in the decision process. It is likely that as many campaigns are won by influencing who votes as by changing minds and preferences. For nominating contests, there are several ways to regulate participation. Of course, formally, the nomination is made by vote of the delegates to the national conventions, but most delegates are committed to a candidate well before the conventions begin. Our task is to assess the impact of the rules that govern who participates in those.

Participation can be influenced by several factors. The qualifications for participation are one factor. We have many rules that disqualify people from participating in politics: lack of citizenship, not being registered to vote, and being a former felon in some states; and states differ in how long one has to live in a state to attain formal residence status. Most of the state parties also require voters to be registered with a party in order to participate in the presidential primaries, either in a closed primary (which permits only those registered with the party to participate in the party's presidential nominating caucus or primary) or in a semi-open (or "modified") primary (which permits independents but not those registered with the opposition party to participate). Open primaries allow any registered voter to participate, but usually with the restriction that voters may vote in only one party's primary.

A further way to regulate the electorate is by making voting more difficult. As the difficulty of participating increases, so does the level of commitment of those who turn out to vote. The requirement to register keeps some people from voting, and making it easier to register does appear to increase turnout.[9] Where requirements for participating are more demanding, we expect those who are less committed to be the first to drop out.

In the nominating contests the caucus format is significantly more demanding than voting in a primary. Participating in a caucus takes more time because people must actually meet and talk about the candidates, and it requires a greater political commitment because the decisions are registered publicly; sometimes one's preferences even have to be defended in front of neighbors and friends. It is much easier, quicker, and less hassle to just vote in a primary that is secret and involves no arguments with one's fellow voters.

Previous research has shown that the more demanding caucuses do, indeed, restrict participation, often to the single digits.[10] Through Super Tuesday in the 2008 contests, the turnout in Democratic caucuses was less than 20 percent of the 2004 vote for John Kerry, compared to 55 percent of the Kerry vote in the primary states.[11] Even in the first states with all the attention focused on them, Iowa's caucus turnout was only 30.6 percent of the 2004 Kerry vote. That compares unfavorably with the higher New Hampshire primary turnout, which was 83.4 percent of the Kerry vote.[12]

The impact on turnout is well established, but studies of the representativeness of primary voters versus caucus voters and of the impact of open versus closed primaries have not yielded consistent findings. Our theoretical expectations are that greater commitment is accompanied by greater political sophistication and stronger ideological positions.[13] Within this framework, in which the more committed tend to be more activist and to be more ideological, some studies have examined the representativeness of primary electorates. These report mixed results, with some arguing that primary electorates are different demographically, being generally of higher socioeconomic status than nonprimary participants, and that they are more ideological.[14] Others have argued that there are only modest or no ideological differences between primary voters and the larger group of rank-and-file party members.[15]

The question is whether more restrictions on participation are associated with greater ideological extremism among those participating. If so, then we would expect caucuses to have the most ideologically extreme participants, followed by closed primaries, semi-open primaries, and finally open primaries. We want to determine whether restrictions on participation make the Democratic participants more liberal and the Republican participants more conservative, given the underlying ideological tendencies of the states' Democrats and Republicans. To address this, my strategy is to regress the mean ideology of the participants (from exit polls) on the ideology of the states' partisans as measured in the aggregate CBS News/New York Times polls described above. The values are not directly comparable, since the ideology question in the CBS News/New York Times polls offer three options and the exit poll data offer five options, but the questions clearly measure the same thing.[16] The impact of rules is gauged by the coefficients for three dummy variables: caucus states, closed primaries, and semi-open primaries, with the effect of open primaries suppressed (and therefore absorbed in the constant).

We anticipate that the ideology of the primary participants will reasonably mirror that of the ideology of the states' partisans. The first regression for each party shows those relationships (see table 2-3). The fit of partisans' ideology with caucus/primary participants' ideology is stronger for Democrats ($R^2 =$

Table 2-3. *Effects of Caucus and Primary Type on Ideology of the Electorates*

Item	Democratic caucus/ primary ideology		Republican caucus/ primary ideology	
State partisan ideology	1.293	1.305	1.730	2.041
	(9.80)**	(9.68)**	(3.58)**	(4.74)**
Caucus		−0.090		0.388
		(1.35)		(4.55)**
Closed primary		−0.035		0.107
		(1.04)		(1.67)
Semi-open primary		0.013		−0.033
		(0.33)		(0.57)
Constant	2.724	2.739	2.995	2.789
	(111.94)**	(96.03)**	(12.39)**	(11.93)**
Number of observations	39	39	27	27
R^2	0.72	0.75	0.34	0.70

Source: 2008 primary and caucus exit polls conducted by Edison Media Research and Mitofsky International for major media outlets.
Notes: Absolute value of t statistics in parentheses.
* significant at 5 percent; ** significant at 1 percent.

.72) than for Republicans ($R^2 = .34$), but that is largely because of the greater variance in state Democratic ideologies.[17] Probably more reflective of the relationships are the slopes, both of which suggest that participants' ideologies are strongly related to those of the larger partisan groups of their states. Ideology is measured with high values being more conservative. Thus we expect that restrictiveness will lead to negative rule effects for Democrats and positive effects for Republicans. Table 2-3 shows essentially that pattern. The coefficients are not individually statistically significant for Democrats, which is not too surprising given that the number of observations is only thirty-nine. However, the pattern of increasing restrictiveness leading to more liberal electorates for the Democrats and more conservative electorates for the Republicans does hold. The only exception is that the semi-open effect has the wrong sign for both parties, but the coefficients also are essentially zero. The pattern of effects is stronger on the Republican side, and jointly the caucus/primary type coefficients are highly statistically significant ($p < .001$), indicating a marked tendency for restrictions on the electorate to produce more conservative participating groups relative to the ideology of the states' Republican identifiers.

The evidence suggests that regulating the electorate leads to more ideo-logically extreme sets of participants relative to the ideological tendencies of the states' partisans. This generalization must be qualified a good bit, however. The media chose not to poll in most of the caucus states; we have only two included, Iowa and Nevada. It is arguable that because these were highly visible primaries (because they were so early in the process), they would have higher turnouts and more diverse electorates. By this logic, if we could have had the polls for the later caucuses, the pattern would have been stronger. There is nothing in the small number of cases, by itself, to lead us to suspect that the pattern would not hold. Nevertheless, the size of the sample is less than ideal.[18]

The analysis here warrants a conclusion that supports the strong theory in political science that, as the costs of participation rise, those less committed are less likely to participate. The most committed also are, typically, the most strongly ideological, and hence the rules do have a measurable effect on the character of the electorates. Caucuses with their high costs of participation, and closed primaries, which exclude those registered as independents and opposition party members, bias their participating electorates relative to the ideological profiles of their state partisans.

Conclusions

The 2008 primaries did more than produce Barack Obama and John McCain as the Democratic and Republican Party nominees. As seems to be typical, the process was messier on the Democratic side, particularly with the issue of front-loading and the drawn-out controversy over how to deal with the Michigan and Florida delegates, who were elected in primaries that did not conform to the rules set by the Democratic National Committee. This alone will send party commissions back to the drawing board to produce yet another set of revisions to the process by which we select our parties' presidential nominees. That will once again raise concerns about the effects of the early states. Iowa and New Hampshire have grown accustomed to their favored position and to the media and candidate attention that has developed. And because of that attention, other states want some of the action. It may be that the drawn-out contest between Obama and Clinton changes the states' calculations. The final states like South Dakota and Montana got more attention and played as big a role as many of the Super Tuesday states. Being last in 2008 did not mean being ignored. Indeed, if California had kept the final slot it held for years, it would clearly have been determinative.

What we have found here is that the early states are not particularly biased. They are a bit more liberal on the Democratic side, and this is due to the conservatism of the southern states, which stand at some ideological distance from the early states (even with South Carolina included). On the Republican side, the early states are a bit more conservative, and there they favor the inclinations of the conservative Republicans of the South. If party rule makers want balance in sequencing, so that liberal or conservative electorates do not have a disproportionate influence in the winnowing process, then some early stage that balances the states (such as was attempted with the additions of Nevada and South Carolina before Super Tuesday) is justified.

In summary, there are detectable early state biases, but they are modest. It would be a mistake, however, to underestimate the importance of modest differences in the composition of the electorate in a process where so much more attention is given to the "winner" of the vote rather than the delegates actually won. On the Republican side, which still uses winner-take-all elections, small differences can have huge practical as well as psychological effects. In short, sequencing matters.

We also examined rules that regulate the electorate. The issues we examined are caucuses versus primaries, and, among primaries, how open should they be. Whether delegates should be selected in caucuses or primaries is interesting theoretically as well as practically. There will almost certainly be criticisms of the use of caucuses. Some of the debate is appropriately over the impact of caucuses on participation; fewer citizens are willing or able to take the time or to incur the combined political and social cost of going through the caucus process. In caucuses a much smaller pool of citizens have a voice in picking the parties' nominees; that much is indisputable. For true democrats who put a premium on the voice of the average citizen, this is itself enough reason to move toward a blanket adoption of primaries.

There are at least two additional issues with the caucuses. One goes back to the fundamental, but really unanswered, question of who should be represented in the primaries. If the nomination is considered to be a *party* nomination, then an argument can be made that only those reasonably committed to the party and to a candidate ought to have a voice in choosing the *parties'* nominees. As the parties have become more polarized, however, the voices of the two parties come from increasingly distant ideological positions, with the likely result that the candidates nominated will be polarized as well. The concern here is that the great middle of the electorate is left unrepresented.[19] If the bulk of the citizenry is in the ideological middle, critics of the caucus system can argue that the structure of picking candidates should encourage, or at least make it possible for, moderate candidates to win. The ideologically rarefied character of the caucus participants trends in the opposite direction.

Another issue, which is less philosophical and more practical, is that much of Obama's lead over Clinton through the nominating season was accomplished because he amassed about a 100-delegate lead, largely in the caucus states, which tend to be small, and which have voted Republican more often than Democratic in the past in general elections. This is a concern of some in the leftist blogosphere, and will likely be an undercurrent in any discussion of "reform" of the process, especially to the extent that Clinton supporters have a role in shaping the party structures.[20] Our data indicate that the caucus electorates are more liberal than the Democratic primary electorates (again relative to their states' partisans), but because they are smaller are quite likely also more committed, either to particular policy concerns or to a candidate, Obama in this instance.

It is not difficult to see the long-run or broader implications for party nominees in this difference. An increase in the use of caucuses would lead to fewer and more ideological groups of citizens participating. This does not mean that the nominees would inevitably be more polarized. Electability plays a large role in voters' calculus,[21] and moderates remain a substantial group among the caucus participants. Nevertheless, on balance, we would expect more ideological candidates to fare better in caucuses.

Finally, there is the issue of whether closed primaries lead to more extreme preferences among participants. The logic here, based on what we know about general election voters, is solid. Partisans are more ideological than independents, and therefore allowing independents to vote in the primaries should yield some moderation in the overall ideological profile of the electorate. The statistical results support this, but show only modest differences. The reason that the results are not stronger may be due to a process of self-selection. Consider the independents in states with an open or semi-open primary who must choose in which party's primary to vote. If voters are sincere, and there is not a great deal of evidence that they are not,[22] then the independents who choose to vote in an open or semi-open Republican primary are probably leaning Republican to begin with; likewise, the independents who vote in the Democratic open or semi-open primaries are probably more liberally inclined than independents generally. If this kind of sincere voting is typical, then it is not surprising that the ideological differences between open, semi-open, and closed primaries are not great. The same logic would apply for opposition party members in open primaries. Republicans choosing to vote in Democratic primaries may already be favorably disposed and thus not be as die-hard conservative as the Republicans staying with their own primary. Vice versa for Democrats.

This does not mean that mischievous strategic voting does not occur, and such behavior understandably worries primary planners who do not want members of the opposite party selecting their party's nominees, especially if the goal is to undermine the party's chances of success in November. The clearest case in the 2008 election was conservative radio talk show host Rush Limbaugh's call for "Operation Chaos." Limbaugh urged his conservative listeners to cross over and vote for Clinton.[23] It appears that this purposeful strategic voting may have changed the actual result in Indiana, where Clinton won by only 14,000 votes. Ten percent of those voting in the Indiana Democratic primary indicated in exit polls that they were Republicans, and most of them said they voted for Clinton. The Republicans who voted for Clinton overwhelmingly also indicated they planned to vote for McCain in the fall, whereas the Republicans voting for Obama planned to stick with that choice in the general election. This is rather clear evidence of organized strategic voting of the kind that supports arguments for closed primaries. However, accomplishing that may be a challenge because it depends on states registering voters by party, which not all of them do.

While this kind of strategic and mischievous voting seems to be rare, the possibility that it could measurably affect who gets selected is a problem for the parties. In 2008 it was the Democrats, but there is nothing to say that commentators on the liberal Air America or in the blogosphere will not urge the same kind of behavior to undermine Republicans in 2012 or beyond. Restricting primaries to at least a semi-open structure would increase the organizational challenges of future incarnations of Operation Chaos.

Thus, while different voices may argue for or against caucuses, or lobby for or against the open primary, our evidence suggests that, as a general matter, measures that make participation more demanding and therefore restrict the pool of participants will also lead to a somewhat more ideologically extreme pool. The extent to which this produces more ideological candidates is uncertain in any particular contest because ideology is only one of several factors that go into the calculus of primary voters' decisions.[24] Nevertheless, more liberal electorates are going to favor more liberal candidates, and more conservative candidates will tend to fare better among electorates thinned down to committed conservatives.

The larger conclusion is that, not surprisingly, rules do matter. The major reforms following the 1968 election constituted a power shift by giving the rank-and-file partisans a much larger say in choosing their party's nominees.

It is arguable that, under the old pre–McGovern-Fraser rules, neither candidates like George McGovern and Jimmy Carter nor a newcomer like Barack Obama would have received the nomination. The newer process is much more open, especially to "outsider" candidates. I have found that, within this huge change, rules of sequence and participation do have an impact. Lots of research has established the importance of first caucuses and primaries. They establish momentum and eliminate candidates quickly, especially second-tier candidates who do not go into these contests seen as leaders. For them, meeting expectations in the early states is tantamount to an early exit. In this context, the slight apparent biases of the early states may play a role. A more conservative set of Democrats in Iowa would probably have netted John Edwards more votes, and our results suggest that Iowa participants would be somewhat less liberal if Iowa were to use a primary rather than a caucus system. Similarly, the high level of conservatism of the Iowa Republican caucusgoers was not an asset to John McCain. Differences in ideology between the Republican electorates in the Iowa caucuses and in the New Hampshire primaries were quite dramatic, and were due as much to format as to the ideological preferences of the Republicans in the two states.

We find, then, that the rules do matter. They are not alone determinative of who wins, because candidate qualities, momentum, perceptions of electability, and idiosyncratic events all play a major role in the outcomes of the caucuses and primaries. We find that the early states' electorates are modestly more ideological than the state electorates that vote later. The question of whether caucuses or primaries, or open or closed primaries, are more representative cannot be answered directly without determining who should be represented. We can say that restricting the electorates leads to more ideological sets of participants. Whether this is good or not depends on one's view of whose voices should have what weight, and the balance to be struck between ideological fidelity and electability.

Notes

1. John H. Aldrich, "A Dynamic Model of Presidential Nomination Campaigns," *American Political Science Review* 74 (1980): 651–69; Byron E. Shafer, "Scholarship on Presidential Selection in the United States," *American Political Science Review* 82 (1988): 955–63.

2. I draw on the published entrance and exit polls for the 2008 presidential caucuses and primaries (called "exit polls" for simplicity here), which were conducted by Edison Media Research of Somerville, N.J., and Mitofsky International of New York City for the National Election Pool. The partners in the enterprise are ABC News, the Asso-

ciated Press, CBS News, CNN, Fox News, and NBC News. I use all the polls from the Democratic elections ($N = 39$) and the polls of Republican participants before it was clear to everyone that John McCain would be the Republican nominee ($N = 27$). I use exit polls for the Democratic contests from Alabama, Arizona, Arkansas, California, Connecticut, Delaware, Florida, Georgia, Illinois, Indiana, Iowa, Kentucky, Louisiana, Maryland, Massachusetts, Michigan, Mississippi, Missouri, Montana, Nevada, New Hampshire, New Jersey, New Mexico, New York, North Carolina, Ohio, Oklahoma, Oregon, Pennsylvania, Rhode Island, South Carolina, Tennessee, Texas, Utah, Vermont, Virginia, West Virginia, and Wisconsin. Exit polls from the Republican contests used in this analysis are from Alabama, Arizona, Arkansas, California, Connecticut, Florida, Georgia, Illinois, Iowa, Louisiana, Maryland, Massachusetts, Michigan, Mississippi, Missouri, Nevada, New Hampshire, New Jersey, New York, Ohio, Oklahoma, South Carolina, Tennessee, Texas, Utah, Virginia, and Wisconsin.

3. Hanna Fenichel Pitkin, *The Concept of Representation* (University of California Press, 1967).

4. V. O. Key Jr., *Politics, Parties, and Pressure Groups* (New York: Crowell, 1958), pp. 180–82.

5. Zero indicates an even balance of Democrats and Republicans; 1.0 would be attained only if all respondents in a state identified as Republicans (–1.0 for all Democrats). For an explanation of the logic and validity of this approach to measuring opinion in the states, see Robert S. Erikson, Gerald C. Wright, and John P. McIver, *Statehouse Democracy: Public Opinion and Policy in the American States* (Cambridge University Press, 1993).

6. The reliability measure here uses the aggregate level reliability test following Erickson and others (1993) and Bradford S. Jones and Barbara Norrander, "The Reliability of Aggregated Public Opinion," *American Journal of Political Science* 40 (1996): 295–309.

7. The number of cases here is small, thirty-nine for Democratic contests and twenty-seven for Republicans; so using a more relaxed measure of significance does not seem unreasonable. If one only wanted statistically significant results, the analysis could have been presented using individual-level data, which would yield highly significant results. However, our story is about the shape of electorates, not individual differences.

8. The Iowa distinctiveness has to be qualified. For some reason, the exit polls offered Iowa Republicans a slightly different menu of choices for the ideology questions, giving just four rather than five options, collapsing "Very Liberal" and "Somewhat Liberal" into just "Liberal." They collapsed the conservative options on the Democratic Iowa entrance ballot as well. This practice was not followed in the remaining states. These small changes in the options given with the ballots may have had a small effect on Iowa's relative placement.

9. Daniel P. Franklin and Eric E. Grier, "Effects of Motor Voter Legislation: Voter Turnout, Registration, and Partisan Advantage in the 1992 Presidential Election,"

American Politics Research 25 (1997): 104–17; Stephen Knack, "Does 'Motor Voter' Work? Evidence from State-Level Data," *Journal of Politics* 57 (1995): 796–811; Raymond E. Wolfinger and Steven J. Rosenstone, *Who Votes?* (Yale University Press, 1980).

10. Thomas R. Marshall, "Turnout and Representation: Caucuses versus Primaries," *American Journal of Political Science* 22 (1978): 169–82.

11. Josh Barro, "Caucus Voters vs. Primary Voters," in *The Barometer: Political Analysis on the 2008 Race* (http://joshbarro.blogspot.com/2008/02/caucus-voters-vs-primary-voters.html [October 28, 2008]).

12. P. Cronin, "Primary versus Caucus: How Millions of Voters Are Systematically Disenfranchised and Election Results Are Skewed" (www.talkleft.com/media/2008caucusreport.pdf [October 28, 2008]).

13. Philip Converse, "The Nature of Belief Systems in Mass Publics," in *Ideology and Discontent*, edited by David E. Apter (New York: Free Press, 1964); Herbert McClosky, Paul J. Hoffmann, and Rosemary O'Hara, "Issue Conflict and Consensus among Party Leaders and Followers," *American Political Science Review* 54 (1960): 406–27; Warren E. Miller, M. Kent Jennings, and Barbara G. Farah, *Parties in Transition: A Longitudinal Study of Party Elites and Party Supporters* (New York: Russell Sage Foundation, 1986).

14. James I. Lengle, *Representation and Presidential Primaries: The Democratic Party in the Post-Reform Era* (Westport, Conn.: Greenwood Press, 1981); Nelson W. Polsby, *Consequences of Party Reform* (Oxford University Press, 1983).

15. Thomas R. Marshall, "Turnout and Representation: Caucuses versus Primaries," *American Journal of Political Science* 22 (1978): 169–82; Barbara Norrander, "Ideological Representativeness of Presidential Primary Voters," *American Journal of Political Science* (1989): 570–87.

16. It is tempting to put these on the same metric by collapsing the "very liberal" and "somewhat liberal" as just "liberal" and the same with the conservative responses. However, we do not know that, for example, some individuals offered the three-option item might say they are "moderate," but if given the five-option item would feel comfortable saying they are "somewhat liberal" since the latter is really the same thing as calling oneself a liberal. Since my purpose is not to establish differences among identifiers and primary participants, this measurement question does not need to be settled here. Without a doubt, both items get at the same underlying attitudinal propensities.

17. The standard deviations for Democratic partisans' ideology scores for the states included in table 2-4 are .11, and .06 for the Republican partisans' ideologies. These reflect well the distribution of the full fifty-state scores with standard deviations of .11 and .07.

18. One approach considered was to explore these relationships in earlier years. Unfortunately, participants in the caucus states beyond Iowa are almost never polled by the News Election Service.

19. Nolan M. McCarty, Keith T. Poole, and Howard Rosenthal, *Polarized America: The Dance of Ideology and Unequal Riches* (MIT Press, 2006); Keith T. Poole and Howard Rosenthal, "The Polarization of American Politics," *Journal of Politics* 46 (1984): 1061–79.

20. See, for example, "Bill Clinton: Caucuses Are 'Killing Us,'" ABC News (www.talkleft.com/story/2008/5/27/92144/7994 [November 6, 2008]); "Obama Won Caucuses, Clinton Won Primaries" (http://thenexthurrah.typepad.com/the_next_ hurrah/2008/02/obama-won-caucu.html [November 6, 2008]); and many more similar discussions on sites such as CaucusCheating.com (http://caucuscheating.blogspot.com/ [November 6, 2008]).

21. Walter J. Stone, "Party, Ideology, and the Lure of Victory: Iowa Activists in the 1980 Prenomination Campaign," *Western Political Quarterly* 35 (1982): 527–38; Walter J. Stone, Ronald B. Rapoport, and Alan I. Abramowitz, "Candidate Support in Presidential Nomination Campaigns: The Case of Iowa in 1984," *Journal of Politics* 54 (1992): 1074–97.

22. Ronald D. Hedlund, "Cross-Over Voting in a 1976 Open Presidential Primary," *Public Opinion Quarterly* 41 (1977): 498–514.

23. Alec MacGillis and Peter Slevin, "Did Rush Limbaugh Tilt Result in Indiana?" *Washington Post*, May 8, 2008, p. A1.

24. John H. Aldrich and R. Michael Alvarez, "Issues and the Presidential Primary Voter," *Political Behavior* 16 (1994): 289–317; Thomas R. Marshall, "Issues, Personalities, and Presidential Primary Voters," *Social Science Quarterly* 65 (1984): 750–60; Barbara Norrander, "Correlates of Vote Choice in the 1980 Presidential Primaries," *Journal of Politics* 48 (1986): 156–66; Stone, Rapoport, and Abramowitz, "Candidate Support in Presidential Nomination Campaigns."

THOMAS E. PATTERSON

3

Voter Participation: Records Galore This Time, but What about Next Time?

The possibility that voter participation might be different in 2008 surfaced in the nation's first nominating contest, the Iowa caucuses. The old participation record was 220,000 voters, set in 2000. Turnout in 2008 was far higher. More than 350,000 Iowans braved the January cold to express their preference for the next president of the United States. In yet another sign of things to come, the youth vote—ballots cast by those under 30 years of age—was three times greater than it had been in 2004.[1]

In percentage terms, Iowa's turnout was hardly earthshaking—only one in six of the eligible adults participated. The Democratic winner, Barack Obama, received the votes of just 4 percent of Iowa's eligible voters. Mike Huckabee, the Republican victor, attracted the support of a mere 2 percent of Iowa adults.

Nevertheless, the 16.3 percent turnout level was easily the highest percentage ever recorded for a presidential caucus, and eight times the historical average for such contests. In fact, the turnout in the Iowa caucuses, at which voters meet and hear short arguments for each candidate before casting their ballots, was higher than the turnout in most of the presidential primaries held in 2000 and 2004.

More than a score of state primary and caucus turnout records were set in 2008. Overall, about 57 million Americans voted in the 2008 nominating elections, which easily eclipsed the 31 million who voted in 2000, the last time both major parties had contested presidential races.

The 2008 nominating contests had unprecedented features, including the candidacies of the first viable woman presidential candidate and the first viable African American presidential candidate. The 2008 contests were also atypical of recent contests in that the outcome was not determined on Super

Tuesday, which meant that residents of states with primaries and caucuses yet to come had reason to go to the polls, thereby driving up turnout. Accordingly, a full accounting of voter participation in presidential nominating elections requires a look not only at the 2008 contests but at earlier ones as well.

Toward a Voter-Centered Nominating Process: 1972–1984

Through the 1968 campaign, presidential nominations were securely in the hands of party leaders. Although about a third of the states held primary elections, most of the national convention delegates were selected through party caucuses controlled by party leaders. In 1952, for example, Senator Estes Kefauver of Tennessee defeated President Harry Truman in New Hampshire's opening primary. Kefauver then went on to win all but one of the other twelve primaries he entered and was the favorite of rank-and-file Democrats in the final Gallup poll before the party's national convention. Yet Democratic leaders rejected Kefauver and chose instead Illinois governor Adlai Stevenson, who was not even a declared presidential candidate. When asked about the significance of the primaries, Stevenson replied: "All [they do] is destroy some candidates."[2]

The party-centered nominating system was shattered by the bitter 1968 presidential election. The country was mired in the war in Vietnam, and senators Robert Kennedy and Eugene McCarthy challenged Lyndon Johnson's bid for a second term by entering the presidential primaries as antiwar candidates. Their strong showing, which was accompanied by one of the highest voter turnout levels in primary election history,[3] persuaded Johnson to drop out of the race. However, Kennedy was assassinated the night of the last primary and McCarthy had angered party leaders with his blistering attacks on President Johnson. On the first ballot, the convention delegates nominated Vice President Hubert Humphrey, who had not entered a single primary. Insurgent Democrats were outraged, and after Humphrey narrowly lost the general election, they engineered a change in the nominating system.

Through its McGovern-Fraser Commission, the Democratic Party adopted rules designed to place the party's rank-and-file voters in charge of the nominating process. State parties were directed to choose their convention delegates through either a primary election or a caucus open to all registered party voters. In its final report, the Commission pointedly stated the goal: "We view popular participation as the lifeblood of the National Convention. . . . We believe that popular participation is more than a proud heritage of our party, more even than a first principle. We believe that popular control of the Democratic Party is necessary for its survival."[4]

The commission expected the sixteen states with primaries to retain them and assumed that the remaining states would comply with the new rules by opening their caucuses to all party registrants.[5] However, Democratic Party leaders in some caucus states were reluctant to open up the caucuses to all comers for fear that insurgents might use the meetings to capture control of the party organization. Six caucus states switched to primary elections in 1972 and seven more switched in 1976, with a dozen more to follow. The state legislatures that authorized these primaries usually applied them also to the GOP, thus binding the Republicans to the new system as well.[6]

In 1972, the first election under the new rules, caucus participation increased. It increased further in 1976 when the news media decided that the caucuses—particularly the first one in Iowa—warranted closer attention.[7] When Iowa Republicans in 1976 repositioned their caucuses just ahead of New Hampshire's first-in-the-nation primary, matching the Democrats' move of four years earlier, journalists flocked to Iowa, raising the interest level of Iowa voters. About 45,000 Iowans participated in the caucuses—a new record for that type of contest.

Nevertheless, participation in caucus states was far lower than in primary states. The 2.5 percent turnout rate in the 1976 Iowa caucuses paled alongside the 33.4 percent who voted in that year's New Hampshire primary. Across all states in 1976, turnout averaged 1.9 percent for the caucuses and 28.2 percent for the primaries.[8]

In the 1972–84 period, the sequencing of the primaries spurred participation. In scheduling their primaries, many states picked an open date—a Tuesday on which their stand-alone primary would be the center of national attention. When Carter won the hard-fought 1976 Democratic race, for example, the primaries started in New Hampshire (February 24), went on to Massachusetts and Vermont (March 2), then to Florida (March 9), and from there to Illinois (March 16), North Carolina (March 23), New York and Wisconsin (April 6), Pennsylvania (April 27), and Texas (May 1). Not until early May did state contests begin to clump together. The schedule was back-loaded.

Back-loading served to bring voters to the polls. As the campaign moved each week to a new state, its voters were treated to an intense campaign that was headline news across the country. The slow unfolding of the schedule also meant that the nominees would not be determined until late in the schedule. In 1976, for example, both parties had contested campaigns—Gerald Ford versus Ronald Reagan on the Republican side, and Jimmy Carter against a host of contenders on the Democratic side—that lasted until the final day of the primaries.

Nevertheless, the average turnout rate in the 1976 primaries, as well as in the 1972, 1980, and 1984 primaries, was lower than in earlier contested primaries. In his study of eleven competitive primary states in the 1948–68 presidential elections, the political scientist Austin Ranney found an average turnout rate of 39 percent.[9] In the first four presidential elections under the McGovern-Fraser Commission rules, the average turnout in contested primaries was slightly less than 30 percent.[10]

The decrease reflected a general decline in voter participation that began after 1960.[11] Moreover, the newer primaries—those instituted in 1972 or later—attracted fewer voters than did the more established primaries. In 1976, for example, the turnout difference between the newer primaries and the long-standing ones was 7 percentage points on average.[12] The older primaries typically received more attention from the press and the candidates.[13]

During this period, a state's positioning in the schedule had little effect on its turnout level. State primaries near the back of the schedule had turnout rates comparable to those near the front.[14]

The Rise of Front-Loading and the Decline in Turnout: 1988–2004

Even though the turnout rate declined somewhat after the adoption of the McGovern-Fraser Commission rules, the total number of Americans who voted in the nominating contests increased substantially. Some 13 million Americans had voted in 1968. The number was 32 million in 1980, owing to an increase in the number of primaries. By 1980, a score of states had replaced their caucuses with primaries, which attracted on average fifteen times as many voters.[15]

The gain was short-lived. The nominating process was changing, not because of any adjustment in the rules, but because of the new system's dynamics. Although the McGovern-Fraser reforms theoretically created a system where the states were of equal importance, save for the number of delegates, the new system in practice favored states with early contests. The early primaries winnowed the field of candidates and bestowed momentum on the winners. The early states also hogged the media spotlight. In 1976, for example, there were 100 stories on the ABC, CBS, and NBC evening newscasts about the New Hampshire primary. Next in line were two contests immediately following it: the Massachusetts primary with fifty-two evening news stories and the Florida primary with fifty such stories. Other state primaries got substantially less coverage.[16]

Unhappy with their position at the back of the pack, a number of states threatened to move their primaries to a leading position.[17] In an effort to accommodate their demands, while also preserving a semblance of order, the national parties reserved the lead spots for Iowa and New Hampshire and created a "window" for the other states. They were free to schedule their contest anytime between early March (later moved to early February) and early June.

Democrats in southern states were the first to respond. In an attempt to offset the influence of opening contests in the North, a few southern states scheduled their 1984 primaries for the same Tuesday in March. When that clustering proved insufficient, all of the southern states except South Carolina scheduled their 1988 contests for the same Tuesday in March. Seven other states also moved their primaries to that date, creating the first bona fide "Super Tuesday"—a single day on which the candidates would compete in a large number of states. It marked a radical change in the calendar. In the 1970s, the halfway point in delegate selection did not occur until May. In 1988 the halfway point was reached in April.

There was no reason why Super Tuesday had to bring the nominating races to a conclusion, but that became its effect. The candidate with the most money, strongest organization, and deepest party support usually dominated the Super Tuesday primaries, bringing the race to an end before all the states had balloted. In the 1988–2004 period there was only one truly suspenseful race after the March primaries—the 1988 Democratic race.[18] Super Tuesday in that race produced a split decision: Jesse Jackson won five southern states; Al Gore picked up five border states and Nevada; and Michael Dukakis carried eight states, including the biggest ones, Texas and Florida. Dukakis's performance on Super Tuesday was pivotal in his successful run for the party's nomination, but it was not immediately clear that he would prevail. In the other nine races in the 1988–2004 period, the nomination was all but locked up on Super Tuesday.

The creation of Super Tuesday resulted in a sharp drop in voter participation. The stacking of primaries on a single day, followed by an abrupt end to the race once the votes were tallied, has had the effect of creating a tiered participation system. The top tier consists of the early states with stand-alone contests. Their voters narrow the field and bestow momentum. The Super Tuesday states constitute the second tier. Although their contests do not get as much individual attention as the opening contests, their voters ordinarily pick the nominees. The third tier consists of the states with contests at the back of the schedule. Their residents get a chance to vote in the presidential con-

Figure 3-1. *Voter Turnout in Contested Individual and Grouped Primaries,
1988–2004*

Percent who voted

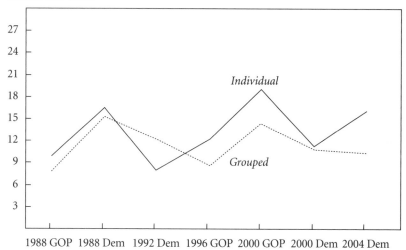

1988 GOP 1988 Dem   1992 Dem   1996 GOP 2000 GOP 2000 Dem 2004 Dem

Source: Committee for the Study of the American Electorate, "2004 Primary Turnout Low:
Grouped Primaries Lower than Individual," March 9, 2004.

test, but their ballots ordinarily do not affect the outcome of the nominating
races.

Over the past two decades, turnout has varied significantly across the tiers.
States with stand-alone early primaries have higher participation rates on
average than states that ballot simultaneously on or around Super Tuesday.
Turnout in the early stand-alone primaries exceeded that of the grouped competitive primaries in every case between 1988 and 2004, with the exception of
the 1992 Democratic primaries (see figure 3-1). On average during this
period, turnout in the stand-alone Democratic and Republican primaries was
one and a half times greater than turnout in the grouped primaries.[19]

This difference reflects the way the campaign is waged in these states. In
those with stand-alone competitive contests, residents get an intense "retail"
campaign in which the candidates travel from one end of the state to the
other. These contests also get intense national news coverage, which include
stories about the state, its people, and its policy concerns. In the grouped-
primary states, the campaign occurs largely through the candidates' televised
ads—"wholesale" politics. Moreover, the news media concentrate on the larger
states in the grouping, largely ignoring the smaller states.

Even so, turnout in the competitive grouped primaries is significantly higher than in the third tier of states—those whose contests are scheduled after the race effectively ends on Super Tuesday. These states essentially ratify the decision made in earlier contests.

Turnout in the late-scheduled contests can be shockingly low. In 2004, for example, Rhode Island's primary attracted only 5 percent of the state's voting-age population. In the 1988–2004 elections, there were a dozen primaries in which the turnout was less than 10 percent—all of them were held after Super Tuesday. The small number of late-scheduled primaries that attract significant numbers of voters typically include important races for statewide or congressional office. One such contest, the 1996 West Virginia GOP primary, attracted 24 percent of the Republican electorate, even though Robert Dole had wrapped up the Republican presidential nomination two months earlier.[20]

Despite such exceptions, primaries held after the nominating race has been settled are not appealing to voters. The 2000 Republican contests, for example, attracted an average of 26 percent of eligible Republicans while George W. Bush's chief rival, John McCain, was still in the race, 18 percent in primaries held within a month of his dropping out, and only 14 percent in subsequent primaries.[21]

The level of primary turnout in the 1988–2004 elections, as well as the turnout for earlier elections, is shown in figure 3-2. As could be expected, turnout was lower when only one party had a contested nominating race, as when George W. Bush ran unopposed for the 2004 GOP nomination. The larger lesson in the data is the steep decline in voting participation after front-loading began in 1988. Before that election, primary turnout averaged 27.6 percent, compared with 20.2 percent thereafter. The 1996 nominating races were decided by the lowest overall (Democratic and Republican primaries combined) turnout rate (17.5 percent) in history, a record that was broken in 2004 when a mere 17.2 percent of eligible voters participated. The 2004 election also established a record low for turnout in a contested Democratic race: 11.4 percent. The 1988 Republican election had the lowest turnout ever for a contested race in that party: 10.0 percent.

Low participation rates meant that the nominees were being chosen by a relatively few voters. In 2004, John Kerry's victories in Iowa and New Hampshire were decisive enough to make him the odds-on favorite for the Democratic nomination. That year, turnout in New Hampshire set a new record, but turnout in the Super Tuesday contests suffered from the widespread belief that Kerry was unstoppable. Barely more than 10 million Americans—roughly 5 percent of the adult population—participated in the 2004 Democratic pri-

Figure 3-2. *Presidential Primary Turnout, 1972–2004*

Percent who voted

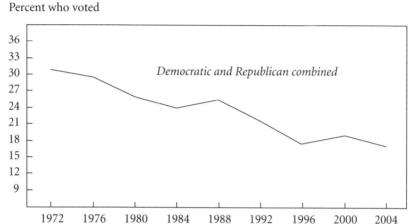

Source: Committee for the Study of the American Electorate, "2008 Primary Turnout Falls Just Short of Record Nationally, Breaks Record in Most States," March 9, 2008.

maries through Super Tuesday.[22] Kerry became the Democratic nominee through the support of somewhat more than half of these voters—less than 3 percent of adults.[23]

The Incredible Turnout Increase: 2008

Compared with recent elections, voter participation in 2008 was extraordinary. Although the turnout rate of 30.3 percent[24] in the primary election states fell short of the modern record of 30.9 percent set in 1972,[25] the number of voters was the highest ever. Roughly 57 million Americans cast a ballot.

The Primaries

Most states—three out of five—set an overall primary turnout record in 2008 (see table 3-1).[26] In Indiana, 36.7 percent of voting-age citizens cast a ballot, easily topping the 28.4 percent who voted in 1976. Rhode Island's 27.0 percent turnout easily topped that state's previous best of 11.5 percent, also set in 1976. Georgia's 32.1 percent turnout was nearly 10 percentage points greater than the 22.8 percent who voted in 1988. Arizona's 24.2 percent turnout was twice that of the state's old record. In fact, so many states set records that it is simpler to list the ones that did not. Among those that fell short of a new high were California, where 41.7 percent turned out, compared with 46.0 percent

Table 3-1. *Voter Turnout in Primary Election States, 2008*
Percent

State	Overall	Democratic	Republican
Alabama	32.1[a]	15.8[a]	16.3[a]
Arizona	24.2[a]	11.1[a]	13.1
Arkansas	26.0	14.9	11.1[a]
California	41.7	23.1	18.6
Connecticut	20.1[a]	14.1[a]	6.0
Delaware	23.2[a]	15.2[a]	8.0[a]
District of Columbia	35.2[a]	33.4[a]	1.8[a]
Florida	29.7	13.8[b]	15.9[a]
Georgia	32.1[a]	16.8[a]	15.3[a]
Idaho	—	no primary	12.0
Illinois	34.3[a]	23.8[a]	10.5
Indiana	36.7[a]	27.9[a]	8.8
Kentucky	28.6[a]	22.3[a]	6.3
Louisiana	19.3	13.6	5.7
Maryland	27.3	19.8	7.5
Massachusetts	38.2[a]	27.3[a]	10.9
Michigan	20.2	8.4[b]	11.8
Mississippi	26.5	20.2[a]	6.3
Missouri	32.6[a]	19.0[a]	13.6
Montana	—	30.0[a]	no primary
Nebraska	18.1	7.4	10.7
New Hampshire	51.9[a]	28.5[a]	23.4
New Jersey	28.9[a]	19.3[a]	9.6
New Mexico	19.2	11.2[a]	8.0
New York	20.5[a]	15.0[a]	5.5
North Carolina	32.7[a]	24.6[a]	8.1[a]
Ohio	40.3[a]	27.5[a]	12.8
Oklahoma	29.4[a]	16.3	13.1[a]
Oregon	39.7	21.7[a]	18.0
Pennsylvania	33.3[a]	24.7[a]	8.6
Rhode Island	27.0[a]	23.6[a]	3.4
South Carolina	30.3[a]	16.5[a]	13.8
South Dakota	28.9	17.1[a]	11.2
Tennessee	26.1[a]	13.8	12.3[a]
Texas	28.6[a]	19.3[a]	9.3[a]
Utah	23.7	7.2	16.5
Vermont	39.4[a]	31.3[a]	8.1
Virginia	26.5[a]	17.7[a]	8.8
Washington	27.3	15.4[a]	11.9
West Virginia	33.4	25.1	8.3
Wisconsin	36.5	26.7	9.8

Sources: CNN, Committee for the Study of the American Electorate, and United States Election Project. Figures calculated by dividing the number of voters in a primary by the number of adults eligible to vote in the state.

a. Record high turnout.

b. Primary not sanctioned by the national Democratic Party.

in 1964; Wisconsin, where 36.5 percent of the voting-eligible population went to the polls, compared with 48.8 percent in 1972; and Maryland, where the participation rate was 27.3 percent, compared with 29.9 percent in 1964.

Tempering the record setting was the fact that many of the new highs occurred in states with a short primary history. Arizona's 2008 primary, for instance, was only the third such contest in the state. Nevertheless, the average turnout rate across all the primaries was 8 percentage points higher than the average for the 1976–2004 period.

The surge is partly attributable to issues that had heightened turnout in the general election four years earlier. In 2004 more than 120 million Americans cast a ballot in the Bush-Kerry race, the highest number on record. Although the turnout rate was below historical highs, it was nonetheless higher than in any election since 1968. Over 60 percent of the population eligible to vote went to the polls in November 2004, motivated by anxiety over the war in Iraq and a weak economy.

These issues carried into the 2008 nominating races, which were compelling for other reasons. For the first time since 1952, neither the incumbent president nor vice president was a candidate, thus ensuring an open race in both parties. The number of announced candidates was exceptionally high— nearly twenty in all. Moreover, two of the candidates represented historical firsts. Barack Obama was the first candidate of his race to have a realistic chance of winning a major-party presidential nomination. Hillary Clinton was his female equivalent—the first woman to have a realistic chance.

Uncertainty about the outcome of the Democratic and Republican races added to the drama. The Democratic lineup, in addition to Obama and Clinton, included John Edwards, the party's 2004 vice presidential nominee, who had a well-funded campaign and a carefully honed campaign message. On the Republican side, John McCain was the early favorite, but he faced strong opposition from GOP conservatives and had trouble raising campaign funds, casting doubts on his viability. McCain did not even seriously contest the Iowa caucuses, becoming the first candidate of either party to skip Iowa and still win the party's presidential nomination.

The first contests lacked the clear-cut outcome they often have. The Democratic and Republican races were unsettled going into Super Tuesday, which included a record-high twenty-three state contests. Super Tuesday helped to clarify the outcome of the Republican race. Although McCain did not run so strongly as to wipe out his competitors, he took a solid lead in the delegate count, which led Mitt Romney to quit the race two days later and forced Mike Huckabee to limp along with limited funding. Even so, Huckabee did not exit

Table 3-2. *Voter Turnout in Caucus States, 2008*
Percent

State	Overall	Democratic	Republican
Hawaii	not tallied[a]	not tallied	not tallied
Alaska	5.0	1.8	3.2
Colorado	5.5	3.5	2.0
Idaho	—	2.1	no caucus
Iowa	16.3	10.9	5.4
Kansas	4.3	1.9	2.4
Maine	not tallied	4.8	not tallied
Minnesota	7.2	5.7	1.5
Nebraska	—	3.0	no caucus
Nevada	9.5	6.9	2.6
North Dakota	5.9	3.9	2.0
Texas	—	7.2	no caucus
Washington	0.9	0.7	0.2
West Virginia	—	no caucus	not tallied
Wyoming	2.5	2.2	0.3

Sources: CNN and United States Elections Project. Figures calculated by dividing the number of caucus participants by the number of adults eligible to vote in the state.

a. The number of caucus participants was not tallied by the state party.

the race until thirty-eight states had voted. Not since 1976 had a Republican race lasted that long.

The Democratic contest also lasted longer than any since 1976, going all the way to the end before Obama prevailed. The Obama-Clinton race was more than a marathon. It was the most resource-intense nominating battle in history. Both candidates were prodigious fundraisers, which enabled them to mount unprecedented television and grassroots campaigns, which heightened public involvement.

The Democratic race spurred the exceptionally high participation rate in 2008. The overall Republican turnout rate of 10.8 percent was on par with other GOP races since 1984, excluding 2004, when turnout dipped because Bush was unopposed. On the other hand, the Democratic primaries had a 19.4 percent turnout rate—the highest since 1972. Twenty-seven of the forty Democratic primaries broke their old record. Only nine of the forty Republican primaries broke a record.

The Caucuses

In 2008, thirteen states held presidential caucuses. Four states (Idaho, Nebraska, Texas, and West Virginia) held a caucus for one party only.

Among the states that used the caucus method for both parties, the average turnout rate exceeded 6 percent, but the level varied widely (see table 3-2). Iowa with its 16.3 percent participation rate was in a class by itself, although Nevada's rate (9.5 percent) was also extremely high by historical standards. The state of Washington, which held primaries *and* caucuses in both parties, had the lowest caucus turnout rate—0.9 percent. Although turnout in the 2008 caucuses set a new record, the average caucus attracted fewer than a fourth as many participants as the average primary election.

Scheduling had a larger effect on caucus participation than it did on primary participation. The Iowa and Nevada caucuses were stand-alone events in advance of Super Tuesday and garnered considerable attention from the candidates and the press. Their turnout level averaged 12.9 percent. The average for subsequent caucuses was less than 5 percent.

Demographic Characteristics of the Primary Electorate

Although the McGovern-Fraser Commission sought a representative party through broad participation in the nominating process, primary electorates have never been fully representative of the party's identifiers, much less of the general population.[27] Better-educated Americans, older Americans, and non-Hispanic white Americans have been disproportionately represented among primary voters.[28]

The 2008 primaries followed the typical pattern in certain respects. Better-educated citizens made up a disproportionate share of the voters in the states' presidential primaries (see table 3-3). In fact, as a state average, individuals with a college degree were overrepresented among primary voters by nearly 20 percentage points.[29] The Republican and Democratic electorates were nearly alike in this respect—college graduates were overrepresented by 18.9 percentage points among Democratic voters and by 20.8 percentage points among Republican voters. Although college graduates constitute only about a fourth of the adult population, they cast nearly half of the primary election votes in 2008.

However, the 2008 primaries were atypical in regard to racial participation. The historical first of Obama's candidacy lured large numbers of black voters to the polls, so many in fact that the percentage of black voters was almost identical to the proportion of blacks in the adult population. This achievement occurred entirely through participation in Democratic primaries, where blacks were overrepresented by an estimated margin of 7.3 percentage points. On the Republican side, they were underrepresented by an estimated 10.8 percentage points. (The GOP primaries had lower turnout, which is why the

Table 3-3. *Demographic Characteristics of the 2008 Primary Electorate*
Percent

Voter characteristics	Democratic electorate	Republican electorate	Total electorate
College graduates	+18.9	+20.8	+19.6
Non-college graduates	−18.9	−20.8	−19.6
White, non-Hispanic	−6.1	+14.8	+2.4
Black	+7.3	−10.8	+0.8
Women	+5.6	−4.9	+1.8
Men	−5.6	+4.9	−1.8
Ages 18–29	−8.6	−12.0	−9.8
Ages 60 and over	+7.3	+11.2	+8.7

Sources: CNN exit polls and U.S. Census Bureau data. Figures based only on primaries where a CNN exit poll was conducted. Figures were derived by calculating the percentages for each state, summing these percentages, and then dividing this sum by the number of states. Figures for the total electorate were derived by weighting the Democratic and Republican electorates in proportion to their overall turnout rates (19.4 percent and 10.8 percent respectively).

Notes: +/− indicates in percentage terms the degree to which a group was overrepresented (+) or underrepresented (−) in the electorate, as an average across the primary states. For each state, census data and exit poll data were used to determine the extent to which a particular demographic group voted in greater or lesser numbers relative to its proportion of the state's vote-eligible adult population. These numbers were then aggregated across the states and divided by the number of states to produce the percentages displayed in the table. Thus the numbers are not based on the U.S. population as a whole but on state-by-state calculations where each state is weighted equally. The figures represent the "average" primary electorate in 2008.

overall figure is not the simple average of the Democratic and Republican primaries.)

Obama's candidacy also attracted considerable interest among young adults. Relative to their numbers in the population, young voters (18–29 years of age) underperformed. They were underrepresented by 9.8 percentage points in the 2008 primaries. However, this proportion is smaller than is ordinarily the case, and is attributable largely to their participation in the Democratic race. Young adults were underrepresented by 8.6 percentage points in Democratic primaries, compared with 12.0 percentage points in the Republican primaries. In contrast, older voters (those 60 and older) were overrepresented by 7.3 percentage points in the Democratic primaries and by 11.2 percentage points in the Republican primaries.

Women were also overrepresented in the 2008 Democratic primaries. After women gained the right to vote in 1920, they were slow to exercise that right.

Even as late as 1960, turnout among women in presidential general elections was nearly 10 percentage points lower than among men. They reached parity with men in 1980, and afterward voted at slightly higher levels in presidential general elections, though not in presidential primaries. In the 2008 primaries, however, women had a marginally higher voting rate than men. Women were overrepresented by an estimated 1.8 percentage points among all voters, an imbalance attributable to the Democratic race, where women were overrepresented by 5.6 percentage points. Clinton's candidacy was undoubtedly a contributing factor.

The Republican electorate was less diverse. As has been true in other recent elections, Republican voters were older, more white, and more male than their Democratic counterparts.

Structural Factors and Participation Levels

Structural factors, including states' position in the nominating schedule, affected participation in the 2008 primaries, though less so than in other recent primaries. Compared with the early stand-alone primaries, turnout declined in Super Tuesday's clustered primaries. Only ten days separated the stand-alone South Carolina primary of January 26 from the twenty-three Super Tuesday primaries of February 5, giving the candidates little time to campaign in those contests. Nor did most of the candidates have the resources to mount extensive campaigns in the Super Tuesday states. Obama was the only candidate to buy televised ads in all of them. The Super Tuesday primaries had an average turnout rate of 28 percent, which was substantially less than the 41 percent average of the earlier stand-alone primaries.[30]

Unlike in other recent primary elections, turnout did not fall after Super Tuesday, even though McCain's victories signaled that the Republican race was nearing its end. Turnout in the post–Super Tuesday primaries averaged 30 percent, owing to the intensity of the Obama-Clinton race. During the post–Super Tuesday period, turnout in the Democratic primaries was 24 percent—roughly three times that of the Republican primaries. Democratic turnout was also higher in the early contests, but by a three-to-two rather than three-to-one margin.

A structural factor that affected turnout in the 2008 primaries was the rule governing voter eligibility. About half of the primaries were closed: that is, participation was restricted to the party's registered voters. The other half allowed any registered voter to participate. In 2008 the open primaries had a 33 percent turnout rate, compared with a 28 percent rate for the closed primaries. Clearly, if greater participation is the goal, the open primary is preferable to the closed primary. On the other hand, the nominating process is designed to choose a *party's* presidential candidate, which is an argument for restricting each party's voters to those registered with that party.

Although presidential primaries are distinctive events, they take place in the context of a state's political culture. Some states routinely have higher turnout rates than other states. When the 2008 primary states are divided into thirds according to their 2004 general election turnout, there is a six-point spread (34 percent versus 28 percent) in primary turnout between the top third and the bottom third. The difference would have been larger except that two of the top-tier states (Connecticut and Delaware, with 2008 primary turnouts of 20 percent and 23 percent, respectively) held closed primaries that were projected to go heavily for Clinton, which dampened turnout. In addition, the surge in the African American vote boosted turnout in several bottom-third southern states. Although South Carolina, Alabama, and Georgia typically have low participation levels, the 2008 primary turnout exceeded 30 percent in each of those states.

What the Future Might Hold: 2012 and Beyond

Participation in the 2008 nominating races will contribute to higher turnout in future elections. The large number of first-time voters augurs well for 2012 and beyond. Studies have found that once citizens cast their first ballot, the odds increase they will participate in subsequent elections.[31]

There is a caveat, however. The McGovern-Fraser Commission's reforms, as Austin Ranney noted, "were consciously designed to maximize participation by persons who are enthusiasts for a particular aspirant *in the year of the convention*."[32] Perhaps more than anything else, this observation speaks to the probable long-term effects of the rise in participation in 2008. The influx of voters in 2008 is attributable to the election's unique features: an unpopular war in Iraq, a wobbly economy, and the historical firsts represented by the Obama and Clinton candidacies. When these influences wane, which will occur as early as the next election, a return to normality is likely.

Turnout variation in primary elections is larger than it is for general elections. Moreover, turnout variation is itself increasing. Sandwiched between the upswings in voting in the 2004 and 2008 presidential elections was a small increase in turnout in the 2006 midterm elections and a downturn in turnout in the 2005 and 2007 local elections—indeed, in 2007 turnout in local elections reached its lowest level in modern times.[33] Today's voters appear more selective than those of earlier generations, choosing to vote or not vote based on their sense of an election's significance rather than out of a sense of personal duty.

Young adults are among the less reliable participants. If Obama had not won the Democratic race, and it was a close call, some of the young people that he brought into the campaign might have sat out the November election. To date, America's young adults have not demonstrated a willingness to participate in election politics whatever the issues, arenas, or candidates. Perhaps that will change if the tone and direction of American politics changes. But the climate of citizenship is different today than in the past, when the nation's schools, families, media, and political institutions nurtured a sense of civic duty and involvement.[34]

In the near future, however, the major problem will be the difficulty of sustaining voter turnout in a nominating process that treats states and their voters unequally. The structure of the presidential nominating system creates what Kathleen Hall Jamieson has called "a primary season of haves and have-nots."[35] Super Tuesday usually marks the end of the competition for all practical purposes, depressing the vote in states that are yet to hold their contests. Unless front-loading is eliminated, the typical participation pattern will be the one in place during the 1988–2004 elections: reasonably high participation at the outset, followed by a sharp drop after Super Tuesday.

The Republican and Democratic parties are aware of the problem, although participation is not their top priority. Above all, they want a process that will yield a viable nominee—one who can win in November. If that can be accomplished through high participation rates in the nominating phase, participation will be embraced. If heightened participation threatens the party's chances in the fall, the party's enthusiasm for it declines significantly, as illustrated by the efforts of some Democratic party leaders to pressure superdelegates to declare their support for Obama as a means of forcing Clinton from the race before the primaries had concluded.

Nevertheless, the national parties are responsive to the concerns of the states, all of which want a meaningful voice in the process. Toward this end, for example, the 1996 Republican National Committee Task Force on Primaries and Caucuses sought to blunt front-loading by granting bonus delegates to any state that scheduled its contest toward the end of the nominating process.[36] The Republican Party's rules also penalize states, including Iowa and New Hampshire, that hold their contest before the earliest allowed calendar date. States that schedule a primary or caucus before this date lose half their convention delegates. Jim Nicholson, a member of the Task Force and later the GOP's national chair, cited participation as the basis for the new formula. "Primaries are a good way to get people involved with the party, and where fewer people vote, the party loses strength."

However, this change has not resolved the front-loading problem. In fact, as the Michigan and Florida Republican primaries in 2008 illustrate, some states are more than willing to forfeit half of their delegates for the opportunity to hold an early contest. In a statement justifying Florida's decision to do so, Governor Charlie Crist said: "Florida's diverse population will be more influential in the presidential primary process."[37]

Nor will any of the widely proposed alternatives to the present nominating system fix the front-loading problem. For a decade, the National Association of Secretaries of State (the organization of state election officials) has tried to persuade the parties to adopt a rotating regional primaries system. Such a system would begin with state contests in one region of the country, then move to a second region, and so on. The order would change with each election, allowing each region to be first in the rotation once every sixteen years. Other objections to this system aside, it is unlikely to give residents of all regions a chance for meaningful participation. A well-funded candidate with name recognition and party support like Dole in 1996 and Bush and Gore in 2000 could easily dominate the first region's contests. Even if the race did not end there, such a candidate would likely sweep the next region's contests. Voters in the remaining regions would effectively be disenfranchised and might feel cheated. It is one thing when a system denies residents of single states a vote, as in the current system, and quite another when a system silences residents of *every* southern, western, midwestern, or northeastern state. The effect would be heightened if a regional favorite were perceived to have lost out because of the order of the voting.

The 2008 nominating elections will undoubtedly be talked about repeatedly as the paradigm of heightened voter participation, as well they should be. Nevertheless, the 2008 contests achieved this remarkable distinction despite a nominating process that in *most* elections produces a large number of "have-nots"—states that are theoretically part of the nominating process but are denied the chance to hold a meaningful contest.

The clustering of state contests early in the schedule is more than just a problem of low turnout in the late contests. It also creates a "silent spring" that affects all Americans, whatever their state of residence. Once the nominations are settled by Super Tuesday, the campaign loses much of its appeal. The conventions are still months away, but the primary races are effectively over, and people lose interest. In 2000, for example, the number of people paying close attention to the campaign was sliced in half within a month after Bush and

Gore locked up the party nominations on Super Tuesday. The same thing happened in 1996. Election interest declined sharply after Dole's win on Super Tuesday and did not rise again until the national party conventions in August.[38] In the 1970s, when the nominating races ended later, citizens remained interested for a longer period. In 1976, for example, interest rose month by month as the campaign moved toward the final early June contests in California, Ohio, and New Jersey.[39] The cost of front-loading, then, also includes a decline in voters' attention to the election, which affects how much they will come to know about the candidates and the issues.

Something better is needed. Participation ought not to rest so heavily on the particulars of a given election. A presidential campaign is America's best chance to mobilize and engage the public. It is an opportunity that ought not to be wasted.

Notes

1. *The 14th Biannual Youth Survey on Politics and Public Service*, Institute of Politics, John F. Kennedy School of Government, Harvard University, April 2008.

2. Quoted in Paul T. David, Ralph M. Goldman, and Richard C. Bain, *The Politics of National Party Conventions* (Washington: Brookings, 1960), p. 296.

3. The Democratic turnout in the 1968 presidential primaries was 24.3 percent of the voting-age population. By comparison, the average Democratic turnout for the 1980–2004 period was half that level. See Curtis Gans, "2004 Primary Turnout Low," report of the Center for the Study of the American Electorate, Washington, March 9, 2005, p. 11.

4. *Mandate for Reform* (Washington: Democratic National Committee, 1970), p. 33.

5. For an overview of the McGovern-Fraser Commission's objectives, see Austin Ranney, *Participation in American Presidential Nominations, 1976* (Washington: American Enterprise Institute, 1977), pp. 1–6.

6. William Crotty and John S. Jackson III, *Presidential Primaries and Nominations* (Washington: Congressional Quarterly Press, 1986), pp. 44–49.

7. Hugh Winebrenner, *The Iowa Precinct Caucuses: The Making of a Media Event*, 2nd ed. (Iowa State University Press, 1998).

8. Ranney, *Participation in American Presidential Nominations, 1976*, p. 20.

9. Austin Ranney, "Turnout and Representation in Presidential Primary Elections," *American Political Science Review* 66 (March 1972): 29.

10. Ranney, *Participation in American Presidential Nominations, 1976*, p. 20; Austin Ranney, ed., *The Elections of 1980* (Washington: American Enterprise Institute, 1981), pp. 353, 364; Jack Moran and Mark Fenster, "Voter Turnout in Presidential Primaries," *American Politics Quarterly* 10 (October 1982): 453–76.

11. Thomas E. Patterson, *The Vanishing Voter* (New York: Vintage, 2003), p. 4.

12. Author's calculation based on available 1976 turnout data.

13. Ranney, *Participation in American Presidential Nominations, 1976,* pp. 26–35.

14. Ibid.

15. Crotty and Jackson, *Presidential Primaries and Nominations,* p. 84.

16. Donald R. Matthews, "Winnowing," in *Race for the Presidency,* edited by James David Barber (Englewood Cliffs, N.J.: Prentice-Hall, 1978), p. 65.

17. Gans, "2004 Primary Turnout Low," p. 5.

18. William G. Mayer, "The Basic Dynamics of the Contemporary Nominating Process," in *The Making of the Presidential Candidates 2004,* edited by William G. Mayer (Lanham, Md.: Rowman and Littlefield, 2004), p. 91.

19. Gans, "2004 Primary Turnout Low," p. 6.

20. Example from William G. Mayer and Andrew E. Busch, *The Frontloading Problem in Presidential Nominations* (Washington: Brookings, 2004), pp. 83–84.

21. Ibid., p. 84.

22. Committee for the Study of the American Electorate (CSAE), "2008 Primary Turnout Falls Just Short of Record Nationally, Breaks Record in Most States," May 19, 2008, p. 1.

23. CNN exit polls, March 2, 2004.

24. Committee for the Study of the American Electorate, "The Primary Turnout Story: Presidential Races Miss Record High," October 1, 2008, p. 1. Figure was derived by calculating the percentages for each state, summing these percentages, and then dividing this sum by the number of states. In other words, the percentage is the average for the state primaries as opposed to an average based simply on voters, which would, for example, have weighted California voters far more heavily than New Hampshire voters.

25. Turnout in contested primaries before the 1972 McGovern-Fraser rules were implemented was also higher than in 2008, but the earlier rates are not fully comparable. There were only a few contested primaries in most election years in the earlier period because candidates for strategic reasons selectively entered or avoided particular primaries. Accordingly, the 1972 election is appropriately regarded as the start of the "modern" era.

26. Committee for the Study of the American Electorate, "2008 Primary Turnout Falls Just Short of Record Nationally," p. 1. The CSAE figures are the basis for the individual state percentages presented in this paragraph.

27. This section is based only on primary election participation. CNN conducted exit polls, which are the basis for the analysis, in only two caucus states, Iowa and Nevada. Exit polls were conducted in more than thirty of the primary election states.

28. See, for example, James L. Lengle, *Representation and Presidential Primaries: The Democratic Party in the Post-Reform Era* (Westport, Conn.: Greenwood Press, 1981); Barbara Norrander, "Explaining Individual Participation in Presidential Primaries," *Western Political Quarterly,* vol. 44 (September 1991), pp. 640–55.

29. It is important to note that the demographic figures cited here are based on state averages, treating each state equally regardless of its population. Thus the percentages refer not to the U.S. population as a whole, but to the average for the primary states. The figures were calculated for each state and the state averages were then determined.

30. For this and subsequent references to the total turnout (Republican and Democratic turnout combined) in state primaries, the data exclude the Michigan and Florida primaries, which were not sanctioned by the Democratic national party, and also exclude those states that held a primary in one party only. For example, Idaho Democrats participated through the caucus method while Idaho Republicans voted in a primary.

31. See Warren E. Miller and J. Merrill Shanks, *The New American Voter* (Harvard University Press, 1996).

32. Austin Ranney, *Curing the Mischiefs of Faction: Party Reform in America* (University of California Press, 1975), p. 153.

33. Local election turnout is harder to track than federal or statewide election turnout because there is no central recording administration. However, numerous localities claimed to have set record lows in 2007 and hardly any reported an upswing in voter participation.

34. Committee for the Study of the American Electorate, "2008 Primary Turnout Falls Just Short of Record Nationally," p. 1.

35. Quoted in "Heavy Campaigning Leads to Better Informed Citizens," *Political Standard* (a publication of the Alliance for Better Campaigns), April 2000, p. 6.

36. Example from William G. Mayer, ed., *In Pursuit of the White House 2000* (New York: Chatham House, 2000), pp. 60–63.

37. Rachel Kapochunas, "Florida Double-Dares National Parties as Jan. 29 Primary Date Is Enacted," *New York Times* website, May 21, 2007.

38. Patterson, *The Vanishing Voter*, p. 113.

39. Thomas E. Patterson, *The Mass Media Election* (New York: Praeger, 1980), p. 68.

KATHLEEN HALL JAMIESON *and*
BRUCE W. HARDY

4

Media, Endorsements, and the 2008 Primaries

Endorsements of candidates were a fixture of the 2008 presidential primary campaign, just as they have been in past primaries. Most research has focused on how newspaper endorsements and statements of support made by prominent political figures affected voting and the outcome of the nominating process. Studies of the effects of newspaper endorsements have produced mixed results. Some have found that newspaper endorsements may influence up to 5 percent of the vote.[1] Others conclude that newspaper endorsements have little[2] or no effect at all on the vote,[3] or only an effect on those less engaged in politics.[4]

Two recent studies of the role of endorsements in the nominating process found significant effects. One that examined "all publicly reported endorsements in a broad range of publications" found that "trial-heat" (head-to-head) poll results and endorsements "are almost equally important predictors of primary outcomes;[5] a second concluded that such polls and endorsements significantly predict votes in both parties during the primaries.[6] Endorsements by groups and unions have been shown to drum up enthusiasm among their members;[7] and when an organization or group stands with a candidate, its members are more likely to embrace the endorsee.[8]

The effects of endorsements should be more pronounced in primary campaigns in which voters confront candidates about whom they know comparatively little.[9] Primaries are intraparty contests where party cues do not reveal important distinctions among candidates. Political communication during this time has a unique opportunity to influence independents and party identifiers alike.

In the 2008 primary season, endorsements abounded. Senator Barack Obama was championed by fellow Democrats Senator Edward Kennedy, Senator Patrick Leahy, Senator Claire McCaskill, Kansas governor Kathleen Sebelius, Senate Majority Leader Tom Daschle, Senator John Kerry, Senator Chris Dodd, former New Jersey senator Bill Bradley, New Mexico governor Bill Richardson, former senator and presidential candidate John Edwards, Caroline Kennedy Schlossberg, and Oprah Winfrey, among others. Obama also received union endorsements from the National Brotherhood of Teamsters (1.4 million members), the American Federation of Government Employees (600,000 members), and the Service Employees International Union (1.4 million members), as well as the Internet-based advocacy group MoveOn.org. The newspapers supporting Obama's candidacy included: the *Boston Globe*, the *Chicago Tribune*, and the *Atlanta Journal-Constitution*.

The candidacy of Senator Hillary Clinton was shored up by endorsements as well. Those in her column included Robert F. Kennedy Jr., former Maryland lieutenant governor Kathleen Kennedy Townsend, former vice president Walter Mondale, Ohio governor Ted Strickland, Pennsylvania governor Ed Rendell, Senator Bill Nelson, former secretary of state Madeleine Albright, U.S. Representative John Murtha, former Nebraska governor Bob Kerrey, the American Federation of State, County, and Municipal Employees (AFSCME) (1.4 million members), and the American Federation of Teachers (AFT) (1.4 million members). Major papers backing Clinton included the *New York Times*, the *Des Moines Register*, and the *Kansas City Star*.

Whereas the ideological signals from the Democratic left, in the form of endorsements of Obama by Senator Kennedy and the liberal advocacy group MoveOn.org, were clear, the signals to conservatives from the right were less so. National Right to Life endorsed Tennessee Republican Fred Thompson. Former New York mayor Rudy Giuliani garnered the support of former presidential contender and conservative religious leader Pat Robertson. Another right-of-center religious leader, Bob Jones III, supported former Massachusetts governor Mitt Romney. And Jerry Falwell Jr. signed on with former Arkansas governor Mike Huckabee. This set of mixed messages from the right signaled the fact that conservatives were clearer about which candidates they opposed than they were about which they favored. None of these endorsers regarded Senator John McCain as a true conservative. Discussion among conservatives centered on which candidate could best appeal to the base created by the candidacy of Ronald Reagan in 1980. The central focus on ideology on the Republican side increased the visibility of endorsements in the media.

During the presidential primaries, candidate endorsements are major campaign events that generate media coverage. In 2008, for example, Senator Kennedy's endorsement of Senator Obama and the endorsement of Senator Clinton by the children of Robert Kennedy received substantial attention from news media, as did the endorsement of Obama by President John F. Kennedy's daughter, Caroline. Greater awareness of endorsements among the electorate is a direct result of media coverage.[10]

The effect of an endorsement can ripple across the pool of alternative contenders as well. A Pew Center for the People and the Press report assessing media effects in 2004 found that endorsements by newspapers "dissuade as many Americans as they persuade."[11] In 2008, a report by the Annenberg Public Policy Center found very small net effects of endorsements, in part because they have the capacity to pull in *and* push away voters.[12] The National Annenberg Election Study revealed, for example, that of those polled between January 25 and February 18, 2008, 7 percent of Americans said that the *New York Times* endorsement of John McCain made them more likely to support the Arizona senator, yet 6 percent said it made them less likely to do so, leaving a net gain of 1 percent. A large majority (83 percent) of respondents reported that knowing of the endorsement made no difference in their level of support.

Although most scholars are interested in a direct effect on voters' intentions, endorsements can be influential in indirect ways as well. When the ideology of an endorser is clear, statements of support or opposition can signal the endorsed candidate's, or referendum's, political bent. This allows voters to make sense of complex ballot resolutions by simply identifying those who back the messages.

The endorsement heuristic was at play in the 2000 primaries when National Right to Life's endorsement of George W. Bush affected perceptions of both Bush and McCain. In the days leading up to the South Carolina primary, National Right to Life endorsed Bush, and the national and state-run Right to Life political action committee ran advertisements painting his main opponent, McCain, as pro-choice. The endorsement of Bush by National Right to Life provided pro-choice voters with a clue, albeit an inaccurate one, that McCain was closer to their point of view and guided pro-life voters toward Bush. National Annenberg Election Survey data showed that in both South Carolina and Michigan, two key primary states, those who want abortion to be legal in all or most circumstances were likely to favor McCain; those who think abortion should be illegal in most or all circumstances were more likely to vote for Bush.[13]

As we outline in this chapter, during the primaries of 2008, endorsements by the *New York Times*, conservatives such as talk radio host Rush Limbaugh and religious leader Dr. James Dobson, and liberal individuals such as Edward Kennedy and organizations such as MoveOn.org influenced public perceptions of the ideological positions of the endorsees.

To determine how the public learns about endorsements and when and how they affected perception of a candidate's ideology in the primaries of 2008, in this essay we focus on three questions: In the primaries of 2008, did media consumption predict voters' knowledge of endorsements? Did endorsements affect voters' perceptions of the political identities of the candidates? And how, if at all, does the effect of endorsements influence people's preferences?

We detail a pathway of influence from media use to knowledge of endorsements to perceptions of the candidates and show how such perceptions influenced opinions about the major candidates during the 2008 primaries. We predicted that media consumption increases people's knowledge of endorsements; that an endorsement influences their perceptions of the candidate by pulling the endorsed in line with the ideological positions of the endorsers and pushing the ideological perceptions of the unendorsed candidate from that of the endorsers; and that perceptions of the ideological identities of the candidates influence vote preferences.

Endorsements and Media Coverage

The effects of endorsements should be more pronounced when few issue distinctions separate the major contenders of one party, as was the case in the 2008 Democratic primaries, or when the ideological identity of the candidates was a central issue, as it was in the Republican contest. The 2008 Democratic primaries provided an environment in which the major contenders agreed on most policy matters. "On the major issues, there is no real gulf separating the two," wrote the *New York Times* about Democratic presidential contenders Clinton and Obama in January 2008. "They promise an end to the war in Iraq, more equitable taxation, more effective government spending, more concern for social issues, a restoration of civil liberties and an end to the politics of division of George W. Bush and Karl Rove."[14] When voters lack knowledge about policy differences among candidates, the signaling power of well-publicized endorsements should be high.[15]

An endorsement cannot matter if voters do not know about it. Some endorsers communicate directly with those affiliated with them. So, for example, in 2008, MoveOn.org's endorsement of Obama was conveyed to its members via e-mail. But the mass media are the vehicle for communicating to those outside the immediate fold. In 2008, some endorsements generated large amounts of coverage in news and other free media. The embrace of Obama by Oprah Winfrey is a case in point.

We begin by assessing the impact of media use and knowledge of candidate endorsements in the primaries of 2008 by turning to data from the 2008 National Annenberg Election Study (NAES) to measure awareness of nine endorsements made during the 2008 primary period.[16] In this survey, self-identified independents were asked about all endorsements, Democrats were asked only about endorsements of the Democratic candidates, and Republicans were asked only about the Republican candidates. The questions asked were: "Do you happen to know whom [Endorser – for example, Ted Kennedy or *New York Times*] endorsed for the [Democratic/Republican] nomination for president?" Specifically, we asked about:

—Oprah Winfrey, who endorsed Obama (79.2 percent correctly identified the endorsee; January 2 to January 6, 2008; $N = 872$).

—Senator Edward Kennedy, who endorsed Obama (69.5 correctly identified the endorsee; January 28 to February 6, 2008; $N = 1,786$).

—Governor Bill Richardson, who endorsed Obama (58.1 correctly identified the endorsee; March 24 to April 2, 2008; $N = 964$).

—the *New York Times*'s endorsement for the Democratic nomination (Clinton) (28.1 correctly identified the endorsee; January 25 to February 5, 2008; $N = 2,105$).

—the *New York Times*'s endorsement for the Republican nomination (McCain) (26.4 correctly identified the endorsee; January 25 to February 18, 2008; $N = 4,072$).

—Senator Joe Lieberman, who endorsed McCain (22.1 correctly identified the endorsee; January 2 to 6, 2008; $N = 863$).

—Dr. James Dobson, who endorsed Huckabee (20.4 correctly identified the endorsee; February 8 to 18, 2008; $N = 1,861$).

—the United Farm Workers, which endorsed Clinton (16.6 correctly identified the endorsee; February 4 to 11, 2008; $N = 1,479$).

—MoveOn.org, which endorsed Obama (15.8 correctly identified the endorsee; February 4 to 11, 2008; $N = 1,479$).

To test the relationship between media consumption and knowledge of endorsements we analyzed nine logistic regression models that included media use measures for television, newspaper reading, and Internet use (see table 4-1).[17] We also included age, gender, race, education, and political ideology as controls. As table 4-1 shows, news media consumption is significantly related to knowledge of endorsements. Only two of twenty-seven relationships between news media use and knowledge of endorsements were

Table 4-1. *Logistic Regressions Predicting Respondents' Knowledge of Candidate Endorsement Endorser/Endorsee*

Item	Oprah Winfrey/ Barack Obama	Edward Kennedy/ Barack Obama	Bill Richardson/ Barack Obama	New York Times/ Hillary Clinton	New York Times/ John McCain	Joe Lieberman/ John McCain	Dr. James Dobson/ Mike Huckabee	United Farm Workers/ Hillary Clinton	MoveOn.org/ Barack Obama
Percentage that correctly identified the endorser	79.2	69.5	58.1	28.1	26.4	22.1	20.4	16.6	15.8
Age n	1.021***	1.044***	1.038***	1.011***	1.010***	1.017***	1.008	1.007	0.991
Gender (female)	0.881	0.777**	0.434***	0.888	0.810***	0.468	1.133	1.018	0.743
Race (black)	1.591	1.101	0.741	1.243	1.229	1.015	0.937	1.195	0.831
Education	1.350***	1.209***	1.178***	1.152***	1.181***	1.108**	1.215***	1.136***	1.202***
Ideology[a]	0.966	0.943	0.973	1.016	1.201***	1.081	1.364***	0.962	0.777**
Television	1.227***	1.138***	1.215***	1.096***	1.114***	1.073**	1.066*	1.143***	1.108***
Newspaper	1.185***	1.083***	1.097***	1.057***	1.065***	1.090***	1.023	1.062**	1.079***
Internet	1.082	1.124**	1.065**	1.069***	1.072***	1.119***	1.052**	1.062**	1.073**
2008 NAES question dates	1/02– 1/06/08	1/28– 2/06/08	3/24– 4/02/08	1/25– 2/05/08	1/25– 2/18/08	1/02– 1/06/08	2/08– 2/18/08	2/04– 2/11/08	2/04– 2/11/08
N	872	1,787	964	2,108	4,071	863	1,858	1,478	1,478
Nagelkerke R^2	0.327	0.265	0.287	0.099	0.124	0.163	0.094	.082	0.133

Source: 2008 National Annenberg Election Survey (NAES).
Notes: Coefficients are odds ratios. *** $p < 0.01$, ** $p < 0.05$, * $p < 0.1$.
a. Conservative coded high.

not statistically significant: newspaper use was not significantly related to knowledge of Dr. James Dobson's endorsement of Huckabee, and Internet use was not significantly related to knowledge of Oprah Winfrey's endorsement of Obama. Television consumption, however, was significantly related to knowledge of all nine endorsements about which we asked.

The relationship between reported television consumption of campaign information during the primaries and knowledge of endorsements is particularly strong for the endorsements that a majority of respondents identified correctly. For example, 79.2 percent of respondents knew that Oprah Winfrey had endorsed Obama. Respondents were 23 percent more likely to know of this endorsement for every additional day that respondents reported getting information from television, controlling for sociopolitical demographic variables. Similar relationships exist for knowledge of Edward Kennedy's and Bill Richardson's endorsements of Obama. More than half of respondents were familiar with their endorsements, and television news use, newspaper reading, and Internet use were all significantly and positively related to recalling that information.

The New York Times endorsements of Senators Clinton and McCain were not as well known as the endorsements by Oprah Winfrey, Senator Kennedy, and Governor Richardson. Yet the three news media use variables in those logistic regression models were significantly and positively related to knowing the name of the candidate endorsed by the New York Times. Media use also predicted whether respondents were aware of Senator Joe Lieberman's endorsement of McCain, Dr. James Dobson's endorsement of Huckabee, the United Farm Workers' endorsement of Clinton, and MoveOn.org's endorsement of Obama. In sum, media consumption is significantly related to knowledge of endorsements in the presence of controls.

Endorsements and Ideological Cues

Endorsements are important because they have heuristic value as predictors of a candidate's ideology. If voters know that certain groups or organizations have endorsed a candidate, they can infer information about the political identity of that candidate. In a primary contest in which few issue distinctions separated Clinton and Obama, the ideological cues implied by endorsements were noteworthy. On February 1, 2008, members of the liberal antiwar advocacy group MoveOn.org voted to give the Illinois senator their group's endorsement. The New York Times reported, "The endorsement by MoveOn.org is the first time the group has weighed in during a Democratic

Table 4-2. *Influence of the Knowledge of MoveOn.org's Endorsement on Respondents' Perceptions of the Democratic Candidates*

Variable	Ideological perceptions of Barack Obama[a]	Ideological perceptions of Hillary Clinton[a]
Age	0.067**	0.059*
Gender (female)	−0.017	0.000
Race (black)	−0.092***	−0.098***
Education	0.193***	0.182***
Ideology[b]	−0.011	0.042
Television	−0.009	0.063**
Newspaper	0.032	0.002
Internet	0.101***	0.095**
Knowledge of MoveOn.org's endorsement	0.065**	0.022
R^2 (percent)	9.2	7.6

Source: National Annenberg Election Study (NAES), conducted from February 4 to 11, 2008; respondents were self-identified Democrats and independents.

Notes: Coefficients are standardized betas: *** $p < 0.01$, ** $p < 0.05$, * $p < 0.1$.

a. Respondents were asked to rate the candidates on a five-point scale ranging from "very conservative" (low) to "very liberal" (high).

b. Conservative coded high.

primary. In a poll of its members, 1.7 million of whom live in the 22 states holding contests next week, Mr. Obama outpaced Mrs. Clinton 70 percent to 30 percent."[18] In accepting the endorsement, Obama acknowledged that it certified his status as an antiwar progressive committed to a new kind of politics. "In just a few years, the members of MoveOn have once again demonstrated that real change comes not from the top-down, but from the bottom-up," noted the Illinois senator. "From their principled opposition to the Iraq war—a war I also opposed from the start—to their strong support for a number of progressive causes, MoveOn shows what Americans can achieve when we come together in a grassroots movement for change."[19]

Such ideological cues can work in two ways: (1) by pulling the ideological perception of the endorsed candidate in line with the ideological perception of the endorser, and (2) by pushing the perception of the unendorsed farther from the perceived ideology of the endorser. Respondents who were aware of MoveOn.org's endorsement of Senator Obama saw him as more liberal than respondents who were unaware of the endorsement (see table 4-2). Controlling for sociopolitical demographic and news media use variables, we see that knowledge of this endorsement influenced perceptions of Obama's ideological dispositions (see table 4-3). Respondents were asked to rate Senator Obama on a five-point scale ranging from "very conservative" to "very liberal." Those who knew about MoveOn.org's endorsement were significantly more likely to see Obama as liberal. Here we see that such knowledge pulls perception of the endorsed candidate into line with the ideological perceptions of the endorser.[20] We did not find, however, that being aware of MoveOn.org's endorsement of Senator Obama pushed perceptions of the ideological dispositions of Senator Clinton toward the conservative end of the ideological spectrum.

Obama also was embraced by Senator Edward Kennedy. Characterized in the press as the "liberal lion" of the Senate, Kennedy had been championing health care reform long before either Clinton or Obama emerged on the national stage. By endorsing the Illinois senator, whose health care plan mandated coverage of children but not of the population as a whole, a distinct point Clinton stressed in debates and ads, Kennedy signaled the credibility of Obama's case that he, like Clinton, stood for universal coverage. The endorsement also underscored the key selling point of the Obama candidacy, his judgment in opposing intervention in Iraq, a position Kennedy had championed in the Senate before Obama's arrival there. Finally, Kennedy's credentials as a stalwart liberal signaled that Obama was ideologically to the left of his main Democratic rival. The ideological telegraphy of that endorsement had the potential to give Obama the advantage of identification as liberal when he needed it with the party's liberal wing in the primaries. The *New York Times* reported that, "When Senator Edward M. Kennedy endorsed Senator Barack Obama's presidential campaign in January, Mr. Kennedy passed the torch of Democratic liberalism, saying it was 'time again for a new generation of leadership.'"[21]

Interestingly, knowledge of Senator Kennedy's endorsement of Obama appears to have increased the perception that Clinton is more liberal as well, going against our push/pull hypothesis of endorsements (see table 4-3). There are two possible reasons for this finding. First, in his endorsement speech for Obama on January 28, 2008, Senator Kennedy did not attack Clinton. In fact he started his speech with, "But first, let me say how much I respect the strength, the work and dedication of two other Democrats still in the race, Hillary Clinton and John Edwards. They are my friends; they have been my colleagues in the Senate. John Edwards has been a powerful advocate for economic and social justice. And Hillary Clinton has been in the forefront on issues ranging from health care to the rights of women around the world. Whoever is our nominee will have my enthusiastic support."[22]

Table 4-3. *Influence of the Knowledge of Senator Edward Kennedy's Endorsement on Respondents' Perceptions of the Democratic Candidates*

Variable	Ideological perceptions of Barack Obama[a]	Ideological perceptions of Hillary Clinton[a]
Age	−0.018	0.028
Gender (female)	−0.063**	−0.037
Race (black)	−0.113***	−0.087***
Education	0.177***	0.200***
Ideology[b]	−0.055**	0.102***
Television	−0.006	0.039
Newspaper	0.067**	0.001
Internet	0.085**	0.083***
Knowledge of Kennedy's endorsement	0.062**	0.107***
R^2 (percent)	10.3	10.1

Source: National Annenberg Election Study (NAES), conducted from January 28 to February 6, 2008; respondents were self-identified Democrats and independents.

Notes: Coefficients are standardized betas: *** $p < 0.01$, ** $p < 0.05$, * $p < 0.1$.

a. Respondents were asked to rate the candidates on a five-point scale ranging from "very conservative" (low) to "very liberal" (high).

b. Conservative coded high.

A second possible reason that knowledge of Senator Kennedy's endorsement is positively related to perceptions of Hillary Clinton as a liberal is that a day after Senator Kennedy made his announcement, the children of Robert Kennedy (Kathleen Kennedy Townsend, Robert F. Kennedy Jr., and Kerry Kennedy) underscored their endorsement of Hillary Clinton in an opinion piece in the *Los Angeles Times*. The simultaneous endorsement of Obama by President John F. Kennedy's brother and daughter propelled both of the former president's liberal family members and their heirs into the news. The Obama campaign's management of the endorsements increased the visibility of both sets of endorsements. As part of the promotional blitz, the Obama campaign doled out interviews to prominent news organizations and placed an op-ed by Caroline Kennedy in the *New York Times*.

In the primaries of 2008, the amount of media coverage attributable to these Kennedy endorsements was increased by the warring op-eds. In the *New York Times*, Caroline Kennedy wrote, "I have never had a president who inspired me the way people tell me that my father inspired them. But for the first time, I believe I have found the man who could be that president—not just for me, but for a new generation of Americans."[23] Writing in the *Los Ange-*

les Times, three of Robert Kennedy's children started their endorsement with: "By now you may have read or heard that our cousin, Caroline Kennedy, and our uncle, Sen. Edward M. Kennedy, have come out in favor of Senator Barack Obama. We, however, are supporting Sen. Hillary Rodham Clinton because we believe that she is the strongest candidate for our party and our country."[24] These endorsements were linked in media reports and created similar identifying signals. The visibility of the two sets of endorsements presumably diminished the likelihood that Senator Kennedy's support for Barack Obama would increase the perception of Hillary Clinton as the more conservative of the two candidates. Our question about people's awareness of Senator Kennedy's endorsement of Obama may also have tapped into people's awareness of Clinton's endorsement by Robert Kennedy's children.

In this case, we do find evidence that perceptions of the endorsee are pulled into line with the ideological stance of the endorser, but we do not find that endorsements have the hypothesized pushing effect. We expect that the push/pull of the ideological perceptions of the candidates will be more pronounced for Republicans because the notion of being a "true conservative," or Reaganesque, appeared in the rhetoric surrounding the GOP 2008 nomination process much more than did the notions of being a "true liberal" in Democratic discussions and news coverage.

During the 2008 primaries, the certifying power of endorsements was on display on the Republican side as well. In the Republican debate of January 24, for example, Senator McCain needed to signal that his original opposition to the Bush tax cuts should be discounted in favor of his 2008 claim that he would make them permanent. He underscored his bona fides as a fiscally conservative supply-sider with an argument from endorsements when, in the January 24 Republican debate, he declared: "I have the support of people like Jack Kemp, people like Phil Gramm, people like Warren Rudman."[25]

Central to the preservation of the ideological enclave of the Republican Party is the voice of conservative radio host Rush Limbaugh.[26] On his radio show, Limbaugh regularly argued against the candidacies of John McCain and Mike Huckabee and tepidly endorsed Mitt Romney. Limbaugh told his audience of 13.5 million that "McCain has been the author of the first official intervention in the first Amendment in this nation's history: McCain-Feingold" (January 7, 2008), and made the case that McCain was a barely disguised liberal. "McCain-Kennedy," intoned Limbaugh, "the most far-reaching amnesty program in American history. McCain-Lieberman—the most onerous and intrusive attack on American industry . . . in American history. McCain-Kennedy-Edwards—the biggest boon to the trial bar since the tobacco settlement" (January 11, 2008). About Huckabee, Limbaugh noted, "You can't trust what he says, changes his positions over and over, say[s] whatever people want to hear" (January 16, 2008). "Governor Huckabee has reversed course on taxes, on illegal immigration. He has reversed course on law and order" (January 21, 2008). The candidate in the race who elicited Limbaugh's respect in the weeks between the New Hampshire primary and Super Tuesday was Romney. If you wanted to know which candidate "more closely embodies all three legs of the conservative stool," said Rush, "you'd have to say that it's Mitt Romney."

During the period between the New Hampshire primary (January 8, 2008) and Super Tuesday (February 5, 2008), Rush Limbaugh began strongly attacking McCain's conservative credentials. Those assaults coincided with listeners' perception of McCain; those who listened to the talk show host were more likely than the nonlistening population—including those who describe themselves as conservatives—to believe that McCain was a moderate. The importance of this finding is magnified by its unexpectedness. Limbaugh had vigorously opposed McCain's bid for the Republican nomination in 2000 and reiterated his disdain for the Arizona Republican in the years between 2000 and 2008. In other words, one would have assumed that any effect Limbaugh could have on his listeners had occurred long before he ratcheted up his anti-McCain rhetoric during the 2008 primaries.

The conservative talk show host, whose audience is estimated to exceed 13.5 million people, escalated his attacks on the Republican contender in the days before and immediately after McCain's victory in the New Hampshire primary on January 8. As part of his arsenal, Limbaugh repeatedly reminded his listeners that the *New York Times* had endorsed McCain. Unsurprisingly we found that Limbaugh's listeners were more likely to know about the endorsement than conservatives not in his audience. Controlling for gender, race, education party identification, and ideology, Limbaugh listeners were 3.94 times more likely than nonlisteners to know that the *New York Times* had endorsed the Arizona Senator for the Republican nomination (see table 4-4). The *New York Times* is a frequent object of Limbaugh's attack on the "liberal media."

Controlling for sociopolitical demographic and news media use variables, we see that people's knowledge of McCain's endorsement by the liberal-leaning *New York Times* editorial page did influence perceptions of McCain's ideological dispositions (table 4-5). Respondents were asked to rate Senator McCain on a five-point scale ranging from "very liberal" to "very conservative." Those who knew about the *New York Times* endorsement were significantly less likely to see McCain as a conservative.

Table 4-4. *Influence of the Knowledge of* New York Times *Endorsement on Respondents' Perceptions of John McCain*

Variable	Ideological perceptions of John McCain[a]
Age	–0.035
Gender (female)	0.038**
Race (black)	0.001
Education	0.071***
Ideology[b]	–0.029
Television	0.020
Newspaper	–0.009
Internet	0.023
Knowledge of *New York Times* endorsement	–0.056***
R^2 (percent)	2.3

Source: National Annenberg Election Study (NAES), conducted from January 25 to February 18, 2008; respondents self-identified as Republicans and independents.
Notes: Coefficients are standardized betas: *** p <0.01, ** p < 0.05, * p < 0.1.
a. Very conservative coded high.
b. Conservative coded high.

An across-time analysis of 639 Limbaugh listeners and 8,077 nonlisteners surveyed by the 2008 National Annenberg Election Survey shows that Rush Limbaugh effectively defined John McCain for his listeners. As outlined in table 4-6, before the New Hampshire primary about half of Limbaugh's listeners said McCain was a conservative. That number dropped almost 12 percentage points after McCain won in New Hampshire. After January 8, the number of Limbaugh listeners who said McCain was a liberal jumped 9 percentage points. During this period, the political perceptions of McCain among non-Limbaugh listeners remained stable. Table 4-7 displays a regression analy-

Table 4-5. *Logistic Regression Predicting Correct Answer to "Do you happen to know who the* New York Times *endorsed for the Republican nomination for president?"*

Variable	Odds ratio
Gender (female)	0.877
Race (black)	0.854
Education	1.192**
Republican	1.069
Ideology[a]	1.110**
Rush Limbaugh listeners	3.942**

Notes: Nagelkerke R^2 (percent) 11.2; ** p < .01; * p < .05.
a. Conservative coded high.

Table 4-6. *Rating of John McCain's Ideology by Limbaugh Listeners and Non-listeners before and after the New Hampshire Primary*
Percent

Respondents' rating of McCain's views	Rush Limbaugh listeners		Nonlisteners	
	Before N = 205	*After* N = 434	*Before* N = 2,721	*After* N = 5,356
Conservative	50.7	38.9	59.3	58.9
Moderate	33.2	35.9	27.5	27.4
Liberal	16.1	25.2	13.2	13.7

Notes: Before N.H. primary = Dec. 17, 2007 to Jan. 7, 2008; after N.H. primary = Jan. 9 to Feb. 6, 2008.
Source: 2008 National Annenberg Election Survey.

sis of the differential impact of Limbaugh listening before and after the New Hampshire primaries—the 95 percent confidence intervals of the two Limbaugh regression coefficients do not overlap, indicating that Limbaugh had a significant impact on perceptions of McCain's ideological disposition after the New Hampshire primary.

Figure 4-1 plots the average ratings of McCain's ideological views among Limbaugh listeners and nonlisteners over time. Immediately after the New Hampshire primary, Limbaugh listeners begin to shift from their view that Senator McCain is a conservative. These results hold after controlling for gender, race, education, party identification, and respondents' own ideology.

Table 4-7. *Regression Analysis Predicting Respondents' Perception of John McCain's Ideological Views*

Variable	Before New Hampshire primary (Dec. 17, 2007 to Jan. 7, 2008)[a]	After New Hampshire primary (Jan. 9, 2008 to Feb. 6, 2008)[a]
Gender (female)	−.053***	.000
Race (black)	−.058***	.002
Education	.137***	.102***
Republican	−.012**	.029**
Ideology[b]	.000	−.069***
Rush Limbaugh listeners	−.049**	−.113***
R^2 (percent)	2.7	3.0

Source: 2008 National Annenberg Election Survey.
Notes: Coefficients are standardized betas: *** $p < 0.01$; ** $p < 0.05$; * $p < 0.1$.
a. Very conservative coded high.
b. Conservative coded high.

Figure 4-1. *Seven-Day Rolling Average Ratings of John McCain's Ideological Views on a Five-Point Scale Where "Very Conservative" = 5 and "Very Liberal" = 1*

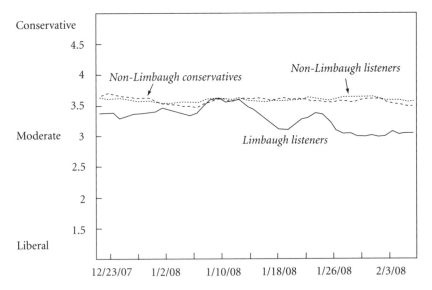

Also on the Republican side, a major endorsement of Mike Huckabee came from Dr. James Dobson, chairman of the board of the conservative group Focus on the Family. Focus on the Family produces an internationally syndicated conservative radio program. Stressing that he was endorsing as a private citizen, Dobson embraced Huckabee and attacked McCain on February 8, 2008, stating that the former Arkansas governor had held "unwavering positions on the social issues, notably the institution of marriage, the importance of faith and the sanctity of human life." At the same time, Dobson reiterated a statement he had issued on Super Tuesday. If McCain were to win the Republican nomination, said Dobson, he would not vote for him in the fall: "His record on the institution of the family and other conservative issues makes his candidacy a matter of conscience and concern for me."[27]

If a voter knew Dr. Dobson as a conservative evangelical Christian and was aware as well that he endorsed Huckabee, this voter might infer that Mike Huckabee's political views are more in line with Dobson's than are the views of the unendorsed contenders. Regression analysis shows that this is what happened (see table 4-8). People's awareness of Dobson's endorsement is positively and significantly related to conservative perceptions of Huckabee's ide-

Table 4-8. *Influence of the Knowledge of Dr. James Dobson's Endorsement on Perceptions of Mike Huckabee's Ideological Views*

Variable	Perceptions of Mike Huckabee
Age	−0.025
Gender (female)	0.081**
Race (black)	−0.015
Education	0.184***
Ideology[a]	0.009
Television	0.046*
Newspaper	0.021
Internet	0.031
Knowledge of Dobson's endorsement	0.176***
R^2 (percent)	9.2

Source: National Annenberg Election Study (NAES), conducted from February 8 to 18, 2008; respondents self-identified as Republicans and independents.

Notes: Coefficients are standardized betas: *** $p < 0.01$, ** $p < 0.05$, * $p < 0.1$.

a. Conservative coded high.

ological disposition. In fact, knowledge of this endorsement produced the second strongest coefficients in the model, behind level of education. Not only did Dobson's endorsement pull perceptions of Huckabee in a more conservative direction, it also pushed perceptions of John McCain, the unendorsed candidate, in a more moderate direction, among self-identified Republicans and among self-identified Protestants. The two regression models outlined in table 4-9 show that, in the presence of controls, both Protestants and Republicans who were aware of Dobson's endorsement of Huckabee were less likely to rate McCain as a conservative than those who were not aware of the endorsement.

Ideological Perceptions and Candidate Favorability

The 2008 primaries demonstrate the capacity of the media to magnify the public's knowledge of endorsements. In both the Democratic and Republican primaries, endorsements by a prominent national newspaper and by prominent liberal and conservative groups and individuals affected voters' ideological placement of candidates. We found evidence during the Republican primaries of 2008 that endorsements can pull voters' perceptions of candidates' ideology in line with the endorser and push perceptions of the unendorsed away.

Table 4-9. *Influence of Knowledge of Dr. James Dobson's Endorsement on Perceptions of John McCain's Ideological Views*

Variable	Self-identified Republicans	Self-identified Protestants
Age	−0.027	−0.023
Gender (female)	0.026	0.065*
Race (black)	0.014	0.003
Education	0.037	0.004
Ideology[a]	0.063*	0.011
Television	0.047	0.033
Newspaper	−0.036	0.058
Internet	0.005	−0.014
Knowledge of Dobson's endorsement	−0.103***	−0.090**
R^2 (percent)	1.6	1.4

Source: National Annenberg Election Study (NAES), conducted from February 8 to 18, 2008.
Notes: Coefficients are standardized betas: *** $p < 0.01$, ** $p < 0.05$, * $p < 0.1$.
a. Conservative coded high.

Such shifts matter because popular perceptions of the ideological stances of candidates shape voters' opinions. To show these relationships empirically, we ran three regression models predicting respondents' favorability ratings of Senators Hillary Clinton, Barack Obama, and John McCain.[28] The influence of the candidates' perceived ideology on their favorability among voters depends on the ideological stance of the voter. The predictor variable tapping the influence of each candidate's perceived ideology was constructed by formulating the absolute difference between respondents' perception of the candidates and their own self-placement on a five-point ideology scale.[29] Greater differences in this variable were negatively related to candidate favorability in the presence of controls in all three models (see table 4-10). The more a voter believes a candidate to be ideologically distant from him- or herself, the less favorably he or she feels about the candidate. As demonstrated in this chapter, candidate endorsements have the ability to influence perceptions of the candidates' ideology. By drawing the endorsed into line with the endorser and possibly pushing the unendorsed out of acceptable bounds, these mediated announcements of support for a candidate can influence voter preference.

Much of the past research on this topic focused on the direct influence of knowledge of endorsements on a voter's choice. In this chapter, we have illustrated that the role of endorsements during the primaries can be complex.

Table 4-10. Regression Model Predicting Candidate Favorability

Variable	Senator Hillary Clinton	Senator Barack Obama	Senator John McCain
Age	−0.003	−0.033***	0.055***
Gender (female)	0.079***	0.014**	−0.029***
Race (black)	0.029***	0.173***	−0.085***
Education	−0.045***	0.112***	0.030***
Democrat	0.235***	0.108***	−0.119***
Republican	−0.170***	−0.123***	0.155***
Absolute difference between respondent's ideological placement and ideological placement of candidate	−0.360***	−0.367***	−0.254***
R^2 (percent)	39.8	31.1	17.8

Note: Coefficients are standardized betas: *** $p < 0.01$, ** $p < 0.05$, * $p < 0.1$.

Endorsements do much more than simply capture votes. Voters use them as cues about the ideological identities of the candidates.

Notes

1. Robert S. Erickson, "The Influence of Newspaper Endorsements in Presidential Elections: The Case of 1964," *American Journal of Political Science* 20 (1976): 207–33; Sidney Hollander Jr., "On the Strength of a Newspaper Endorsement," *Public Opinion Quarterly* 43 (1979): 405–07; Timothy B. Krebs, "The Determinants of Candidates' Vote Share and the Advantages of Incumbency in City Council Elections," *American Journal of Political Science* 42 (1998): 921–35.

2. Michael G. Hagen and Kathleen H. Jamieson, "Do Newspaper Endorsements Matter? Do Politicians Speak for Themselves in Newspapers and on Television?" in *Everything You Think You Know about Politics and Why You're Wrong,* edited by Kathleen H. Jamieson (New York: Basic Books, 2000).

3. Robert E. Hurd and Michael W. Singletary, "Newspaper Endorsement Influence on the 1980 Presidential Election Vote," *Journalism Quarterly* 61 (Summer 1984): 332–38; Tim Counts, "Effects of Endorsements on Presidential Vote," *Journalism Quarterly* 62 (Autumn 1985): 644–47.

4. John P. Robinson, "Interpersonal Influence in Election Campaigns: Two Step-Flow Hypotheses," *Public Opinion Quarterly* 40 (1976): 304–19.

5. Marty Cohen, David Karol, Hans Noel, and John Zaller, "Polls or Pols? The Real Driving Force behind Presidential Nominations," *Brookings Review* 3 (Summer 2003): 36–39.

6. Wayne P. Steger, "Who Wins Nominations and Why? An Updated Forecast of the Presidential Primary Vote," *Political Research Quarterly* 60 (2007): 91–99.

7. James G. Gimpel, "Packing Heat at the Polls: Gun Ownership, Interest Group Endorsements, and Voting Behavior in Gubernatorial Elections," *Social Science Quarterly* 79, no. 3 (1998): 634–48.

8. Peter F. Burns, Peter L. Francia, and Paul S. Herrnson, "Labor at Work: Union Campaign Activities and Legislative Payoffs in the U.S. House of Representatives," *Social Science Quarterly* 81 (2000): 507–16; Ronald B. Rapoport, Walter J. Stone, and Alan I. Abramowitz, "Do Endorsements Matter? Group Influence in the 1984 Democratic Caucuses," *American Political Science Review* 85 (1991): 193–203.

9. J. David Kennamer and Steven H. Chaffee, "Communication of Political Information during the Early Presidential Primaries: Cognition, Affect, and Uncertainty," *Communication Yearbook* 5 (1982): 627–50; Michael Pfau, Kathleen E. Kendal, Tom Reichert, Susan A. Hellweg, Waipeng Lee, Kyle J. Tusing, and Theodore O. Prosise, "Influence of Communication during the Distant Phase of the 1996 Republican Presidential Primary Campaign," *Journal of Communication* 47 (1997): 6–26; Samuel L. Popkin, *The Reasoning Voter: Communication and Persuasion in Presidential Campaigns*, 2nd ed. (University of Chicago Press, 1994).

10. R. Lance Holbert, "Intramedia Mediation: The Cumulative and Complementary Effects of News Media Use," *Political Communication* 15 (2005): 447–61.

11. See "Pew Internet and American Life Project," 2004 (http://people-press.org/reports/pdf/200.pdf [October 30, 2008]).

12. See "Endorsements Don't Sway the Public—with a Few Exceptions," 2008 (www.annenbergpublicpolicycenter.org/Downloads/Releases/NAES 2008/EndorsementsRelease_March5_final.pdf [October 30, 2008]).

13. Jamieson, ed., *Everything You Think You Know about Politics and Why You're Wrong*.

14. Editorial, "Primary Choices: Hillary Clinton," *New York Times*, January 25, 2008, p. A24.

15. Scott Keeter and Clif Zukin, *Citizen Learning in Presidential Nominations* (New York: Praeger, 1983).

16. The National Annenberg Election Survey (NAES) is conducted each presidential election by the Annenberg Public Policy Center of the University of Pennsylvania. It was the largest academic election survey conducted during the 2008 campaign. It included between 45,000 and 50,000 rolling cross-section telephone interviews (one interview per respondent) and almost 100,000 web interviews (including up to five interviews with the same person) as the campaign evolved. The first web wave began in October 2007; the final interviews were completed following the general election,

November 4, 2008. National Annenberg Election Surveys also were conducted in 2000 and 2004. The 2008 survey, as with past NAES polls, examined a wide range of political attitudes about candidates, issues, and the traits Americans want in a president. It also placed a particular emphasis on the effects of media exposure through campaign commercials and news from radio, television, newspapers, and the Internet. In addition the survey measured the effects of other kinds of political communication, from conversations at home and on the job to various efforts by campaigns to influence potential voters. The data analyzed in this chapter come from the telephone rolling-cross sectional survey and not the web panel.

17. Media use was measured by asking respondents: (1) "Thinking now about the past week, how many days did you see information on broadcast or cable television about the 2008 presidential campaign? This includes seeing programs on television, on the Internet, your cell phone, iPod, or PDA." (2) "Still thinking about the past week, how many days did you read a newspaper for information about the 2008 presidential campaign? This includes reading a paper copy of the newspaper, an online copy, or a newspaper item downloaded on your cell phone, iPod, or PDA." (3) "How many days in the past week did you see or hear information about the 2008 presidential campaign on the Internet; this may include accessing the Internet through your cell phone, iPod, or PDA.

18. Jeff Zeleny and Patrick Healy, "Obama Wins Endorsement of MoveOn.org," *New York Times*, February 2, 2008, p. A12.

19. See "MoveOn Endorsement Throws Progressive Weight behind Barack Obama," MoveOn.org Press Release, 2008 (http://moveon.org/press/pr/obamaendorsementrelease.html [October 30, 2008]).

20. Ibid.

21. Katie Zezima, "Standing in for Kennedy, Obama Embraces Legacy," *New York Times,* May 26, 2008, p. A10.

22. Transcript available at http://my.barackobama.com/page/community/post/samgrahamfelsen/CGVRs.

23. Caroline Kennedy, "A President Like My Father," *New York Times*, January 27, 2008, p. WK18.

24. Kathleen Kennedy Townsend, Robert F. Kennedy Jr., and Kerry Kennedy, "Kennedys for Clinton," *Los Angeles Times,* January 29, 2008, p. A21.

25. John McCain, "Transcript: The Republican Debate," *New York Times*, January 24, 2008.

26. Kathleen Hall Jamieson and Joseph N. Cappella, *Echo Chamber: Rush Limbaugh and the Conservative Media Establishment* (Oxford University Press, 2008).

27. See "Influential Social Conservative, James Dobson, Endorses Huckabee for President," 2008 (Foxnews.com/2008/02/08 [October 30, 2008]).

28. Exact question wording: "Now for each of the following people, please tell me if your opinion is favorable or unfavorable using a scale from 0 to 10. Zero means very

unfavorable, and 10 means very favorable. Five means you do not feel favorable or unfavorable toward that person." "Hillary Clinton," "Barack Obama," "John McCain."

29. Exact question wording: "Generally speaking, would you describe your political views as (1) Very Conservative, (2) Somewhat Conservative, (3) Moderate, (4) Somewhat Liberal, or (5) Very Liberal?"

WILLIAM G. MAYER

5

Superdelegates:
Reforming the Reforms Revisited

"In the future everyone will be world-famous for fifteen minutes."
—Andy Warhol, 1968

Had Andy Warhol been a political scientist studying the presidential nomination process, he might have reformulated his oft-quoted dictum to read: Every delegate selection rule, no matter how arcane, will become world-famous in at least one nomination contest. Every four years, the Democratic and Republican national parties each promulgate a long and detailed set of rules governing the composition and selection of national convention delegates. In general, these rules are carefully studied by a very narrow slice of campaign managers, consultants, political activists, and reporters, while the vast majority of Americans—even those who follow politics rather closely—remain entirely unaware of them. Yet every so often the special circumstances of a particular nomination race make one of these rules unexpectedly significant and controversial. Suddenly, it becomes apparent that one of these rules might have a critical impact on who will win a party's presidential nomination—and that not everyone approves of the rule. This in turn sets off a mad scramble among the nation's reporters and commentators to explain how the rule works and why in the world it was ever created.

In 2008 it was the superdelegates' turn in the spotlight. In mid-February, millions of ordinary voters and even many campaign reporters suddenly realized that there was a special class of delegates who were not selected in primaries or caucuses, who were not pledged in advance to vote for a particular candidate—and who might well hold the balance of power in the tightly contested race between Hillary Clinton and Barack Obama. This chapter provides a broad overview of the whole superdelegate issue: What are superdelegates, who fits into this select group, why was this class of delegates created, and what role have they played in past nomination contests?

Besides their role in the 2008 Democratic nomination race, superdelegates merit our attention for another reason. The contemporary era in presidential nominations, according to almost all scholars and commentators, began in the late 1960s and early 1970s, when a special Democratic commission, the Commission on Party Structure and Delegate Selection, entirely rewrote the rules used by that party to select its national convention delegates. The new rules were instantly controversial, and over the next decade and a half numerous attempts were made to "turn back the clock"—to reform the reforms. Yet surprisingly little came from all the clamor. In the end, most of the new rules were left untouched; in a few cases the changes were, if anything, pushed even further in the direction initially sought by party reformers.[1]

The most conspicuous exception—indeed, perhaps the only real exception—is superdelegates, which were added to the Democratic rules in 1982 in an effort to make sure that more party leaders and elected officials served as national convention delegates. Two and a half decades after their creation, when there is once again widespread criticism of the presidential nomination process, it is worth taking a close look at this important episode in the recent history of party reform.

What Are Superdelegates?

Superdelegates—or unpledged party leaders and elected officials, as they are formally designated in the Democratic Party's national rules—are automatic or ex-officio delegates. That is to say, they become delegates to the Democratic National Convention not by winning these slots in primaries and caucuses, but because they hold a leadership position in government or in the formal party organization. In 2008 the superdelegates were of five basic types:[2]

—all members of the Democratic National Committee;

—all Democratic members of the U.S. House of Representatives and the U.S. Senate;

—all Democratic governors;

—all former Democratic presidents and vice presidents, former Democratic majority leaders of the Senate, former Democratic speakers of the House, and former chairs of the Democratic National Committee—a group sometimes referred to as "distinguished party leaders";

Table 5-1. *Number and Composition of Superdelegates at the 2008 Democratic National Convention*

Superdelegate type	Number	Percent
Democratic National Committee members	441	10.0
U.S. senators and representatives	280	6.3
Governors	27	0.6
Distinguished party leaders	23	0.5
Add-on unpledged	82	1.9
Total	853	19.3

Source: *2008 Democratic National Convention—Delegate/Alternate Allocation,* provided to the author by the Democratic National Committee and updated to reflect restoration of the Florida and Michigan delegates.

—a small number of unpledged "add-on" delegates, based on the number of votes each state had on the national committee.[3]

In total, as shown in table 5-1, superdelegates accounted for 853 votes at the 2008 Democratic national convention, or about 19 percent of the total convention votes.

The Origin of the Superdelegate Rule

Like most of the distinctive features of the contemporary presidential nomination process, the story of superdelegates begins with the Democratic Party reforms of the late 1960s and early 1970s. During the bitter and divisive Democratic convention of 1968, partly as a concession to the opponents of Hubert Humphrey, the delegates approved a vaguely worded resolution that, as eventually interpreted, authorized a commission to rewrite the delegate selection rules for the 1972 convention. Though commissions are often dismissed as a way of "studying" a problem in order to avoid acting on it, the Commission on Party Structure and Delegate Selection—more commonly known as the McGovern-Fraser Commission, for the two men who served as its chairmen—met or even exceeded the expectations of its most fervent supporters. In just four years, the commission succeeded in putting together a comprehensive set of recommendations that entirely recast the ground rules for delegate selection, got these recommendations accepted by the Democratic National Committee, and then compelled fifty different state parties to abide by their provisions. The result has been justly described as "the greatest systematic change in presidential nominating procedures in all of American history."[4]

Table 5-2. *Participation of Major Democratic Elected Officials as Delegates at Democratic National Conventions, 1956–84*
Percent

Year	Governors	U.S. Senators	U.S. Representatives
1956	70	69	28
1960	85	72	44
1964	79	72	50
1968	92	67	36
1972	67	35	15
1976	44	18	15
1980	74	14	14
1984	83	62	66

Source: Howard L. Reiter, *Selecting the President: The Nominating Process in Transition* (University of Pennsylvania Press, 1985), table 4.5, p. 66.

The broad charge to the McGovern-Fraser Commission was to ensure that "all Democratic voters" had a "full, meaningful and timely opportunity to participate" in the selection of national convention delegates.[5] The commission, whose membership and staff substantially underrepresented party regulars,[6] interpreted this to mean, among other things, that delegate selection rules should no longer give any kind of privileged role or special advantages to party leaders or long-time party activists. One of the commission's new delegate selection guidelines (C-2) explicitly banned automatic or ex-officio delegates. Other rules prohibited proxy voting (B-1) and nonpublic slate-making procedures (C-6), and set severe limits on the number of delegates that could be chosen by state party committees (C-5).[7]

The net effect of these rules was a sharp decline in the presence of major Democratic officeholders at the party's national conventions.[8] Table 5-2 shows figures compiled by political scientist Howard Reiter on the percentage of Democratic governors, U.S. senators, and U.S. representatives who served as convention delegates.[9] All three time-series show a significant drop-off between 1968 and 1976. For example, from 1956 to 1968, on average 70 percent of the Democratic members of the U.S. Senate were voting delegates at the national convention. But this number fell to 35 percent in 1972, and then to 18 percent in 1976.

For reasons that are explored more fully later in this chapter, many Democrats and nonpartisan commentators believed that the reduced number of elected officials and party leaders serving as convention delegates was negatively affecting the workings of the presidential nomination process as well as the Democratic Party's performance in government. Between 1973 and 1986, the Democratic Party established a regular series of reform commissions to reconsider, revise, and/or extend the work of the McGovern-Fraser Commission. In 1977 and 1978 the Commission on Presidential Nomination and Party Structure (the Winograd Commission) was the first to take up the issue of party leader participation. After decisively voting down a proposal that would have given automatic delegate slots to a sizable list of party and elected officials, the commission settled on a considerably more restrained proposal. Specifically, the Winograd Commission recommended—and the Democrats incorporated into their 1980 delegate selection rules—the creation of a new category of delegates, called *pledged* party leaders and elected officials.[10] The size of each state's convention delegation was increased by 10 percent, with the additional seats filled by various types of party leaders. "Priority of consideration" was to be "given to, among others, Democratic Governors, followed by State Party Chairs and Vice Chairs and other members of the Democratic National Committee, United States Senators and United States Representatives." But—and this was the key point—these new delegates all had to indicate in advance (in writing) which of the announced presidential candidates they intended to support, a pledge that was binding at the national convention unless the candidate specifically released them from it. Moreover, the pledged party leader and elected official seats were to be allocated among the presidential candidates in the same percentages as the delegates who had been selected in the state's primary or caucus-convention system.[11]

This rule, in slightly modified form, is still part of the Democrats' delegate selection process. To clarify how the new rule worked, suppose there were a state that had 100 ordinary or "base" delegates and that these delegates were chosen via a primary, with the result that Jimmy Carter won sixty delegates and Edward Kennedy received forty. That state would get ten pledged party-leader delegates (10 percent of 100), six of whom would have been pledged to support Carter, four to vote for Kennedy.

This system does not entirely preclude the selection of uncommitted party-leader delegates. If there were an uncommitted option on the state primary ballot and enough people checked it or pulled the appropriate lever, some of the party-leader delegates might go to the convention uncommitted. But most voters are unwilling to take the trouble to vote in a primary or attend a caucus just to indicate that they are still undecided, with the result that, except in unusual circumstances, only a tiny percentage of the primary or caucus vote is cast for "uncommitted." On average, between 1980 and 2004, just 2.7 percent of the total Democratic primary vote was uncommitted.[12]

In practice, then, party leaders and elected officials could take advantage of these new delegate slots only if they were willing to commit to one of the major presidential candidates well in advance of the national convention— something that many elected officials in particular were reluctant to do in hotly contested, divisive races. Party leaders also had to hope that the voters in their state shared their candidate preference in sufficient numbers. If all of a state's major elected officials endorsed Jimmy Carter but Edward Kennedy won the primary, many of these officials would go without convention seats. Notice finally that while the new rule might have enabled more party leaders to become delegates, it prevented these new delegates from having any impact at all on the outcome of the presidential nomination contest. The preferences of the party-leader delegates were required to be exactly the same as those of the delegates selected in primaries and caucuses—so it was the primaries and caucuses that *completely* determined which candidate prevailed.

The data in table 5-2 suggest that the Winograd Commission's reforms had only a limited impact on the number of party leaders and elected officials at the 1980 Democratic convention. Although there *was* an increase in the number of Democratic governors in attendance (all twenty-three of the governors at the 1980 convention were elected as part of the 10 percent add-on),[13] the percentages of U.S. senators and representatives actually declined a bit between 1976 and 1980.

Had the Democrats won the 1980 presidential election, it is possible that they would have rested content with the Winograd Commission's timorous handiwork. As the subsequent narrative makes clear, the notion of awarding automatic delegate slots to major party leaders never fit very well with the egalitarian, participatory ethos that has been dominant in the contemporary Democratic Party. The outcome of the 1980 elections, however, created a set of conditions that were almost uniquely favorable to pushing the counter-reforms a critical step further. The very scale of the Democratic debacle—they lost not only the presidency in 1980, but also thirty-three seats in the House of Representatives and control of the Senate for the first time in twenty-six years—set off a mad scramble for "party renewal" in every direction. In particular, Jimmy Carter's overwhelming defeat by a Republican candidate once widely thought to be unelectable seemed to confirm all of the critics' worst fears about the system wrought by McGovern-Fraser. Carter had won the 1976 Democratic nomination in spite of a notable lack of previous governmental experience and a conspicuous lack of support among other Democratic leaders, even his fellow governors. And just as the skeptics had predicted, Carter spent the next four years giving the impression of a man who was simply out of his depth, who however personally decent and intelligent he might have been, never gave the sense that he had mastered the job of being president. The way to remedy this problem, according to many observers, was to incorporate a greater element of "peer review" into the presidential nomination process: to give other elected officials and party leaders a greater voice in selecting the party's presidential standard-bearer. The left wing of the Democratic Party, which might otherwise have resisted the attempt to roll back past reforms, was further weakened by the 1980 congressional elections, which had sent a large number of great liberal icons (including George McGovern) into political retirement.

It was against this background that in July 1981, Charles Manatt, the new chairman of the Democratic National Committee, announced the formation of the party's fourth nomination reform commission in twelve years: the Commission on Presidential Nomination, better known as the Hunt Commission, for its chairman, Governor James B. Hunt Jr., of North Carolina.[14] Both Manatt and Hunt strongly supported making special efforts to increase the participation of party leaders. As the commission's staff director would later note, both men "stressed in all of their early announcements that this item would head the commission's agenda."[15] (The commission's formal mandate merely said that "the role and number of Party and elected officials in the nominating process" was one of ten issues for the commission to consider.)[16] At one point, indeed, Hunt, the AFL-CIO, and the Association of Democratic State Chairs all endorsed a plan in which 30 percent of the 1984 convention seats would have been set aside for uncommitted party-leader delegates.

But this sweeping proposal ran into opposition, partly on philosophical grounds, even more from feminists, who pointed out that most party leaders were men, and that even if more women were included among the pledged delegates, the uncommitted delegates, who might in some instances play a critical role in convention bargaining and decisionmaking, would be overwhelmingly male. As was often true of the Democrats' reform commissions, the rule writing was also affected by the ambitions of prospective candidates for the party's next presidential nomination. Allies of Walter Mondale, who expected to benefit from the superdelegate provision, supported the initiative; commission members looking out for the interests of Edward Kennedy opposed it.

So in the end a compromise was reached. As often happens with a compromise, the final rule was complicated. "Approximately 550 slots" were to be allocated to party and elected officials, who were *not* required to indicate which presidential candidate they supported.[17] (This was in addition to the 10 percent add-on of pledged party leaders, which had been retained from the 1980 rules.) The chair and vice chair of every state and territorial party would become automatic delegates, for a total of 114 delegates. Next, the Democratic Caucus of the U.S. House and the Democratic Conference of the U.S. Senate would select up to three-fifths of their members as delegates. The remaining superdelegate slots would be filled by the state parties (no precise mechanism was spelled out), with Democratic governors and "large-city mayors" to receive top consideration, followed by statewide elected officials, state legislators, members of the Democratic National Committee, and the remaining members of Congress (see table 5-3). Though the new type of delegate was referred to in the Democratic rules as "unpledged party and elected official delegates," a critic of the proposal called them "superdelegates" and the latter name stuck.[18]

After taking into account the 1982 election results, which increased the number of Democrats in Congress, there were 568 superdelegates at the 1984 Democratic National Convention, or 14.4 percent of the total convention membership (see table 5-4).

Superdelegate Rules, 1988–2008

Once included in the Democratic delegate selection rules, superdelegates have remained there ever since, though as summarized in table 5-3, the specific rules changed a bit between 1984 and 1996. The thrust of the changes was both to expand the number of superdelegates and to make their selection less discretionary. After 1984, the state parties had little role in determining which specific party leaders and elected officials became superdelegates. Automatic delegate status was extended to all members of the Democratic National Committee in 1988. (The state party chairs and vice chairs who were made superdelegates in 1984, it should be noted, are also members of the national committee.) The proportion of Democratic members of Congress who became superdelegates was increased from three-fifths in 1984 to four-fifths in 1988, and then to 100 percent in 1996. As shown in table 5-4, the result has been to push the superdelegates' presence in the national convention from 14 percent in 1984 to 19 percent in 2008.

Behind these statistics, however, lies a somewhat more tangled story. In the lead-up to the 1988 and 1992 nomination races, a significant effort was made to cut back on the number of superdelegates or eliminate them entirely. In both cases, the drive against the superdelegates was spearheaded by the losing candidates from the previous nomination cycle. In 1984, both Gary Hart and

Table 5-3. *Composition of Democratic Superdelegates, 1984–2008*

1984
- All chairs and vice chairs of state Democratic parties
- 3/5 of the Democratic members of the House and Senate
- Approximately 260 other delegates, chosen by the state parties, with priority given to (a) Democratic governors and large-city mayors; and (b) statewide elected officials, state legislators; members of the Democratic National Committee; members of Congress not previously selected; and other state, county, and local elected and party officials

1988–1992
- All members of the Democratic National Committee
- All Democratic governors
- 4/5 of the Democratic members of the House and Senate
- All former Democratic presidents, former Democratic vice presidents, former Democratic majority leaders of the U.S. Senate, and former Democratic speakers of the U.S. House of Representatives

1996–2008
- All members of the Democratic National Committee
- The Democratic president and vice president, if applicable
- All Democratic members of the House and Senate
- All Democratic governors
- All former Democratic presidents, former Democratic vice presidents, former Democratic majority leaders of the U.S. Senate, former Democratic speakers of the U.S. House of Representatives, and former chairs of the Democratic National Committee
- About eighty other "add-on" delegates selected by the state convention, the state committee, or the state's district-level delegates

---

Source: Compiled from the delegate selection rules for the Democratic National Convention, 1984–2008.

Jesse Jackson were convinced that the rules had given an unfair advantage to Walter Mondale. While the former vice president had received just 38 percent of the primary vote, he nevertheless won a majority of the delegates. Several different party rules came under attack, but prominent among them was the superdelegate provision. As we will see later in this chapter, superdelegates overwhelmingly endorsed Mondale and played an important role in putting him over the top. Jackson wanted to eliminate the superdelegates entirely; Hart more modestly wanted to cut their number approximately in half.[19]

Table 5-4. *Superdelegates at the Democratic National Convention, 1984–2008*

Year	Number of superdelegates	Total number of delegates	Superdelegates as a percentage of all delegates
1984	568	3,933	14.4
1988	645	4,162	15.5
1992	772	4,288	18.0
1996	777	4,298	18.1
2000	802	4,399	18.5
2004	802	4,322	18.6
2008	853	4,419	19.3

Source: Based on delegate allocation data provided by the Democratic National Committee.

In the end, the Mondale campaign agreed to support a report from the convention rules committee that established yet another party reform commission, called the Fairness Commission. Reflecting the divergence in opinion between the Jackson and Hart forces, one resolution approved by the convention required the commission to "examine the prospect of eliminating the . . . category of unpledged official delegates at future conventions" on the grounds that they did not "reflect the demographic composition" of the Democratic electorate. A second resolution said that "the Commission should formulate and the DNC should adopt delegate selection rules" for the 1988 convention "that will take into account . . . the recommendation to reduce the number of unpledged party and elected official delegates to not more than 5 percent of the total delegates . . . plus each State Party Chair and Vice Chair."[20]

The Fairness Commission was duly created in June 1985, but it proved from the beginning to be a considerably more moderate body than Jackson, in particular, had envisioned.[21] Unlike its predecessors, the Fairness Commission was composed largely of members of the Democratic National Committee. Its chairman, Donald L. Fowler of South Carolina, said that "the 1984 rules worked pretty well and there was no reason to change a lot."[22] An adviser to the commission described a "general consensus" among party leaders that "the party has got to stop mucking around with the nominating process."[23] While granting some minor concessions to Jackson on other issues, the Fairness Commission actually recommended a slight *increase* in the number of superdelegates, a recommendation that was easily approved by the full national committee in March 1986 and thus incorporated into the delegate selection rules for 1988.

As things turned out, Gary Hart was not much of a factor in the 1988 Democratic nomination race, his campaign having imploded over a sex scandal in May 1987. But Jackson actually increased his share of the primary vote—from 18 percent in 1984 to 29 percent in 1988—and clearly believed that he deserved more for his showing than a prime-time speaking slot at the convention. Having been burned four years earlier by agreeing to leave matters up to a reform commission, this time Jackson took a more direct approach: he sought a convention rules report that would actually write his favored rules into the Democratic Party charter, thus making it considerably more difficult, though not impossible, to rescind.

Jackson's specific proposal was to deny superdelegate status to all Democratic National Committee members except state party chairs and vice chairs, thereby reducing the total number of superdelegates by about 250. And to the chagrin of many party leaders, the Dukakis campaign agreed to this. The Dukakis campaign's reasoning was similar to the reasoning of the Humphrey campaign in 1968 and the Mondale campaign in 1984. They were looking for a way to appease Jackson and his followers. Jackson sought numerous changes in the party platform—but these changes would have pushed the platform quite far to the left and might therefore have cost Dukakis a considerable number of votes in the general election. By contrast, making concessions on future rules was virtually costless. As *Congressional Quarterly* noted at the time, "Either [Dukakis] would be president in 1992—and therefore a likely favorite for renomination regardless of the rules—or he would be a defeated presidential nominee who would likely be on the political sidelines." David Price, former staff director of the Hunt Commission, had a less flattering description: "Candidates meet their short-term needs but sell out the long-term interests of the party."[24]

Had Jackson chosen to take automatic delegate status away from a different group, his gambit might have succeeded. As it was, Jackson had targeted the one group—the Democratic National Committee—that had the authority to amend the party charter in between conventions.[25] And in September 1989, the DNC did exactly that—voting to make all DNC members superdelegates once again.[26]

A Word about the Republicans

To this point, this chapter has dealt entirely with superdelegates and rules reform debates in the Democratic Party. This is no accident: over the past four decades, changes in the rules of the presidential nomination process were

Table 5-5. *Participation of Major Republican Elected Officials as Delegates at Republican National Conventions, 1956–84*
Percent

Year	Governors	U.S. Senators	U.S. Representatives
1956	72	53	12
1960	94	49	18
1964	88	48	23
1968	88	56	31
1972	80	50	27
1976	69	57	37
1980	74	63	40
1984	87	54	43

Source: Howard L. Reiter, *Selecting the President: The Nominating Process in Transition* (University of Pennsylvania Press, 1985), table 4.6, p. 68.

usually initiated first and more completely in the Democratic Party; certainly the Democrats' internal deliberations have attracted more controversy and media attention. But the Republicans have also made changes in their national delegate selection rules; and though they have left more discretion and control in the hands of state parties, many of the changes are quite similar to those adopted by the Democrats. Particularly relevant to the subject of this chapter, between 1976 and 2000 the Republican delegate selection rules included an explicit ban on ex-officio delegates: "There shall be no automatic delegates to the national convention who serve by virtue of party position or elective office."[27] As shown in table 5-5, however, whether because the Republicans are a less ideologically divided party,[28] or because as the more conservative party they have a greater respect for party elders, the GOP experienced nothing like the Democrats' sharp decline in the presence of party leaders in attendance at their national conventions.[29]

This is where matters stood until the 2000 Republican National Convention, when the party added a provision to its delegate selection rules that reads superficially as if it authorizes superdelegates—and has sometimes been interpreted as such.[30] The regulation in question is Rule 13(a)(2), which grants convention membership to "the national committeeman, the national committeewoman and the chairman of the state Republican Party of, each state and American Samoa, the District of Columbia, Guam, Puerto Rico, and the Virgin Islands."[31] In 2008, after taking into account the penalties incurred by states whose primaries or caucuses preceded the national party's scheduling rules, this gave automatic convention seats to 153 delegates, or about 6 percent of the convention total.

In practice, the RNC convention delegates are a mixture of pledged and unpledged delegates. As David Norcross, who in 2008 was chairman of the RNC's Standing Committee on Rules, explains, the national committee members and state party chairs "are bound by state party rules and are not free to 'freelance' unless state party rule so provides." For example, in 2008, Norcross served as co-chair of the Mitt Romney campaign in New Jersey—but even if Romney had remained an active presidential candidate, Norcross, as the Republican National Committeeman from the Garden State, would have had to vote for McCain at the 2008 convention, because McCain won New Jersey's winner-take-all primary.[32] According to information provided by the Republican National Committee, forty-four states and territories did *not* bind their RNC delegates, though a number allowed their state conventions to adopt binding resolutions.[33]

Have Superdelegates Mattered?

Besides providing a good vantage point for observing the struggles and fault lines of the Democratic presidential party over the last several decades, superdelegates are worth studying because, as noted earlier, they represent the only major attempt that has been made to roll back the Democratic rules reforms of the early 1970s. To what extent have superdelegates succeeded in fulfilling the goals of those who created them?

While increasing the number of party leaders at national conventions was thought to contribute to the presidential nomination process in a number of ways, its principal objective was to reintroduce an element of peer review. The case for peer review was stated particularly well by the late Nelson Polsby in a book that was written while the Hunt Commission was conducting its deliberations:

> Peer review is a criterion which entails the mobilization within the party of a capacity to assess the qualities of candidates for public office according to such dimensions as intelligence, sobriety of judgment, intellectual flexibility, ability to work well with others, willingness to learn from experience, detailed personal knowledge of government, and other personal characteristics which can best be revealed through personal acquaintance.... Since the sort of information involved in peer review is never likely to be spread widely in the population at large, the build-

ing of this criterion into the process of candidate selection presumably entails an enlarged role of experienced politicians. . . . There are some things that Presidents must do that people exposed to candidates only through the intermediation of the news media are unable to inform themselves about.[34]

The nomination system that existed between 1912 and 1968 has often been called the "mixed system," since it tried to incorporate the opinions of both ordinary voters, through primaries, and party leaders, who controlled large blocs of uncommitted convention delegates. The McGovern-Fraser Commission dramatically enlarged the first of these, while almost eliminating the second. In this way, critics charged, the new "plebiscitary system" made possible the nomination of candidates like George McGovern and Jimmy Carter, who had little support among regular party leaders or other elected officials.

How has the system worked since the advent of the superdelegates? A strong case can be made that nothing quite like the triumph of Jimmy Carter has occurred in any Democratic nomination contest since 1980. Whatever else may be said of the Democratic presidential nominees since then, they have been men of substantial experience who were generally well regarded by other party leaders. Whether the Democrats have avoided a repetition of the McGovern problem—nominating a candidate too liberal to be an effective general election candidate—is a more debatable proposition. Their quadrennial protestations notwithstanding, Democratic presidential nominees since 1980 have been, in general, a very liberal group—on some issues, such as abortion and gay rights, considerably to the left of the positions McGovern had embraced. And in some cases—1988 is a good example—that perception probably cost the party a considerable number of votes. The relevant issue here, however, is one of relative rather than absolute placement—and at least according to the American National Election Studies, no subsequent Democratic presidential candidate has been perceived to be as far out of the mainstream as McGovern was.

The more important question is whether the superdelegates had anything to do with either of these outcomes. And there is little reason to think so. A more plausible explanation is that McGovern's and Carter's nominations were the product of a variety of special circumstances, particularly the fact that the postreform nomination process was then new and untried; as the process has become better understood, it has usually given the nomination to the pre-race front-runner.[35]

Putting 2008 aside for the moment, the only Democratic presidential candidate between 1984 and 2004 who may have owed his nomination to the superdelegates was Walter Mondale in 1984. Those who have studied this nomination contest have usually singled out two points where superdelegates gave a critical boost to the Mondale campaign.

The first occurred relatively early in the campaign. In 1984 the selection of the House superdelegates by the House Democratic Caucus was held unusually early in the election year: on January 25 and 26, more than three weeks before the Iowa caucuses. The Mondale campaign, which believed it had substantially more support among House members than any of the other candidates, hoped to use a victory in the caucus as a way of acquiring a burst of momentum that would help push the campaign to further triumphs in Iowa and New Hampshire, as well as enhance its aura of inevitability.[36]

The first part of the plan worked perfectly. Of the 164 House members who were selected as superdelegates, sixty-seven supported Mondale, according to a poll by *Congressional Quarterly*. The former vice president's nearest competitor, John Glenn, was endorsed by just thirteen (fifty-eight were uncommitted).[37] But if Mondale's campaign managers truly hoped that "a House caucus victory [would] carry as much weight as a first-place finish in Iowa or New Hampshire," they were sadly mistaken.[38] Though Mondale breezed to a large victory in Iowa—he had long been favored there—it was Gary Hart, with the support of just five House superdelegates, who scored an upset win in New Hampshire, whose residents seemed notably unimpressed by Mondale's support among party leaders.

Eventually, Mondale recovered from this unexpected setback, and according to some observers it was his continuing lead in the delegate count, based on his dominance among superdelegates, that helped get him through the dark times. As one Democratic official noted several months later, "I don't think Mondale would have survived if he had not had the super delegates. . . . They were one of his anchors at a time he was close to adrift. They allowed him to keep his credibility and his frontrunner status."[39] Well, maybe—but I am skeptical. In going over the press coverage of the three or four weeks after the New Hampshire primary, I can find little evidence that the delegate counts played much role in forming popular or journalistic assessments. Nobody thinks New Hampshire is important because of the delegates available there. What mattered was the fact that Mondale was handily defeated in a state where he had once appeared to be way ahead of the pack—and then lost the Maine caucuses and a nonbinding primary in Vermont. And what finally helped him turn the tide was plainly not the superdelegates, but the fact that he managed to win two major southern primaries on Super Tuesday, closely followed by victories in Illinois, Michigan, and New York.[40]

A far stronger case can be made for the benefit that Mondale derived from superdelegates at the end of the primary season. As Hart and Mondale slugged it out through the long primary season, the Mondale campaign repeatedly claimed that on June 6, the day after the final day of primaries, the former vice president would announce that he had secured the 1,967 delegates necessary to clinch the Democratic nomination. But again, things didn't turn out quite as they expected. The district-level winner-take-all rules used in California turned a narrow Hart victory in the popular vote into a 205 to 72 thrashing in the California delegate count. As of early morning on June 6, Mondale was still about forty votes shy of the majority he had promised.

To get the final necessary votes, the Mondale campaign turned to the siz-able bloc of uncommitted superdelegates. After several hours of frantic phone calling, Mondale acquired just enough commitments to put him seven votes above the critical threshold in the semi-official count maintained by United Press International. As the New York Times headlined a story on the next day's front page, "Democratic Leaders Put Mondale on Top in a Day of Decision."[41]

What would have happened if the superdelegates had not been available? By every objective measure, Mondale would still have been in an advantageous position to win his party's nomination. He had won more primary votes than either Hart or Jackson and had a large lead among ordinary (non-super) del-egates. There were also a small number of state conventions yet to be held, in states thought to be congenial to Mondale.[42] That said, the Mondale cam-paign received a great psychological and political boost from being able to claim the nomination right after the final day of primaries, without opening an extended period of delegate hunting and challenges to the delegates it had already won. In the end, according to a painstaking analysis conducted by political scientist Priscilla Southwell, Mondale won 52 percent of the votes cast by non-superdelegates in the convention balloting held in mid-July. But even that narrow margin occurred only after a lot of delegates originally commit-ted to one of the other candidates had switched to Mondale as the party's nominee apparent.[43]

As ambiguous as the record is in 1984, this is actually the *strongest* case that can be made for the influence of superdelegates on the outcome of a Demo-cratic nomination race. In other years, one candidate so thoroughly domi-nated the primaries, and ended the primary-and-caucus season with such a substantial majority of the delegates, that the superdelegates were pretty clearly irrelevant to the final result. In 1988, for example, Michael Dukakis won 43 percent of the primary vote, compared to 29 percent for Jesse Jackson, his nearest opponent. Even more decisively, of the final thirteen primaries, when Dukakis and Jackson were the only candidates still left in the race, Dukakis won twelve of them, the lone exception being the District of Columbia. By the night of June 8, the last day of primaries, Dukakis had amassed 2,264 delegates, well over the 2,081 needed to clinch the nomination.[44] Not even Jackson, a notoriously poor loser, claimed that he would have won under a different set of rules. Similar stories could be told about the victories of Bill Clinton in 1992, Al Gore in 2000, and John Kerry in 2004.

Did a lead among the superdelegates help any of these candidates in their efforts to win the primaries? The evidence actually suggests just the opposite: After 1984 the tendency was for superdelegates in contested nomination races to remain uncommitted until one candidate had emerged as the popular favorite in the primaries. In 1988, for example, a *Congressional Quarterly* survey of the congressional superdelegates conducted in late April, after Dukakis had clearly established himself as the odds-on favorite to win the Democratic nomination, found that just fifty-one of 250 delegates (20 percent) openly supported Dukakis, 19 percent backed one of the other candidates, and 60 percent were still uncommitted.[45] Similarly, in 1992 the House Democratic Caucus selected the House superdelegates on March 13, three days after Clinton swept to victory in six southern primaries. According to a tabulation by *Congressional Quarterly*, 73 percent of the superdelegates were uncommitted, while just 22 percent endorsed Bill Clinton.

It is against this background that one must analyze the controversy over superdelegates that took place during the Democratic nomination contest of 2008. Superdelegates first started to receive substantial press attention in early February, when an unexpectedly close outcome in the February 5 Super Tuesday voting made clear that there would be no early knockout victory for either Hillary Clinton or Barack Obama, and that the fate of the Democratic nomination might therefore rest with the large bloc of uncommitted party leaders and elected officials. As it happened, this concern with the superdelegates coincided with a string of ten consecutive primary and caucus victories by Obama, which gave him a clear if narrow lead in both the popular vote and the media delegate counts. And this, in turn, led to a critical difference of opinion between the two campaigns over how the superdelegates should approach their task. Obama argued that superdelegates should follow the will of the voters, and that "it would be problematic for the political insiders to overturn the judgment of the voters." Clinton, by contrast, claimed that "superdelegates are, by design, supposed to exercise independent judgment," particularly on such matters as which candidate would make the better chief executive and who would be the stronger general election candidate.[46]

As the campaign progressed, it soon became apparent that most superdelegates sided with Obama on this key issue, that they were reluctant to play a role in the presidential nomination process that would open them to charges of being "antidemocratic." As House Speaker Nancy Pelosi declared on a Sunday morning talk show in mid-March, "If the votes of the superdelegates overturn what's happened in the elections, it would be harmful to the Democratic Party."[47] Recognizing the difficulty to be faced, the Clinton campaign later tried to make the argument that the New York senator had actually received more popular votes than Obama, but this claim required a number of questionable statistical manipulations—such as counting the votes in Michigan, where Obama wasn't even on the ballot, and ignoring caucus states, where Obama had shown particular strength—and as a result never caught on as a valid measure of popular sentiment. Had there been a clear, compelling reason to question Obama's fitness as candidate or president, some superdelegates might have been willing to brave the public furor—but the Clinton campaign was never able to establish such a rationale. Though Obama had a noticeable lack of previous experience in government, Clinton's was not obviously more substantial; and most poll matchups between the Democrats and the likely Republican nominee, John McCain, showed Obama running slightly but consistently better than Clinton.

Whatever the exact mixture of motivations, Clinton's once substantial lead among the superdelegates quickly began to narrow. As shown in table 5-6, in early February, on the eve of Super Tuesday, Clinton had a two-to-one lead among those superdelegates who had announced a preference for one of the candidates. By mid-February, Obama had gained the backing of about forty more superdelegates, while Clinton's support had declined. By early May, most media delegate counters were reporting that a small plurality of the superdelegates now favored Obama. Meanwhile, the remaining primaries were playing out about as expected: Though Clinton won a majority of the primaries held after March 1, including those in Texas, Ohio, and Pennsylvania, the Democratic Party's insistence that states divide their delegates in direct proportion to the primary vote ensured that she made little progress in the now-critical delegate counts. On May 20, the Obama campaign announced that it had secured a majority of the delegates available in primaries and caucuses.[48] With leads among both types of delegates, Obama clinched the Democratic nomination on June 3, and Hillary Clinton, recognizing the inevitable, dropped out of the race and endorsed Obama several days later.

For the purposes of this chapter, what is most noteworthy is the very limited role that superdelegates played in deciding the 2008 Democratic race.

Table 5-6. *Declared Preferences of Democratic Superdelegates in the 2008 Nomination Race*

Date	Clinton	Obama	Undecided or no answer
February 2	204	99	493
February 17	189.5	142.5	463
March 14	221	201.5	372.5
April 6	221	209	364
May 9	264	266	265

Source: Based on delegate counts conducted by the *New York Times*.

Though a plurality of them ultimately supported Obama, it would be misleading to say that, in some meaningful sense, they "gave him the nomination." All the superdelegates really did in 2008 was ratify a decision already reached in the primaries and caucuses. There is no compelling evidence that the superdelegates provided a meaningful, independent source of judgment on the merits of the candidates.

Conclusion

At one level, the moral of this story is that superdelegates have had less impact on Democratic presidential nominations than their proponents had hoped or their opponents had feared. There *is* evidence that superdelegates gave a valuable assist to Walter Mondale in 1984. The six Democratic contests since then, however, would have played out almost exactly as they did even if there had been no superdelegates. All of this helps explain, of course, why so many Americans were, at least until quite recently, entirely unaware that they even existed.

On a larger scale, the most striking lesson of the superdelegate saga concerns the difficulty of turning back the clock on political reform. Institutions are constituted as much by expectations and behavior patterns as by laws and rules; and once those expectations have changed, repealing the laws may not undo the effects of reform. In the current case, the American public, in both parties, has spent the past four decades learning that presidential nominations are determined by their preferences as expressed in primaries and caucuses. The result is that even when a group of uncommitted delegates has the theoretical capacity to influence the outcome of a closely contested nomination race, they are reluctant to exercise that power.

The dominant American view of political parties is that they are essentially public entities and should therefore be controlled by the ordinary processes of democracy. This view was nicely summed up in a letter to the *New York Times* in February 1981, when the Democrats were first beginning to deliberate about the various superdelegate proposals. A member of an earlier Democratic reform commission complained that, however one might defend such proposals in practical terms, they denigrated "the right, in a democratic society, of the people to select the Presidential nominee, a right no less fundamental than the right of the people ultimately to choose the President himself in a national election."[49]

However "self-evident" this proposition might seem to many Americans, most other democracies do not accept it. Elsewhere in the world, political parties tend to be regarded as private organizations, whose internal decisions and procedures are open only to formal party members. In explaining this latter point of view to undergraduates, I have often posed the issue this way: Imagine two people. One is a long-time Democratic Party activist who has worked in her local organization for twenty years, contributed to party causes and candidates, and held a variety of party positions. The other is an 18-year-old college student who became excited about Barack Obama six weeks ago. Should these two people have the same level of influence on the Democratic presidential nomination decision?

It is a striking indication of how far the democratic spirit pervades American political culture that, in all of the recent controversy over the superdelegates, I cannot find a single, sustained attempt to defend the proposition that party leaders and elected officials deserve a larger role in what is clearly the most important decision that American parties make. Absent such a philosophical defense, it was inevitable that superdelegates would decline to render the kind of independent judgment the Clinton campaign had hoped for.

One question that was often asked during the 2008 nomination season concerned the future of superdelegates: After all the controversy, would the Democrats simply decide to abolish them? The answer, it now seems clear, is that they will survive—but only because they have so little real effect.

Notes

1. For example, the McGovern-Fraser Commission guidelines merely *urged* state parties to "adopt procedures which will provide for fair representation of minority views on presidential candidates." See Commission on Party Structure and Delegate Selection [the McGovern-Fraser Commission], *Mandate for Reform* (Washington:

Democratic National Committee, 1970), Guideline B-6, p. 44. By 1992, however, all states were *required* to allocate both district and at-large delegates in accordance with the "expressed presidential preference or uncommitted status of the primary voters or . . . the convention and caucus participants." See *Delegate Selection Rules for the 1992 Democratic National Committee* (Washington: Democratic National Committee, 1990), Rule 12, p. 10.

2. See *Delegate Selection Rules for the 2008 Democratic National Convention* (Washington: Democratic National Committee, 2006), Rule 9.

3. The precise formula is one unpledged add-on delegate for every four votes on the Democratic National Committee. See *Call for the 2008 Democratic National Convention* (Washington: Democratic National Committee, 2007), Article I (I).

4. Byron E. Shafer, *Quiet Revolution: The Struggle for the Democratic Party and the Shaping of Post-Reform Politics* (New York: Russell Sage, 1983), p. 28. For a detailed exploration of the ways that nomination politics has changed since the 1950s and 1960s, see Michael G. Hagen and William G. Mayer, "The Modern Politics of Presidential Selection: How Changing the Rules Really Did Change the Game," in *In Pursuit of the White House 2000: How We Choose Our Presidential Nominees*, edited by William G. Mayer (New York: Chatham House, 2000), pp. 1–55. For an argument that recent changes in the nomination process have been driven by other forces, see Howard L. Reiter, *Selecting the President: The Nominating Process in Transition* (University of Pennsylvania Press, 1985).

5. See Commission on Party Structure and Delegate Selection, *Mandate for Reform*, p. 9.

6. See Shafer, *Quiet Revolution*, chap. 3; and Austin Ranney, "The Political Parties: Reform and Decline," in *The New American Political System*, edited by Anthony King (Washington: American Enterprise Institute, 1978), p. 238.

7. For a complete list of the guidelines, see Commission on Party Structure and Delegate Selection, *Mandate for Reform*, pp. 38–48.

8. It has also been widely assumed that there was a significant, parallel decline in the number of national convention delegates holding formal positions in national, state, and local Democratic Party organizations, but I know of no one who has actually compiled data on this issue.

9. A slightly different set of numbers was reported in Commission on Presidential Nomination and Party Structure (the Winograd Commission), *Openness, Participation and Party Building: Reforms for a Stronger Democratic Party* (Washington: Democratic National Committee, 1978), p. 18. Part of the discrepancy is explained by the fact that Reiter recorded the number of elected officials serving as *delegates*, whereas the Winograd Commission counted the number who served as *delegates or alternates*. But in some cases Reiter's figures are actually higher than those of the Winograd Commission, rather than lower. I use Reiter's data partly because previous experience has taught me to trust his work, partly because his time series extends to 1984, while the Winograd Commission's ends in 1976.

10. This label was not actually used until 1984, when it became necessary for the rules to distinguish the pledged party-leader delegates from the unpledged superdelegates.

11. See Commission on Presidential Nomination and Party Structure, *Openness, Participation and Party Building*, p. 50.

12. Based on data from *Guide to U.S. Elections*, 5th ed., vol. 1 (Washington: CQ Press, 2005). Uncommitted here means all votes cast for "uncommitted," "no preference," uninstructed delegates, and "none of the names shown." Data for the 2008 primaries are not yet available.

To stack the deck even further against the selection of uncommitted party-leader delegates, the Democratic rules in 1980 (and in subsequent years) had at least a 15 percent "threshold" requirement: candidates or uncommitted preferences received no delegates at all unless they received at least 15 percent (and sometimes more) of the vote in a state or congressional district. Thus a statewide uncommitted vote of 5 or even 10 percent might not yield a single uncommitted delegate, unless the vote was concentrated in a relatively small number of districts.

13. Thomas E. Mann, "Elected Officials and the Politics of Presidential Selection," in *The American Elections of 1984*, edited by Austin Ranney (Washington: American Enterprise Institute, 1985), p. 102.

14. My account of the Hunt Commission draws especially on David E. Price, *Bringing Back the Parties* (Washington: CQ Press, 1984), pp. 166–71; Mann, "Elected Officials"; Elaine Kamarck, "A History of 'Super-Delegates' in the Democratic Party," unpublished manuscript; and contemporary coverage in *Congressional Quarterly Weekly Report* and the *New York Times*.

15. Price, *Bringing Back the Parties*, p. 166.

16. For the full text of the mandate, see Commission on Presidential Nomination, *Final Report* (Washington: Democratic National Committee, 1982), pp. 60–61.

17. The phrase "approximately 550 slots" is taken from the Hunt Commission's *Final Report*, p. 6. The precise number of superdelegates was equal to (a) 400, apportioned among the states according to the same formula used to compute their base delegations; plus (b) any additional slots needed to bring the number under (a) in each state equal to the number of Democrats holding the offices of governor, U.S. senator, U.S. representative, and mayor of a city over 250,000 in population; plus (c) two per state for the chair and vice chair of the state party. See *Delegate Selection Rules for the 1984 Democratic National Convention* (Washington: Democratic National Committee, 1982), Rule 7(D).

18. The critic was Susan Estrich, who went on to manage Michael Dukakis's presidential campaign in 1988. See Kamarck, "A History of 'Super-Delegates,'" p. 2.

19. On the 1984 preconvention maneuvering, see "Democratic Nominating Rules: Back to Drawing Board for 1988," *Congressional Quarterly Weekly Report*, June 30, 1984, pp. 1568–69; and Warren Weaver Jr., "Democratic Panel Yields to Jackson Backers," *New York Times*, June 27, 1984, p. A23.

20. The text of both resolutions is reprinted in *The Charter and the Bylaws of the Democratic Party of the United States* (Washington: Democratic National Committee, 1991), pp. 25–29.

21. My account of the Fairness Commission draws on Rhodes Cook, "Many Democrats Cool to Redoing Party Rules," *Congressional Quarterly Weekly Report*, August 24, 1985, pp. 1687–89; Cook, "Democrats Alter Rules Slightly in Effort to Broaden Party Base," *Congressional Quarterly Weekly Report*, October 26, 1985, pp. 2158–59; Cook, "Harmony Is In, Bickering Out as Democrats Consider Rules," *Congressional Quarterly Weekly Report*, March 1, 1986, pp. 509–10; and Cook, "Brushing Aside Complaints, DNC Approves Rules for 1988," *Congressional Quarterly Weekly Report*, March 15, 1986, p. 627.

22. Quoted in Cook, "Democrats Alter Rules," p. 2158.

23. Thomas E. Mann, as quoted in Cook, "Many Democrats Cool," p. 1687.

24. Both quotations appear in Rhodes Cook, "Pressed by Jackson Demands, Dukakis Yields on Party Rules," *Congressional Quarterly Weekly Report*, July 2, 1988, p. 1799. For further coverage of the agreement, see E. J. Dionne Jr., "Democrats Agree on Rules to Select Nominee in 1992," *New York Times*, June 26, 1988, p. A20.

25. See *Charter*, Article 12, Section 1. Charter amendments instituted by the national committee require two-thirds approval, while the national convention can amend the charter by majority vote.

26. See Andrew Rosenthal, "Democrats Vote to Rescind Part of Dukakis-Jackson Pact," *New York Times*, September 29, 1989, p. A12.

27. See *The Rules of the Republican Party*, Rule 32(a)(7).

28. On this point, see William G. Mayer, *The Divided Democrats: Ideological Unity, Party Reform, and Presidential Elections* (Boulder, Colo.: Westview, 1996).

29. See the data in Reiter, *Selecting the President*, table 4.6, p. 68.

30. Unlike the Democrats, the Republican Party's national rules are framed entirely by their national conventions, with no vehicle for changing them in between conventions. Thus the delegate selection rules adopted by the 2000 convention did not apply until the 2004 nomination.

31. See *The Rules of the Republican Party as Adopted by the 2000 Republican National Convention* (Philadelphia: Republican National Convention, 2000), p. 12. The ban on automatic delegates remains in effect for all other delegates. See Rule 15(b)(7). In 2004, the Northern Mariana Islands was added to the list of territories whose top party officials are automatic convention delegates.

32. David Norcross, communication with the author, July 14, 2008.

33. See *Republican National Committee, 2007–2008, Rule No. 15(e) Delegate Selection Overview Summaries for Presidential Primaries, Caucuses, and Conventions* (www.gop.com/images/Press_State_Summaries.pdf [July 17, 2008]).

34. Nelson W. Polsby, *Consequences of Party Reform* (Oxford University Press, 1983), pp. 169–70.

35. For an extended version of this argument, see William G. Mayer, "Forecasting Presidential Nominations," in *In Pursuit of the White House: How We Choose Our Presidential Nominees*, edited by William G. Mayer (Chatham, N.J.: Chatham House, 1996), esp. pp. 60–64.

36. See Diane Granat, "Most House Democrats Lean to Front-Runner Mondale in 'Superdelegate' Selection," *Congressional Quarterly Weekly Report*, January 21, 1984, pp. 89–92.

37. See "Democratic Delegate Count," *Congressional Quarterly Weekly Report*, February 11, 1984, p. 254.

38. Granat, "Most House Democrats," p. 89.

39. As quoted in Mann, "Elected Officials," p. 109.

40. For a good account of Mondale's recovery—an account that does not mention his lead among the superdelegates—see Jack W. Germond and Jules Witcover, *Wake Us When It's Over: Presidential Politics of 1984* (New York: Macmillan, 1985), chaps. 8 and 9.

41. David E. Rosenbaum, "Democratic Leaders Put Mondale on Top in a Day of Decision," *New York Times*, June 7, 1984, p. A1.

42. See Germond and Witcover, *Wake Us*, p. 324.

43. Priscilla L. Southwell, "The 1984 Democratic Nomination Process: The Significance of Unpledged Superdelegates," *American Politics Quarterly* 14 (January–April 1986): 75–88.

44. Based on the delegate count maintained by the Associated Press, as reported in *Congressional Quarterly Weekly Report*, June 11, 1988, p. 1582.

45. Based on data reported in "Members Who Will Be 'Superdelegates' at the Democratic National Convention," *Congressional Quarterly Weekly Report*, April 23, 1988, pp. 1092–93.

46. Both quotes are taken from Adam Nagourney and Carl Hulse, "Neck and Neck, Democrats Woo Superdelegates," *New York Times*, February 10, 2008, p. A1.

47. Quoted in Adam Nagourney and Jeff Zeleny, "For Democrats, Increased Fears of a Long Fight," *New York Times*, March 16, 2008, p. A1.

48. Adam Nagourney and Jeff Zeleny, "Obama Declares Bid 'within Reach' after Two Primaries," *New York Times*, May 21, 2008, p. A1.

49. Letter from Nora Engel, *New York Times*, February 9, 1981, p. A18.

MELANIE J. SPRINGER *and* JAMES L. GIBSON

6

Public Opinion and Systems for Nominating Presidential Candidates

Increasingly, political pundits, policymakers, and the media have critiqued the methods used by political parties in the United States to nominate presidential candidates. The complicated selection process is widely regarded as disorderly, chaotic, and irrational. Commentary about the selection system during the 2008 presidential primary season was no exception. Some have claimed that "the presidential primary system is broken."[1] Specific concerns about the current system center on the short-term and long-term ramifications of front-loading, questioning whether small and unrepresentative states, like Iowa and New Hampshire, should have such a disproportionately influential role in the process, and the seemingly important differences between the qualities a candidate needs to win a primary election and those necessary to secure a victory in November.

Although these concerns bear heavily on the actors directly involved in the primary process, little is known about public attitudes toward these institutional mechanisms. Perhaps rooted in the view that the American mass public is too uninformed to be able to form preferences about such institutions, public opinion scholars have rarely questioned ordinary people about their views regarding presidential nomination systems. That said, decisionmakers and policy reformers often claim that the American public wants to change the system, and in some cases that they prefer Reform X to Reform Y. Yet there is little systematic evidence to support these claims. This is a significant lacuna, especially as reform proposals gain momentum and serious conversations about changing the presidential selection system begin to take shape.

In this chapter we strive to systematically evaluate the preferences of the American public with respect to the presidential primary system, and to assess public opinion about current reform proposals. We are motivated by the possibility that while the candidate selection systems used in the United States are complex, the public may have real, informed opinions about the process. Previous work has suggested that reforming the primary process is not something Americans care about, but the issue has recently become vastly more salient in the wake of grievances during the 2008 elections; furthermore, as serious reform discussions begin to take place, it will be necessary to consult the public. Even if the masses do not appreciate every intricacy of the state-by-state selection system, important differences might exist in the public's broad preferences about the goals and intentions of the process itself. Individuals may differ in their commitment to policies that lead to different outcomes. Specifically, some may prefer systems that emphasize solidarity, winnability, or representation; others may value diversity or inclusiveness. Furthermore, because we are gauging public opinion about a distinctly partisan process, it seems reasonable to expect differences to exist between partisan groups, and even with respect to strength of partisanship. In this chapter we strive to understand these preferences and differences and discuss how to incorporate the public into reform discussions.

Our findings indicate that, contrary to the existing literature, the American public is reasonably informed about the presidential nomination process, but they are divided over whether the current system is performing adequately. While this division seems to be related to partisanship to some degree, preferences appear to be governed more by strength of partisanship than by type of partisanship. Specifically, we found that those who strongly identify with either party are more satisfied with the current system than weak party identifiers. In addition, an overwhelming desire for greater inclusiveness seems to permeate opinions about presidential selection processes. In particular, the most popular reform proposal, a single nationwide primary, is regarded as the system that would most enhance broader participation in the nomination process. This suggests that the American mass public would prefer reform guided by the principle of inclusiveness; however, they are also reasonably satisfied with the status quo, contrary to the sentiments expressed by the media and policy reformers.

The Current Presidential Selection System

The system currently used in the United States to select presidential candidates is extraordinarily complex. This complexity is due, at least in part, to the

Table 6-1. *2008 Presidential Candidate Selection Method by State*

Party	Primary	Caucus
Republican	AL, AZ, AR, CA, CT, DE, DC, FL, GA, ID, IL, IN, KY, MD, MA, MI, MS, MO, NE, NH, NJ, NM, NY, NC, OH, OK, OR, PA, RI, SC, SD, TN, TX, UT, VT, VA, WA, WV, WI	AK, CO, HI, IA, KS, LA, ME, MN, MT, NV, ND, WA, WY
Democratic	AL, AZ, AR, CA, CT, DE, DC, FL, GA, IL, IN, KY, LA, MD, MA, MI, MS, MO, MT, NH, NJ, NY, NC, OH, OK, OR, PA, RI, SC, SD, TN, TX, UT, VT, VA, WV, WI	AK, CO, HI, ID, IA, KS, ME, MN, NE, NV, NM, ND, WA, WY

extreme fragmentation in authority over the presidential nomination process. To varying degrees, this process is controlled by the elected branches of the federal government, the federal courts, the national political parties, the state political parties, the elected branches of the state governments, the state courts, and presumably, in less systematic ways, by other influential political actors and elites. Although reforming the process with its tiered, and somewhat unclear, structure of authority will present its own set of challenges, merely understanding the process is quite demanding. At least two aspects of the current system seem to be especially problematic: (1) understanding the selection method used by the parties in any given state, and (2) realizing the consequences of timing in the election cycle. As shown in tables 6-1, 6-2, and 6-3, there is quite a bit of variation on both of these dimensions.[2]

Table 6-1 documents the impressive variation in the state-by-state methods used to select presidential candidates in 2008. The two parties are free to choose whether to hold a primary or a caucus in each state. In many states, the two parties use the same selection method. For example, both the Republican Party and the Democratic Party hold primary elections in Arizona, California, Pennsylvania, and many other states. In some states, however, the two parties use different methods. For example, in Louisiana, the Democratic Party holds a primary election, and the Republican Party has a caucus. In Nebraska, the Democratic Party has a caucus and the Republican Party holds a primary. These variations complicate voting processes and delegate allocation for party members across the nation, making both the process and the outcome somewhat confusing to the average voter.

More significant, at least to reformers, is the variation in the timing of presidential selection contests. In particular, the issue of front-loading is at the center of many current reform debates. Front-loading is "the concentration of primaries and caucuses at the beginning of the delegate selection season."[3] Because individual states want to be influential in determining the presidential

Table 6-2. *2004 Presidential Primary and Caucus Dates*

Party	January and February	March and April	May and June
Republican	DC, IA, NH, MO, ND, OK, TN, WI	CA, CT, GA, OH, MD, MA, NY, RI, VT, FL, LA, MS, TX, WA, IL, SC, CO, KS, PA, NV	IN, NC, AZ, UT, WY, NE, WV, DE, ME, AR, KY, OR, AK, MI, NC, ID, AL, NM, SD, HI, VA, MT, NJ
Democratic	DC, IA, NH, AZ, DE, MO, NM, ND, OK, SC, MI, WA, ME, TN, VA, NV, WI, HI, ID, UT	CA, CT, GA, OH, MD, MA, MN, NY, RI, VT, FL, LA, MS, TX, KS, IL, AK, WY, NC, CO, PA	IN, NC, NE, WV, AR, KY, OR, ID, AL, NM, SD, MT, NJ

Table 6-3. *2008 Presidential Primary and Caucus Dates*

Party	January and February	March and April	May and June
Republican	IA, WY, NH, MI, NV, SC, FL, ME, AL, AK, AZ, AR, CA, CO, CT, DE, GA, IL, MA, MN, MO, MT, NJ, NY, ND, OK, TN, UT, WV, KS, LA, WA, DC, MD, VA, WA, WI	OH, RI, TX, VT, MS, PA	IN, NC, NE, WV, KY, OR, ID, HI, MT, NM, SD
Democratic	IA, NH, MI, NV, SC, FL, AL, AK, AZ, AR, CA, CO, CT,DE, GA, ID, IL, KS, MA, MN, MO, NJ, NM, NY, ND, OK, TN, UT, LA, NE, WA, ME, DC, MD, VA, HI, WA, WI	OH, RI, TX, VT, WY, MS, PA	IN, NC, NE, WV, KY, OR, ID, MT, NM, SD

nominee, it is in their interest to hold their primaries as early as possible. This leads to the compression of primaries toward the beginning of the nomination season (whenever that is). Further, many reformers have criticized New Hampshire and Iowa's "first-in-the-nation" status for allowing these small, homogeneous, and unrepresentative states to dominate early media and campaign attention, invariably skewing their effect on campaigns and fueling momentum for some candidates over others. As a result, several states are jockeying to hold their elections at the beginning of the primary calendar too, in order to gain more influence over the outcome.[4] This sort of leapfrogging exacerbates concerns about timing and advantage in the presidential selection process.

As the opportunistic rationale for front-loading and leapfrogging caught on with the states, the trend has accelerated. Primary and caucus dates have changed dramatically from 2004 to 2008—that is, over just one presidential election cycle (see tables 6-2 and 6-3). Most notably, in 2008 more than twenty states held primaries or caucuses on February 5, making so-called Super Tuesday the most crowded primary day in American history. While some say that front-loading is creating a sort of unintentional, de facto, national primary day, just letting the process unfold on its own has consequences as well. Front-loading not only elongates the primary process; it also dramatically affects media and candidate attention in states, exacerbates the "horse-race" character of the selection process, and seems to further advantage front-runners. In the absence of successful reform initiatives, front-loading, and its consequences, are expected to become even worse in 2012.

Reforming the Current System

In response to several undeniable flaws in the current presidential candidate selection process, many contend that radically reforming the system is essential because it has "spun out of control."[5] The overwhelming sentiment in the media and among political officials is that the "political parties must fundamentally reform the dysfunctional presidential primary system. We need a better process in 2012—one that empowers all Americans."[6] Further, in an engaging article, "Vote Early, Count Often," Jonathan Soros wrote that "the system we use to select the major-party presidential nominees in this country is badly broken . . . we must change the way we select candidates."[7]

These complaints have not gone unnoticed. In fact, bipartisan discussions are currently under way, and several reform proposals are being circulated to restructure the presidential selection process before the 2012 election. In general these plans seek to revise the temporal ordering of primary voting, the geographic organization of the vote, and the clustering of voting according to large and small states. Specifically, these reform proposals include: a National Primary Election Day, the Delaware Plan, the American Plan, the Rotating Presidential Primary Plan, and the Regional Lottery Plan.

With the adoption of a single national primary election day, all states would hold their primary or caucus on the same day. This plan was first introduced in 1913 by Woodrow Wilson. Although it has not gained much national momentum since then, with the increase in front-loading American primaries seem to be moving in this direction. Proponents of national primary reform tout it as simplifying an unnecessarily complicated primary process and infusing an inherent fairness into the system by allowing all fifty states to hold elections on the same day.[8] As Jonathan Soros suggests, "The only solution that treats every voter equally would be to establish a true national primary, with every state voting on the same day."[9] This plan strives to level the playing field for primary voters and to increase inclusiveness and participation in the selection process. Despite these advantages, however, critics worry that a national primary election day would nationalize the campaign. They argue that a nationalized primary system would minimize the contact that voters have with the candidates, since states would have to compete for attention before Election Day, and it could disproportionately help candidates who can raise enough money to wage a national campaign from the outset.[10]

The Delaware Plan, in contrast, would maintain the traditionally staggered primary season. Under this reform, supported by Delaware Republican state chairman Basil Battaglia in 2000, the states would be grouped into four pods according to population size, as determined by the decennial census.[11] The smallest thirteen states would hold their primaries or caucuses first, followed by the next smallest thirteen, then the twelve medium-sized states, and finally the twelve largest states. Small states such as Delaware and North Dakota would hold primaries or caucuses in February or March, and the process would continue until the largest states, including California, Texas, and New York, voted in May or June. States could choose between having a primary or a caucus, and each state could schedule the election at any time during its appointed month. Individual states could also choose to hold elections later in the nomination calendar, although they could not hold them earlier. By letting the small states go first, the Delaware Plan aims to give small states an opportunity to play an important role in the nomination process, thereby fostering better representation and inclusiveness. The plan would also lengthen the process overall, but in an intentionally systematic way; however, some complain that this system would create four mini–national campaigns with many of the same disadvantages associated with having a single national primary day. In addition, large states might still vote too late to affect the outcomes, which would presumably be unsatisfactory to those states and their voters.

There is also the American Plan (sometimes known as the California Plan or the Graduated Random Presidential Primary System), which is designed to begin with contests in states with small populations.[12] Similar to the Delaware Plan, the system features a schedule consisting of ten two-week intervals during which randomly selected states could hold their primaries. In the first interval, states with a combined total of eight congressional districts would hold their primaries or caucuses. This is approximately equal to the total number of congressional districts in Iowa and New Hampshire.[13] Any state, or combination of states, amounting to a total of eight congressional districts could be in the first round of primaries and caucuses. In the second period (two weeks later), the eligibility number would increase to sixteen, and every two weeks the combined size of the contests would grow by eight congressional districts, until a combination of states totaling eighty congressional seats (nearly one-fifth of the total) would be up for grabs in the tenth and last interval toward the end of June. Because the biggest states are much more populous than the other states, this baseline design would allow California, which has fifty-three districts, to vote no earlier than the seventh interval. To put California on equal footing with the other populous states, the order of rounds four through ten would be staggered, and the four most populous states would be eligible to vote by the fourth of ten rounds. Since only 11 percent of the American electorate would vote in the first three intervals, large states would enter into the selection process early enough to have as meaningful an input as any other state.

Alternatively, in 2000 the National Association of Secretaries of State (NASS) recommended the Rotating Presidential Primary Plan. Under this proposal, the United States would be divided into four regions—Northeast, Midwest, West, and South—each with roughly the same number of voters in the Electoral College, based on the previous census. Primaries to select convention delegates would be grouped by region. Eastern states would hold their primary elections in March, southern states in April, midwestern states in May, and western states in June. Primaries in each state would be scheduled near the first Tuesday in March, April, May, or June, and not all of the states in a region would hold their primaries on the same date. In the following presidential election year, the regions would rotate; for example, if the plan is adopted for the 2012 election, then in 2016, the southern states would hold their elections first, followed by the midwestern states, the western, and then the eastern states. A critical caveat, and perhaps a fatal blow to this plan, is that Iowa and New Hampshire would be exempt from the system and retain their leading positions in the process.[14]

Both the American Plan and the Rotating Presidential Primary Plan offer systematic procedures for how the selection process would unfold and strive to increase inclusiveness and fairness. Interestingly, a similar plan has also been the subject of national legislation.[15] On July 31, 2007, Senator Amy Klobuchar introduced S. 1905, the "Regional Presidential Primary and Caucus Act of 2007," in the U.S. Senate; and on September 6, 2007, Representative Alcee Hastings introduced H.R. 3487, "Regional Presidential Primary and Caucus Act of 2007," in the U.S. House.[16] Both bills provide for a rotating schedule for the regional selection of delegates to a national presidential nominating convention. Like the Rotating Presidential Primary Plan, these bills propose to divide the United States into four regions of specified states (including the District of Columbia) for holding presidential primaries in each presidential election year. The bills also require the four successive presidential primaries to be held on the first Tuesday of March, April, May, and June, ending on the sixth day following such Tuesday. Unlike the Rotating Presidential Primary Plan, however, the Election Assistance Commission (EAC) would conduct a lottery by March 1, 2010, to select the region in which the first primary would be held. The EAC would also create a rule for subsequent election cycles so that the same region would not vote first during every presidential election season. The bills further specify that when a state decides to hold a caucus, the caucus should take place during the period in which its region is scheduled to hold a primary. If adopted, this legislation would apply to any primary or caucus held in 2012, and during each presidential election year thereafter.[17]

In *A More Perfect Constitution*, Larry Sabato goes even further than calling for national legislation by advocating a constitutional amendment to create a regional lottery system.[18] According to Sabato, "Congress should be constitutionally required to designate four regions of contiguous states (with contiguity waived for Alaska and Hawaii and any other territories that might one day become states)."[19] The Regional Lottery Plan would divide the United States into four regions, identical to those in the Rotating Presidential Primary Plan. States in each region would hold their nominating events in successive months, from March through June. This is similar to the plan proposed by the NASS, but the order of the regions holding nominating events would be determined by an American election lottery, and there would be no lead-off states. According to Sabato, the lottery would be run by a five-member nonpartisan part-time election lottery commission appointed by an organization such as the National Association of Secretaries of State.

Sabato's Regional Lottery Plan has many of the same advantages as the Rotating Presidential Primary Plan; its main difference is the lottery used to determine the order in which each region will participate in the nominating process. Because candidates would not know more than a few months before an election which region would lead off the contest, "homesteading," or targeting key states, could be eliminated and candidates would be forced to focus equally on all areas.[20] In addition, according to Sabato, "The establishment of a U.S. Election Lottery, to be held on New Year's Day of the presidential election year, would yield fairness and also add an element of drama to the beginning of a presidential year." The proposal "would [also] 'repeal' the nonexistent constitutional right to go first that Iowa and New Hampshire have appropriated for themselves."[21] In doing so, Sabato's plan is designed to foster increased national interest in the process while systematically increasing the organization and fairness of the system.

These reform proposals provide an array of creative options for fixing the selection system. The plans differ on several dimensions, such as one-person one-vote, inclusiveness, and respect for the federalist tradition (and each has its own set of biases). Although some of the proposals seem even more complicated than the current system, each seeks to spread out the candidate selection contests over several months, increase procedural fairness, and reduce the negative effects associated with front-loading. While it may be hard to determine all of the consequences and ramifications of the proposed reforms, especially over the long term, each strives to remedy some of the perceived ills associated with the current selection system. Before serious system reform takes place, it will be important to include the public in the discussion. The result of these reforms bears heavily, of course, on the selection of candidates for the highest elected office in the country. So the questions arise: Are Americans concerned about the current system? And if given the choice, what reform strategy would they choose? The rest of the chapter strives to answer these questions.

What Do We Know about Public Views of the Current System?

The conventional wisdom, albeit grounded in limited empirical evidence, regarding the American public's position on the presidential selection system and potential reform initiatives is summarized by three relatively straightforward conclusions.

First, "reforming the presidential nomination process is just not something that most Americans care much about."[22] At least when asked in the American National Election Studies (ANES) survey, "What do you think is the most important problem facing the country?" no one has ever listed the presidential nomination process as the country's most important problem.[23] This may not be the best way to judge the public's level of concern about the system, but some maintain that one of the reasons that national reform proposals have not been successful in the past is "the public's general lack of concern with the issue."[24] Specifically, if the public does not care about reforming the presidential selection system, then elected officials, motivated mainly by concerns about reelection, will not pursue it; it would simply not provide much Election Day payoff. Of course, reforming the selection process may become more salient to voters as they reflect on the drama and uncertainty the 2008 primary season delivered.

Second, generally speaking, "the public supports public participation in, and control of, the presidential selection process, and is considerably more skeptical about, if not downright hostile toward, proposals that seek to increase the power of party leaders or other elite groups."[25] Despite the fact that the primary process is inherently a party operation, some would argue that this generalization about the American public's preference reflects their long-standing support of democratic institutions and processes, and their pronounced ambivalence about political parties and party bosses.

Third, Americans support a national primary system "because it seems to be the most direct and overtly democratic system available."[26] This characterization suggests that if the American public were given a choice between reform proposals, or a choice between change and the status quo, the public would overwhelmingly favor a national primary. Consequently, as front-loading continues and the system increasingly resembles a national primary, the masses may become more content with the current selection process.

In summary, previous work on the subject commonly characterizes the American public as not being interested in the primary process or in reforming it. If they were concerned, scholars suggest that they would want the public to have more power over the process than the parties; and if given the choice, they would prefer a single national primary to virtually any other alternative. Yet this is not the picture portrayed by the media or by reformers, and the basis for these conclusions does not seem particularly well founded. We therefore began our study by searching for recent polls in which Americans were asked what they thought about the presidential nomination process, quite apart from the specifics of the 2008 contest and the candidates.

This exhaustive search located only a single Fox News/Opinion Dynamics Poll, from September 2007, which asked the public whether the tradition of New Hampshire having the first primary election in the nation should continue.[27] A national sample of registered voters ($N = 900$) responded: 41 percent said "keep the tradition," "42 percent said "time to change the tradition," and 17 percent said "don't know." The only other "recent" survey on mass opinions about primary reform was conducted in July 2000, when a CBS News/*New York Times* poll asked a sample of registered voters ($N = 954$) whether "a new nominating system based on state population (where the smallest states could begin to hold their primaries in February, the small states in March, the medium-sized states in April, and the biggest states in May) would be a better system than the one we have now, or not?" To this, 40 percent of respondents said the new system would be "better," 38 percent said "not better," and 22 percent responded "don't know."[28]

Thus we know very little about current public preferences toward presidential nomination systems and current reform proposals; yet any of the current reform proposals would dramatically affect the process by which American voters select candidates for the presidency. Further, the issue seems particularly salient in the wake of the 2008 primary contests. As such, we think it is imperative to systematically consider the public's views on presidential candidate selection systems. Although the American people may not have opinions on all of the intricacies of the process, they probably do have opinions about whether the system works and about the principles that ought to guide its reform.

Public Opinion and Presidential Nomination Systems

We are not sanguine about the depth of knowledge ordinary people have about the presidential nomination process, and questioning people about structures that they have never thought about is unlikely to produce very useful answers. We therefore conceptualize institutional preferences somewhat differently from prior research. In particular, we distinguish among three preferences: (1) most concretely, people's opinions of, and preferences for, specific institutional structures; (2) more abstractly, the expectations people hold for such structures; and (3) more abstractly still, people's institutional expectations as derived from their larger political and social values.

We know that people's evaluations of the objectives of institutions vary. Some may expect nominating institutions to build solidarity and to lessen intra-party conflict. Others may want institutions that produce winners. Still others may be concerned with representation, in all of its manifestations, including symbolic representation. We posit that individuals form their preferences for institutional structures according to the goals they hold for such institutions. Namely, they prefer particular institutional structures that they perceive to match the objectives they have for the system. Finally, at the highest level of abstraction, we can imagine that people differ in the degree to which they emphasize (and prefer) the majoritarian institutions of democracy over institutions associated with liberalism and minoritarianism. Other values may also influence people's attitudes toward presidential nominee selection systems.

Thus, at the most conceptual level, we hypothesize that values give rise to, and are associated with, the expectations citizens hold for institutions in the governmental system, and that preferences for specific institutional structures reflect these expectations. Of course, we recognize that citizens may not be able to map their expectations onto specific institutional structures. We therefore hypothesize that political knowledge is key to linking institutional preferences and various types of psychological attributes. We further recognize that exogenous variables may influence this entire process. For instance, strong partisans are likely to feel quite differently about presidential selection systems than weak partisans. White Americans likely hold views that are different from those of minority Americans.

Finally, an important advantage of this conceptualization of the structure of attitudes is that it allows us to query people about both their opinions directly and the precursors to those opinions. To the extent that people do not have specific institutional preferences, we adjust the inquiry to focus on the next higher level of abstraction. Our supposition is that, at the level of political and social values, virtually everyone will be able to respond to our queries.

Analysis

In order to evaluate public perceptions about presidential candidate selection systems, we conducted a telephone survey of a nationally representative sample of Americans in November and December of 2007 (see appendix 6A for details about the survey). Because individuals' knowledge about the presidential selection process is central to our study and to the conclusions we can draw, we began by trying to determine how knowledgeable the American people are about presidential candidate selection systems. We asked respondents to characterize their level of awareness about "discussions over how we select presidential candidates in the United States" on a scale ranging from "have never heard of" to "very aware." The replies indicate that the presidential candidate selection systems are reasonably salient to the American people: 38.6 percent of respondents claimed to be very aware of discussions about the systems, another 45.1 percent said they were somewhat aware, and only 5.7 percent admitted to not having heard about the issue. Although the presidential selection process is not among the most pressing social and political problems facing the American people, the issue is far from obscure.

Of course, self-declared awareness of an issue is nothing more than a self-declaration, so we also examined the degree to which Americans are *informed* about presidential candidate selection systems. We asked the respondents if they knew which state "traditionally is the first to nominate candidates for president," offering them a list of options that included New Hampshire, California, and New York. A majority of respondents (56.4 percent) correctly identified New Hampshire as the first state to nominate; 17.6 percent admitted that they did not know the answer to the question. When asked to select a definition of the term "caucus," knowledge was considerably less widespread.

Only 20.6 percent correctly identified a caucus as a "small meeting of voters to discuss and choose candidates." A plurality (39.3 percent) thought the term applies to "a statewide convention in which all party members come together." In comparison to election system–specific knowledge, one-third of the respondents (33.7 percent) knew that when the U.S. Supreme Court decides a case "the decision is final and cannot be reviewed."[29] While awareness of the presidential candidate selection systems and political knowledge are correlated ($r = .32$), these data suggest that substantive information about selection systems is probably fairly limited (or that people know about aspects of the selection systems about which we did not ask).

In addition to gauging the public's interest in, and knowledge about, the selection system, we sought to determine the degree to which the American people are satisfied with the current presidential candidate selection system. Here we see substantial divisions among the respondents, with 41.7 percent unhappy with the system to at least some degree, and 53.3 percent happy to at least some degree (only 5.0 percent did not know how happy they are with the current system). Practically no relationship exists, however, between satisfaction with the selection system and awareness of it (nor is there a connection between satisfaction and political knowledge), so instructing people on the intricacies of the presidential candidate selection systems is unlikely to make them feel more satisfied with the current system.

From this, our broad conclusion is that the American people are divided on whether the current system is performing adequately. Interestingly, this division is related to partisanship to some degree. For instance, 64.5 percent of those identifying themselves as Republicans are happy with the current presidential candidate selection systems; this figure dips to 51.9 percent among Democrats, and falls to 47.5 percent among those identifying themselves as independents. More generally, some relationship exists between the strength of one's party identification and satisfaction with the presidential candidate selection systems ($r = .13$, $p < .000$). Among stronger party identifiers of either party, 60.4 percent are at least somewhat satisfied with the current presidential candidate selection systems, while only 38.8 percent of the weak party identifiers hold comparable opinions.[30]

Thus it appears that dissatisfaction with the presidential nominee selection systems currently used in the United States is not overwhelming. Moreover, satisfaction with the current system predominates among those most concerned with parties—the strong partisans. So, contrary to the claims of reformers and journalists, perhaps the current system is not entirely broken in the eyes of the American people.

Support for Candidate Selection System Reforms

To gauge public opinion about the reforms being discussed after the 2008 primary season, we asked our respondents about four variants. Figure 6-1 reports the questions and responses.[31]

The data reveal varying degrees of support for these reform proposals. As has been true in other surveys of this sort, the idea of a single national primary election draws the support of a majority of the American people.[32] A majority also prefers that New Hampshire not be allowed to open the nomination season. The other reform ideas attract less than majority support. In general, the respondents are somewhat discriminating in the reform plans they support, with only 12.0 percent supporting all four ideas and 12.9 percent supporting none of them.[33]

Partisan differences in support for these various reforms are not great. Some exceptions exist, however. For instance, on the question of the tradition of allowing New Hampshire to go first in the presidential candidate selection process, 42.8 percent of the Republicans and 49.0 percent of the independents support change, while the figure for the Democrats is 56.7 percent. In general, those most aware of the presidential candidate selection process resist this change, although even at the highest level of awareness a plurality rejects the idea that New Hampshire should always go first. Still, it is perhaps noteworthy that, on the most popular reform proposal, the nationwide primary, Democrats and Republicans support the idea at roughly the same level (with independents being somewhat more supportive), and favoring a national primary is entirely unrelated to the strength of party attachments and the degree of awareness of the selection system debate.[34]

These reform proposals, while fairly widely discussed among the political cognoscenti, must appear to the respondents to be quite cumbersome, and we do not doubt that many believe that "the devil is in the details." Consequently, we asked the respondents about some specific principles or criteria on which reform plans ought to be based. Figure 6-2 reports the degree to which the respondents judge these factors to be either important or very important.

The respondents rated each of these criteria as important, and, indeed, except for the last item, a majority rated each as "very important." Nearly everyone is willing to cede small states more influence than their numbers warrant, and everyone wants a predictable and fair system. The item on which there is the least agreement (although it still draws the support of a large majority of the respondents) has to do with punishing states that manipulate the selection system. We wonder whether—given the debacles in Michigan

Figure 6-1. *Support for Presidential Candidate Selection System Reforms*

Percent favoring reform

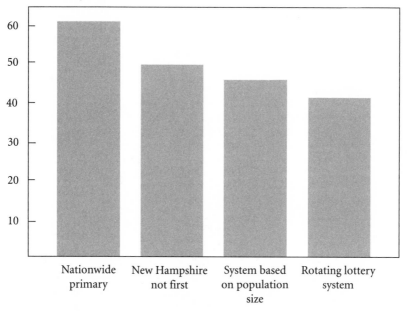

Proposed reform

Source: Weidenbaum Center Survey on Presidential Selection System Preferences, 2007.

The questions read:

1. It has been suggested that presidential candidates be chosen by the voters in a single nationwide primary election instead of by the present system in which the states use different processes at different times of the year. Would you strongly favor, favor, oppose, or strongly oppose this?

2. For many years the state of New Hampshire has held the first presidential primary election in the nation. Do you think the tradition of New Hampshire having the first primary should continue, or do you think it is time to change the tradition and allow other states to hold their primary elections before New Hampshire?

3. Some people have proposed the parties adopt a new nominating system based on the size of the state's population. The smallest states could begin to hold their primaries in February, the small states could begin in March, medium-sized states could begin in April, and the biggest states could begin in May. Do you think this would be a much better, better, worse, or much worse system than the one we have now?

4. It has been proposed that four individual regional primaries be held in different weeks during a presidential election year with the order rotating through a lottery system. Does this sound like a very good idea, a good idea, a poor idea, or a very poor idea?

Figure 6-2. *The Importance of Various Criteria for Proposed Changes in Selection Systems*

Percent regarding criterion as important

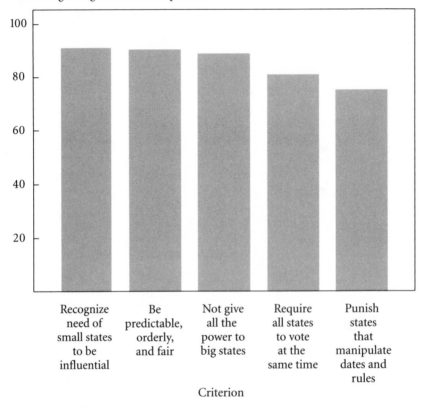

Source: Weidenbaum Center Survey on Presidential Selection System Preferences, 2007.

The question reads:
In terms of any changes to the current system by which the [DEMOCRATIC/REPUBLICAN] parties select their nominees for the presidency, how important is it that the system:

—not give all the power to the big states like California, New York, and Texas
—be more predictable, orderly, and fair
—recognize that the small states need to have some influence over the outcome
—require that all states vote at the same time
—punish those states that manipulate the date on which they hold the primary so as to give the state more influence over who is nominated

Note the criteria above are listed in the order in which they appear in the figure.

and Florida in 2008—opinions today would be as forgiving of the states that cheat (or are made to cheat). We also note that the opinions of Democrats and Republicans are virtually identical on this issue. Because these criteria are consensually supported by the American people, few systematic differences exist with regard to partisanship, political knowledge, or other dimensions.

We recognize that the items reported in figure 6-2 border on being platitudes. We therefore sought to investigate the preferences people employ in judging presidential candidate selection systems using more demanding questions about the objectives desired from such systems. These are the criteria by which presidential selection systems should be judged. Because the responses represent the preferences of the respondents, even if they have no information about the actual systems, these questions are easy for ordinary people to answer. The questions and criteria about which we queried the respondents are reported in the bottom portion of table 6-4. These questions were tailored to the respondents according to their professed party identification in an earlier question, with independents being randomly assigned to hear questions about the Democrats or the Republicans.

Nearly all respondents rated "candidate winnability" and "including all states in the process" as important criteria for a selection system, and two-thirds of respondents rated them as very important. As noted by the correlation with party identification, partisan differences on the weight attached to the capability of winning and state inclusiveness are trivial. However, strong partisans place considerably more emphasis on winnability than weak partisans (see the correlation with strength of party identification), even while a preference for inclusiveness is not associated with state involvement.

A second group of criteria is widely supported, though not by a consensus of the respondents. For instance, a majority prefers that minorities be given a voice in the process, although this is less true of Republicans and more characteristic of strong party identifiers. Most do not want big states to dominate the process, and this view is more common among strong party identifiers (both Republicans and Democrats).

A third group of criteria are supported, or strongly supported, by only a minority (but often a plurality) of the respondents. For instance, only 45.5 percent prefer that the candidate be ideologically pure, and conversely, 44.9 percent favor ideological diversity. Solidarity needs (feeling good) are scored as the least important by our respondents, although strong party identifiers are more likely to express a need for in-group solidarity. Across all of these criteria, only a few substantial partisan differences are observed. The strongest is on ideological diversity, which Republicans are considerably more likely to rate as

Table 6-4. *Respondents' Preferences for a Presidential Nominating System*

	Percentage who said criterion is "very important"	Mean	Standard deviation	N	Correlations	
Criterion					*Party identification*	*Strength of identification*
Makes all states feel involved	66.1	3.56	.70	1,414	−.03	.07
Candidate capable of winning	66.0	3.55	.73	1,411	−.03	.29
Gives minorities a voice	58.6	3.45	.77	1,409	−.12	.14
Reflects majority preferences	54.9	3.39	.79	1,406	.03	.09
Does not reflect big state interests	52.8	3.32	.86	1,409	−.04	.14
Favors ideological diversity	44.9	3.29	.77	1,410	−.17	.17
Favors regional diversity	44.7	3.28	.77	1,411	−.11	.15
Ideologically pure	45.5	3.20	.89	1,413	.04	.19
Makes people feel good to be in party	47.8	3.18	.97	1,413	−.10	.34

Source: Weidenbaum Center Survey on Presidential Selection System Preferences, 2007.
Note: The criteria are presented in rank order according to the mean response.
The question reads:
Now we would like to ask you to think a bit more about the process by which the [DEMOCRA-TIC/REPUBLICAN] parties select the person to be their candidate to be the president of the United States. Please tell me how important it is that the system the [DEMOCRATS/REPUBLICANS] use to select a nominee for president who:
—makes all states—including the small states—feel like they are part of the candidate selection process
—is capable of winning the election for president
—gives minorities a voice in the process
—reflects strictly the preferences of the majority, based on the simple rule that one person should have one vote, no more, no less
—does NOT simply reflect the interests of the big states, like California, New York, and Texas
—recognizes the need for ideological diversity on the [DEMOCRATIC/REPUBLICAN] ticket
—recognizes the need for regional diversity on the [DEMOCRATIC/REPUBLICAN] ticket
—is ideologically pure and won't compromise on the issues
—makes people feel good to be a [DEMOCRATIC/REPUBLICAN]

Note the criteria above are listed in the order in which they are reported in this table.

unimportant. Only 35.0 percent of the Republican respondents rated ideolog-ical diversity as very important; in comparison, 58.0 percent of the Democrats rank diversity highest on the scale. Generally, however, Democrats and Repub-licans do not differ greatly in the priority they assign to these criteria.

Strength of party identification (irrespective of which party the respondent supports) is far more likely to affect support for the selection system criteria. Strong partisans are more likely to assert that solidarity and winnability are important, as for example in the finding that 82.3 percent of the strongest par-tisans believe the capability of winning is of utmost importance, compared to only 42.7 percent of nonpartisans. Similarly, strong partisans are far more likely than nonpartisans to stress solidarity criteria (64.5 percent versus 24.1 percent, respectively). Significant differences are also found on nearly all other criteria, with the exception of "reflecting majority preferences" and "making all states feel involved in the process." The key conclusion from this analysis is that the criteria one seeks to maximize in selection system preferences dif-fer markedly according to the degree of one's attachment to a political party.

To what degree do these criteria represent more abstract and general pref-erences for a candidate selection system? We address this question via a factor analysis of the responses reported in table 6-4. When subjected to common fac-tor analysis, the items reported in table 6-4 produce a unidimensional struc-ture.[35] The continuum seems to represent a range from inclusiveness to exclusiveness. At one end of the continuum is the preference for regional diver-sity, giving minorities a voice, the need for ideological diversity, and giving small states influence and not allowing big states to dominate. All of these preferences seem to reflect a desire to include more people and interests in the selection system. At the other end is the statement about strictly adhering to majority preferences, ideological purity, and winnability. In light of the find-ing of unidimensionality, we have created an index that indicates the degree of emphasis on criteria of exclusion or inclusion. In some sense, this continuum ranges from "big tent" preferences for broad party participation to a desire for relative party purity, perhaps so that parties can actually stand for something.

Analysis of the factor scores reveals that strong partisans give considerably more emphasis to inclusiveness: $r = 0.28$. With the full seven-point measure of party identification, the beta coefficient is 0.34. This relationship is depicted in figure 6-3, which demonstrates that strong partisans of either party are more in favor of inclusiveness than independents and weak partisans, and that even controlling for strength of party identification, Democrats favor inclusiveness (slightly) more than Republicans. Perhaps the most interesting

Figure 6-3. *Partisanship and Support for Inclusiveness in Nominee Selection Systems*

Average score on preference of inclusiveness

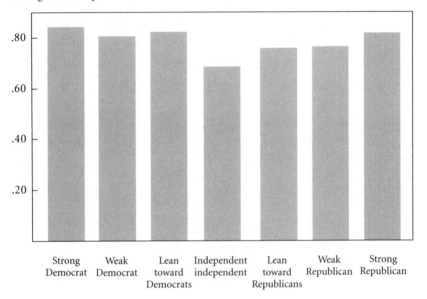

Party identification

Source: Weidenbaum Center Survey on Presidential Selection System Preferences, 2007.

aspect of this figure is the strong priority partisans attach to inclusiveness versus purity.

Connecting Selection System Criteria with Reform Preferences

Finally, we return to the question of support for specific reforms, and in particular, the degree to which individuals who favor more or less inclusiveness support each of the reform alternatives. By examining the connection between the desire that systems be inclusive and the specific reform proposals, we can get some purchase on whether different reform proposals are associated in the minds of Americans with greater degrees of inclusiveness. We observe only a modest relationship between support for inclusiveness and favoring a national primary (see figure 6-4). Among those with the strongest preferences for inclusiveness of presidential nominee selection systems, a clear majority (64.3 percent) support a national primary. This figure dips to a bare majority among those who place the least amount of emphasis on selection system

Figure 6-4. *Relationship between Inclusiveness and Support for a National Primary*

Percent favoring a national primary

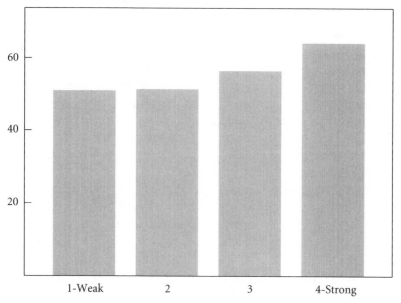

Preference for inclusiveness in selection systems

Source: Weidenbaum Center Survey on Presidential Selection System Preferences, 2007.

inclusiveness. Whatever the actual operation of a national primary system, the American people tend to think of it as a system through which greater and broader participation in the nomination process should be enhanced.

Conclusion

Reforming the presidential selection process will have major, lasting consequences for presidential politics in the United States. In listening to this sample of the American people, we find, contrary to the conventional wisdom, that the issue of primary reform is important to the public, that Americans are aware of the current reform discussions, and that they are reasonably informed about the specifics of the system. We do not contend that this issue compares in salience to substantive policy matters such as the economy or the war in Iraq, but Americans seem to care about how presidential nominees are selected.

The current system of nominating presidential candidates has garnered a lot of criticism from the so-called elite sectors of the population. However, our findings reveal that the American people are more satisfied than dissatisfied with the status quo, and partisans exhibit the highest levels of satisfaction with the current system. This is not to say that the populace at large rejects all of the proposals for reform, but except for implementing a national primary, there is not a great deal of public support for any of the reform plans being discussed. Most Americans do not support the primacy of New Hampshire and Iowa in the current nomination system, but otherwise, dissatisfaction is far from rampant. What the American people do want is a nominating system that is more inclusive rather than one that imposes barriers to participation. A national primary was favored on precisely such grounds. As in so many areas of American politics, ordinary people want to enhance their participation rather than circumscribe it.

Perhaps the most important finding of this research is that, while Democrats and Republicans do not differ a great deal in their preferences, strong and weak partisans do. Moreover, strong partisans favor inclusiveness considerably more than weak partisans, which is perhaps surprising. The picture that emerges from our analysis is not one of the dogmatic party activist seeking to maximize ideological objectives, but is instead one of the "big tent" partisan. Of course, ours is not a study of activists; it is a study of ordinary people. Furthermore, strong partisans may favor inclusiveness primarily as a means toward an end: winning, which strong supporters of both parties want dearly. Nonetheless, partisans seem to be pragmatic.

It is perhaps surprising that many Americans support both a direct primary system and the principle that small states ought to be given disproportionate influence in the nominating process. A direct primary connotes one-person, one-vote, whereas the current state-dominated system gives vastly more influence to citizens of small states than to those of large states. We doubt that most Americans recognize this conflict; but a strict system of voter equality seems not to be the most preferred institution from the viewpoint of most people.

We conclude by noting that implementing any sort of reform of the current system is not going to be an easy task. In particular, reformers must decide who the relevant constituency or "public" is when making a decision about changing the process. Our work reveals that there is not a unified public in the reform discussion, so reformers must decide whose preferences matter in the conversation. Should they just listen to the views of partisans? Are nonpartisans and independents irrelevant? While we did not find noticeable cleavages between partisan groups, except perhaps on dimensions of pre-ferred inclusiveness, there are widespread differences in the preferences of individuals with different strengths in partisanship. This suggests that any reform proposal must begin not with a snapshot of the views of the American people in toto, but by canvassing party supporters.

In addition, we need to think further about the role that the parties should play in the reform debate. The tenuousness of the political parties' public or private status as institutions has real consequences for this process. The long-standing tension between party politics, public involvement, and inclusiveness remains implicitly at the root of the reform discussion. This difference will have to be reconciled in order to credibly advocate for or against particular reform proposals.

Finally, this chapter obviously is only an initial foray into the etiology of public preferences on presidential nominating systems. We have established that most people do have such preferences, but more research ought to be con-ducted to determine how these preferences are grounded in larger political attitudes and values. It seems from the findings presented here, for instance, that Americans want more than a system that maximizes the influence of their individual votes. Instead, they seem willing to dilute their own influence in order to enhance inclusiveness and perhaps even fairness. Nominating sys-tems seem to have symbolic importance for the American people, rather than merely instrumental significance. Understanding how values get implemented in policy choices is the most important next step in this research agenda.

Appendix 6A: Survey Details

This survey is based on a nationally representative sample, including an over-sample of African Americans. The survey, conducted by SRBI, was fielded on November 19 to December 16, 2007 (before the 2008 primary season began). Computer Assisted Telephone Interviewing (CATI) was used. Within households, the respondents were selected randomly. The interviews averaged around eighteen minutes in length. In the main survey, the AAPOR Cooperation Rate #3 was 41.4 percent and the AAPOR Response Rate #3 was 24.5 percent,[36] which is somewhat below average for telephone surveys these days,[37] and most likely reflects the decision not to pay the respondents for participating in the survey. For the African American over-sample, the Cooperation Rate #3 was 53.1 percent and the Response Rate #3 was 33.4 percent. The black over-sample consists of two portions. A total of 156 interviews were completed via standard random digit dialing (RDD) methods, with respondents drawn from telephone exchanges with an African American population of 15.0 percent or more (which represents a population including 72 percent of African Americans in the United States). The second portion of the black over-sample (N = 264) was drawn from African American households identified in earlier RDD surveys (SRBI/Time polls). Owing to random selection of respondents within households, the respondent in the early survey was not necessarily selected for the interview in this project. From the RDD over-sample, the SRBI/Time polls respondents, and the African Americans in the primary RDD sample, 502 African Americans were interviewed. In all portions of the total sample, up to twelve calls were made to contact the respondent. The final data set was subjected to some relatively minor post-stratification and was also weighted to accommodate variability in the size of the respondents' households. The initial questionnaire was subjected to a formal pretest, and, on the basis of the results, was significantly revised. According to the estimates of the interviewers, 80.4 percent of the respondents were friendly and interested in the survey (another 17.2 percent were cooperative but not particularly interested), and 85.4 percent were rated as having a good understanding of the questions being asked.

Notes

1. "The Primary Problem," *New York Times*, September 2, 2007.

2. Of course, there is even more variation in the type of primary (that is, open or closed) used by the parties. This has important consequences for candidate selection, but is beyond the scope of this chapter.

3. William G. Mayer and Andrew E. Busch, *The Front-Loading Problem in Presidential Nomination* (Washington: Brookings, 2004), p. 2.

4. Of course, there is always some degree of uncertainty about what position in the primary calendar will be the most influential, as we observed during the Democratic nomination process in 2008.

5. "Stop the Madness Proposal Would Bring Sanity to Primary System," *Dallas Morning News*, September 21, 2007.

6. Bob Graham, "How to End the Gridlock," *Washington Post*, January 30, 2008.

7. Jonathan Soros, "Vote Early, Count Often," *New York Times*, October 30, 2007.

8. Jessica Taylor, "Fixing the Primary Scramble: Q&A with Ryan O'Donnell," *National Journal*, November 1, 2007.

9. Soros, "Vote Early, Count Often."

10. Taylor, "Fixing the Primary Scramble."

11. See University of Virginia, Center for Governmental Studies, "The Nominating Process," from the Report of the National Symposium on Presidential Selection titled *Presidential Selection: A Guide to Reform*, 2008 (www.centerforpolitics.org/reform/report_nominating.htm [November 2, 2008]).

12. The American Plan is touted by Thomas Gangale in *From the Primaries to the Polls: How to Repair America's Broken Presidential Nomination Process* (Westport, Conn.: Praeger, 2008).

13. The description in the text follows that in University of Virginia, Center for Governmental Studies, "The Nominating Process."

14. On April 2, 2008, the Republican National Committee's rules panel voted 28–12 for the "Ohio Plan," which is very similar to the Rotating Presidential Primary Plan. The Ohio Plan preserves early slots for smaller states, including Iowa and New Hampshire, and rotates "pods" of larger states quadrennially in later slots. The plan calls for Iowa, New Hampshire, South Carolina, and Nevada to hold their contests in mid-February. After that, there would be a several-day window for nineteen other small states to hold contests. The remaining states would then vote by region in three groups, or "pods," in March and April. The three groups would rotate every four years. This plan was discussed by the full RNC in August 2008. See Ralph Z. Hallow, "RNC Looks to Fix 2012 Primaries," *Washington Times*, April 3, 2008.

15. Historically, under the American federalist system, the states have maintained nearly unilateral control over the election systems within their borders; however, national reform proposals seeking to change election laws are not completely unprecedented. Apart from federal legislation regulating election conduct and enfranchise-

ment during the Civil Rights Movement, the U.S. Congress and President Clinton enacted the National Voter Registration Act in 1993. Most famously this legislation created the "motor voter" program enabling individuals to register to vote at Department of Motor Vehicles offices and other government agencies. This is to say that efforts toward national legislation are reasonably viable; however, reforming the primary system might present a different set of hurdles for government officials since, apart from being under the domain of the states, primary elections are under the control of the political parties themselves.

16. Senate bill S. 1905 was read twice and referred to the Committee on Rules and Administration, where committee hearings were held. House bill H.R. 3487 was referred to the House Committee on House Administration. No further action has taken place on either bill.

17. This is not the first attempt at federal legislation of this kind. On September 6, 2007, Senate bill S. 2024, the "Fair and Representative Presidential Primaries Act of 2007," was introduced by Senator Bill Nelson. Similarly, in the House, H.R. 1523, "The Interregional Presidential Primary and Caucus Act," was introduced by Representative Sander Levin on March 14, 2007. These bills sought to divide the United States into six regions of specific states to provide for interregional primary elections and caucuses, according to a certain order. In the Senate the bill was read twice and referred to the Committee on Rules and Administration. In the House, the bill was referred to the House Committee on House Administration, and no further action was taken.

18. Larry J. Sabato, *A More Perfect Constitution: Twenty-Three Proposals to Revitalize Our Constitution and Make America a Fairer Country* (New York: Walker, 2007). While a constitutional amendment might seem extreme, Sabato suggests that it is necessary, over and beyond usual legislative action. As he notes, "Congress has some power to intervene in the state-based, party-centered nominating process, yet the federal legislature would be highly unlikely to step into that briar patch. Presidential nominating reform has never been a priority for Congress, in part because of the traditional rights of the states and parties to organize this sector of politics" (p. 129).

19. Ibid., p. 131.

20. University of Virginia, Center for Governmental Studies, "The Nominating Process," 2008.

21. Sabato, *A More Perfect Constitution*, pp. 132–33.

22. Mayer and Busch, *The Front-Loading Problem in Presidential Nominations*.

23. Ibid., p. 126.

24. Ibid., p.139.

25. Ibid., p. 128.

26. Ibid., p. 129.

27. Fox News/Opinion Dynamics Poll, September 2007. The survey was conducted by Fox News, September 25–26, 2007, and the methodology was chosen by Opinion Dynamics. Data provided by the Roper Center for Public Opinion Research, University of Connecticut.

28. CBS News/*New York Times* Poll, July 2000. The survey was conducted by CBS News/*New York Times*, July 13–16, 2000. Data provided by the Roper Center for Public Opinion Research, University of Connecticut.

29. These three items are used in our analysis as measures of general political knowledge. Only 6.6 percent of the respondents got all three questions correct; 26.9 percent answered none of them correctly. Thus, this turned out to be a fairly difficult test of political knowledge. For recent revisionist evidence on the political information held by the American people, see James L. Gibson and Gregory A. Caldeira, *Citizens, Courts, and Confirmations: Positivity Theory and the Judgments of the American People* (Princeton University Press, 2009).

30. Of course, some of this difference is due to the fact that political knowledge is related to the strength of party attachments ($r = .11$) and awareness of the presidential candidate selection systems ($r = .16$).

31. We were somewhat surprised by the relative infrequency of "don't know" replies in response to these questions. Across the four reforms shown in figure 6-1, the percentage of respondents without an opinion is 8.1, 16.3, 22.7, and 9.1, respectively. We are particularly impressed by the finding that nearly all Americans hold an opinion on whether a national primary should be used for selecting presidential candidates.

32. See, for example, Mayer and Busch, *The Front-Loading Problem.*

33. This conclusion is reinforced by the finding that support for the various reforms is not strongly intercorrelated. The strongest relationship we observe is between support for a system based on population size and a rotating lottery system ($r = .22$).

34. We find some relationship between favoring a national primary and political knowledge, with those most knowledgeable being least likely to favor the idea. Still, even among those with the highest level of knowledge, a plurality (48.4 percent) supports the reform.

35. The conventional criterion for identifying substantively important factors is that an eigenvalue must exceed 1.0. The second factor extracted in this analysis has an eigenvalue of 1.023, which just barely exceeds the criterion. When the solution is treated as two-dimensional and rotated using oblique criteria, the two factors are correlated at .88, which indicates of course that they are practically indistinguishable and of no value (owing to multicollinearity) as separate measures in any of our analyses. Moreover, in the unidimensional, unrotated solution, all factor loadings exceed .30, so interpreting the structure as unidimensional is reasonable.

36. American Association for Public Opinion Research, *Standard Definitions: Final Dispositions of Case Codes and Outcome Rates for Surveys* (Ann Arbor, Mich.: 2000).

37. A. L. Holbrook, J. A. Krosnick, and A. M. Pfent, "Response Rates in Surveys by the News Media and Government Contractor Survey Research Firms," in J. Lepkowski and others, eds., *Telephone Survey Methodology* (New York: Wiley, forthcoming).

LARRY J. SABATO

7

*Picking Presidential Nominees:
Time for a New Regime*

Even a cursory glance at the presidential primary process reveals fundamental flaws that undermine the democratic process, disfranchise some voters and cede too much power to others, increase the cost of elections, and extend the duration of campaigns. One of the basic difficulties is that the Constitution gives no guidance and sets no rules for the nominating process. Of course, the Founders had no need to design a more precise presidential nominating system since, in 1787, they believed neither in political parties nor in mass democracy. But we do, and the Constitution has not grown with our vision of an acceptable electoral process.

The current schedule for presidential primaries and caucuses is something of a mess, giving too much power to an unrepresentative few with undue influence over the party nominees. Because it would require uprooting entrenched interests, Congress, the parties, and the states usually refuse to address reform of the nominating system.

The essential problem—that the Constitution neglects the crucial role politics and parties play in the process of American elections—has never been corrected. Strange as it may seem in today's political climate, the Founders preferred to think of themselves and their contemporaries as statesmen, not vulgar politicians, and in the statecraft of their times there was remarkably little formal role for politics. In his farewell address, George Washington cautioned the new nation against "the potent engines, by which cunning, ambitious, and unprincipled men will be enabled to subvert the power of the people and to usurp for themselves the reins of government."[1] Skeptical though he was of the value of political parties, even Washington and his immediate successors eventually realized that politics and its institutions were necessary tools of statecraft. Moreover, they were necessary for a successful republic. Ultimately, Adams and Jefferson helped to create rival political parties. Their Electoral College deadlock in the 1800 presidential contest led to a constitutional amendment that acknowledged the inevitable political relationship between the president and vice president. Citizens grew impatient with elite rule and began demanding the opportunity to cast popular ballots for the president to instruct their electors. And the American system, in fits and starts and with the occasional piecemeal constitutional adjustment, adapted to include these political changes.

Nevertheless, real constitutional adaptation has yet to catch up to the evolution of politics from a reluctant avocation of "public-spirited gentlemen" to the multibillion-dollar industry in a wealthy, diverse, polyglot, ever-changing, twenty-four-hour-news-driven, Internet-saturated continental republic. The omission of modern politics from the Constitution and its amendments poses endless difficulties for regulating the structure of presidential selection, the manner of congressional elections, electioneering law, and campaign finance reform, none of which can be effectively addressed without the inclusion of thoughtful provisions in a new twenty-first-century Constitution. It is often said that our political inadequacies are better handled through statutory means, so smaller, less permanent corrections can be made over time. And this point has some merit. Of course, any constitutional amendments affecting the political system *should* be kept only as specific as absolutely necessary to address the ills described in this chapter. In keeping with the principles of federalism, congressional and state statutes ought to supplement constitutional mandates.

Still, any serious attempt at widespread political reform depends on constitutional retooling. As much as states try to chip away at the ossified political interests that partly control American elections, their successes will be few and far between. Ingrained interests would fight and probably stop most, and perhaps all, of the reforms outlined here. Broad-based change requires a widespread political mandate, the most effective mechanism for which lies in the Constitution. Considering the ubiquity and power of such ingrained interests, there seems to be only one sure method to avoid endless conflict with all the incumbents, wealthy groups and individuals, special interest groups, even specific states (think Iowa and New Hampshire in the presidential selection process) that have a stake in blocking political reform. The solution: bypass the markets of political power altogether. What we need exceeds the strength of the occasional statute or referendum, and we ought to begin by overhauling the inadequate methods we employ for picking a president.

The Origins of Political Species

Once avoided in their entirety by the Founders and the Constitution, political parties have become the sine qua non of American democracy. Woodrow
Wilson was not the first, but he was perhaps the most prescient and insight-
ful American president to acknowledge the essential role political parties play
in the functioning of both elected branches of republican government—the
institutions that undergird the American experiment through a seemingly
fragile system of checks and balances. He wrote:

> Government is not a machine, but a living thing. . . . No living thing can
> have its organs offset against each other as checks, and live. . . . The way
> in which the several branches of the federal government have been sep-
> arately organized and given efficiency in the discharge of their own
> functions has only emphasized their separation and jealous indepen-
> dence. . . . It is for that reason that we have had such an extraordinary
> development of party authority in the United States and have developed
> outside the government itself so elaborate and effective an organiza-
> tion of parties. [The political parties] are so absolutely necessary to hold
> the things thus disconnected and dispersed together and give some
> coherence to the action of political forces.[2]

Wilson further suggested that the political milieu subjects government to the
same evolutionary forces to which Darwin attributed natural selection. Parties evolve to meet the organizational needs of government. But unlike most
species, which seek on some level to maximize reproductive fitness, political
parties seek not just to endure, but to prevail. They want to win, and part of
winning involves the other team losing, thereby encouraging parties to maximize changes that serve *their* needs with little or no regard to the needs of the
citizenry. It is difficult to blame political parties, which fundamentally are
and always have been state-based, for behaving self-interestedly, especially
when no federal constitutional guidelines exist to regulate them. Nor would
it be wise to trust state legislatures or state party committees to enact sufficient
reforms; these succumb to the same self-interested gridlock that political parties do, not to mention the difficulty of arranging uniform reform throughout the country.

Despite the appearance that national political parties maintain a firm control over state party committees, it is the second group that actually sets most
of the rules for presidential selection, such as whether a primary or a caucus
is held in a particular state, and how those events are to be run. With no one

on the national level truly in charge, fifty state political parties compete for the privilege to be first, or second, or tenth, in the presidential selection process every four years. Such squabbling has become so intense at times that the Democratic Party and the Republican Party in some states have failed to agree on a common date for a primary or caucus, subjecting voters in those states to two separate nomination campaigns and two separate elections. In other words, the state parties, which dwell within a sort of legal no-man's-land of national organization but state-based operation, frequently promote individual party interests over national interest. Fortunately for the American electorate, Supreme Court Chief Justice John Marshall established the precedent that the federal Constitution supersedes state constitutions. Even though this does not always mean that federal powers supersede state powers (for example, if the enumeration of powers does not seem to support the exercise of federal power), it does allow us to impose a sort of federal intelligent design on state political parties. And only the Constitution can achieve this aim.

In 1968 candidates competed in sixteen presidential primaries, in a manageable schedule spread out over three months, from March to June.[3] Voters had ample time to evaluate the candidates, and the candidates had enough time between contests to adjust their message if needed. Such a relatively leisurely schedule allowed for midcourse corrections in the selection of a nominee; enough time between contests to let the momentum of the first primary winner diminish, so voters in the next state could take a fresh look at the contenders. By contrast, in 2004 there were thirty-six primaries, plus the contests in D.C. and for "Americans abroad," between January and June. At least a year of intense, headline-grabbing maneuvering preceded a six-month period of equally intense politicking. By 2008 the number of presidential primaries had expanded to thirty-nine, plus territorial contests in Puerto Rico, American Samoa, the Virgin Islands, and Guam.

As if that schedule weren't grueling enough, the 2008 primaries exhibited a phenomenon known as "front-loading," when a majority of states rush to hold their primaries as early as possible, in order to maximize their political impact and significance for candidates. Hastening a particular state's primary contest has its rewards: Candidates pour millions of dollars into advertising and local staff operations, compounded by the millions media outlets spend tracking candidates and, in turn, showcasing the more picturesque spots in the state. Knowing that all state political organizations tend to act self-interestedly, it's hardly a mystery why states clamor to go first in the primary contest lineup. The problem here arises when the states crowd so closely together that little time exists between contests, so the winner of the first battle often wins the second and the third, and the entire nomination choice depends more on momentum than carefully considered individual choices. Some call it a "steamroller," others a "slingshot," but the effect is clear: a lightning-quick nomination of that initial victor. Although the 2008 Democratic marathon between Senators Hillary Clinton and Barack Obama was an exception to the rule, the primaries scheduled later in the calendar usually become pro forma events, with low voter turnout and little media attention. To add insult to injury, the already crowned candidates do not even show up to campaign. Moreover, the front-loading means that the candidates must start their campaigns a full year or two before the first nomination contest, in order to become known around the country and raise the huge sums needed to compete. This elongation of the full-throttle campaign is welcomed only by political consultants and other paid election staffers, certainly not by the average voter, who grows bored and frustrated with the permanent campaign.

By the 2008 presidential election season, forty states had scheduled contests (including both primaries and caucuses) before March. To put that in some historical context, only one state primary occurred before March in 1980. With only a few modern exceptions (1976 on the Republican side and 1984 in the Democratic contest), presidential nominees are known well in advance of the party conventions, and typically, the first few primaries and caucuses virtually determine the winners. Even in 2008, when Obama and Clinton fought to a virtual tie during the regular season, the nomination was rapidly resolved after the final primaries in early June, when it became clear that Senator Obama had sufficient delegates to secure the nomination.

Let's take a closer look at 2008. On the Republican side, only three contests mattered for Senator John McCain. McCain leveraged his long-standing popularity in New Hampshire to produce a stunning comeback after having been written off a few months earlier, when his campaign, finances, and staff collectively imploded. It was simple chance—and New Hampshire's bulldoggedness in maintaining its first-in-the-nation status—that saved McCain. After receiving 37 percent of the vote in New Hampshire, McCain went to South Carolina on January 19 and received an even lower 33 percent, just enough to edge out former Arkansas governor Mike Huckabee. Next up was Florida, where McCain held on to defeat former Massachusetts governor Mitt Romney by yet another narrow margin, 36 to 31 percent. For all practical purposes, the Republican nomination had been determined by a third of the party's voters in this unrepresentative trio of states.

The 2008 Democratic side could not have been more different. Barack Obama and Hillary Clinton fought for every last delegate. The process that began in the snows of Iowa on January 3 would not end until the prairie states of South Dakota and Montana had voted on June 3. The grueling schedule of state primaries and caucuses was haphazard and made little sense. A gargantuan national contest of twenty-two Democratic states on February 5, dubbed "Super Duper Tuesday," was supposed to be the finale to a month-long nomination battle. Instead, it became merely another way station that included a gap of about six weeks with no significant contests between Ohio and Texas on March 4 and Pennsylvania on April 22.

The parties, ideological opposites, thus demonstrated polar opposites in nomination politics in 2008, and neither process was exemplary. The Republicans determined their nominee all too quickly, with three states having disproportionate influence and the unfair winner-take-all system pushing the party to a premature conclusion. The Democrats, underlining their party's long-held obsession with an excruciating degree of fairness, forced their two leading candidates through an obstacle course stretching over fifty states and four territories. With the rules mandating that the top candidates would evenly split the delegates in many congressional districts unless one candidate secured a massive majority (usually more than 63 percent), the practical effect was that Clinton or Obama could win a large state by a technical landslide (more than 55 percent) and net only a few more delegates than the landslide loser. This guaranteed an exhausting, marathon fight to the finish— exciting for all campaign observers, to be sure, but not necessarily in the party's or the public's interest.

Considering the accelerating pace of primary politics, the explosion of private funding propelling candidates for year-long campaigns, and the constant clamoring of states to hold primaries earlier and earlier, what is to be done to restore our conception of popular democracy in presidential selection? Despite attempts by the Republicans in 2000 and the Democrats in 2008 to establish some reasonable reordering of the early contests and also to slow front-loading, the 2008 primary season revealed how ineffective such attempts at reform have been.

Few want to go back to the bad old days when party "bosses" chose presidential candidates in smoke-filled rooms. (Yes, the bosses did reasonably well by selecting nominees such as Franklin Roosevelt, but they also picked the disastrous Warren G. Harding.) Primaries and caucuses are fundamental to our conception of popular democracy in presidential selection. But there is such a thing as ineffective and poorly organized popular democracy.

Every attempt to bring order out of chaos has failed, and there have been many attempts to do so.[4] At the GOP Convention in Philadelphia in 2000, where George W. Bush was nominated for president for the first time, national Republican leaders tried to pass a plan to give states incentives to hold later primaries and caucuses in an attempt to slow front-loading, but the plan failed to pass muster with the convention delegates.[5] For 2008, the Democratic National Committee attempted to bring about some reasonable reordering of the early contests by designating a couple of more diverse small states to go first, but the attempt to dilute the impact of Iowa and especially New Hampshire was less than successful.[6]

Democrats chose Nevada, where Latinos are a prominent minority, and South Carolina, where African Americans often constitute a majority of the primary electorate, to join Iowa and New Hampshire at the starting line in January 2008. Not to be excluded from such a coveted position, Florida and Michigan inserted themselves into January as well, disregarding warnings from the Democratic National Committee not to do so. This prompted the DNC first to refuse to seat delegates from either state, and then eventually to compromise by seating half of the apportioned delegates.

Naturally, such changes in the schedule did not sit well with the state parties of Iowa and New Hampshire, both of which had grown accustomed to their anointed position as presidential kingmakers. Both states insisted that they would go first—party rules be damned; and in the end, the parties capitulated to the states' demands. Similar attempts at reform no doubt will be met with similar failure. And much of the problem can be fairly labeled "Iowa and New Hampshire."

A foreign observer might assume that Iowa and New Hampshire have some constitutional mandate always to lead the primary season. As it happens, the Constitution includes no such provision. Nevertheless, these two states, which together constitute a mere 1.4 percent of the U.S. population (and about 40 percent of their residents are rural—double the national proportion), continue to be one of the most glaring obstacles to an equitable, well-distributed primary schedule. Initiated in 1920, the New Hampshire primary solidified its power in 1952 when it strongly influenced President Harry Truman's decision not to seek reelection and led to Dwight Eisenhower's successful bid for the GOP nomination. Further, the New Hampshire primary reinforced its influence in 1968.[7] That year, New Hampshire toppled yet another incumbent when Minnesota senator Eugene McCarthy lost narrowly to President Lyndon Johnson in the Democratic primary, hastening LBJ's decision not to seek another term.[8] Iowa, on the other hand, first gained special significance in

1972, when George McGovern used it to propel himself to an ill-fated Democratic nomination. Iowa can also be credited—or blamed, if you like—for the nomination of a relatively unknown former Georgia governor, Jimmy Carter, in 1976.[9]

Put simply, why should two tiny, heavily white, disproportionately rural states have a staggeringly powerful and electorally imbalanced say in the making of the next president? Answering that question is easy enough: They shouldn't. Answering the question of how and why these two states managed to so deeply entrench themselves in the American political process is a bit more complex, and it deserves further explanation.

Imagine an event that every four years produced tens of millions of dollars in additional revenue for local businesses, showcased every pristine locale, and focused the attention of politicians and policymakers on individuals important to local industry. Such are the benefits for Iowa and New Hampshire for the months that precede the primary contests in both states—a virtual bonanza for local businesses and future federal spending promises. All the candidates—and thus the eventual president—learn all about their problems and needs, an educational process that cannot hurt the states in the spending decisions of the next administration. Plus, the elected president knows he will have to start his reelection effort in the same two states—further incentive to assist them. The presidential selection process is a gravy train for the Hawkeye and Granite States, and they know it. The citizens of the leadoff states take their job as presidential screeners seriously, but then again, what state given this important task would not?

Now, imagine trying to tell these states to forgo the benefits of early contests for the sake of national fairness. Few states—or local political parties, for that matter—would be eager to consider primary schedules that omitted such abundant benefits. The presidential candidates fully understand the stakes of the game, and the absurdity of it. Michael Dukakis, the 1988 Democratic presidential nominee, had this to say about Iowa: "I spent 85 campaign days in the state of Iowa alone. Now, Iowa is a great state . . . and they did very well by Mike Dukakis. But, 85 full campaign days in one state . . . really doesn't make a hell of a lot of sense, does it?"[10] No, it doesn't.

Moreover, the average African American plus Hispanic/Latino population of Iowa and New Hampshire is only 3.6 percent, while the national minority population is 24.6 percent. Even if one were to assume, incorrectly, that the two states are somehow representative of their Northeast and Midwest regions, the burgeoning South and West (containing 55 percent of the country's people) are mainly left out of the critical opening window of presidential selection.

Clearly, Iowa and New Hampshire have managed to secure an incredibly lucrative franchise that they will, understandably, try to protect at all costs. And without a constitutional solution—that is, a constitutional requirement determining primary schedules—there simply is no way to fix a problem that seems to get worse every four years. Even if national party committees wanted to orchestrate a tentative fix, their methods would be ineffectual at best and counterproductive at worst. Their arsenal of punishment includes such terrible fates as giving delegates bad hotels and seating at the party conclaves or, a bit more consequentially, as we saw in 2008, depriving states of some delegates if they insist on disobeying national party regulations. But a handful of lost delegates pales in comparison to the publicity generated by early primaries.

The truth is that Iowa and New Hampshire are determined to do whatever is necessary to keep their contests first.[11] New Hampshire even has a law that requires the secretary of state to do everything in his or her power to keep it that way, and Secretary William Gardner has threatened, if needed, to move the New Hampshire primary back into the calendar year *before* the presidential election to fulfill his mandate. No doubt Iowa would do the same. And we think the process takes too long already?

The Senate held hearings in July 2008 to consider a package of bills designed to overhaul the presidential election system. Florida senator Bill Nelson has introduced several bills, co-sponsored by his colleague Michigan senator Carl Levin (not coincidentally, two legislators from the states that rebuffed DNC scheduling rules in 2008), the centerpiece of which is a constitutional amendment to abolish the Electoral College. Among the other bills discussed was a plan to eliminate the current primary schedule and create a rotating regional system. Few political observers believe these changes have any reasonable chance of being passed by Congress or voluntarily implemented by the states or parties in time for the 2012 election.[12]

Partly to uphold the values of federalism, and partly because many members of Congress fantasize about running for president some day, the federal legislature would be highly unlikely to step into this briar patch.[13] For one thing, many members of the congressional delegations from Iowa and New Hampshire would be willing to self-immolate on the Capitol steps to stop congressionally sponsored reform, and they would likely be joined by any colleagues who believe their own presidential ambitions might be at stake. (It's a rare senator who doesn't wake up in the morning and see a presidential portrait in the mirror.)

The only possible comprehensive solution to the problem of presidential primary reform is likely to be a constitutional one. Considering the circum-

stances in which the Founders designed the original version of the system—
a pre-party, pre-popular-democracy age—the necessity of constitutional
reform is self-evident. The guiding principle can be one that all citizens, and
indeed all states, can readily embrace: Every state and region ought to have
essentially an equal chance, over time, to influence the outcome of the parties'
presidential nominations, and thus the selection of presidents. Simple equity
demands that all of us, regardless of our state of residence, should have the
opportunity to significantly influence the selection of presidential nominees
by filling one of the coveted early voting slots.

Long-term equity is the first crucial component of reform. Reducing front-
loading is the second. Beyond the equal-influence-over-time rule, the presidential selection process also ought to enable the states to spread out the
contests over several months, thereby reducing front-loading and low voter
turnout in the primaries that follow. In most recent cycles, the nominations
have been all but decided by the first few weeks of voting, leaving large majorities of voters and states effectively disfranchised. In 2000, for example, both
Vice President Al Gore and Governor George W. Bush had all but clinched
their parties' nominations before thirty-three states, including many of the
largest, had even held their primaries. Understandably, this fact led an alien-
ated public to tune out the process before they could become fully engaged.

In recent cycles, so much attention, money, and energy goes toward the first
few weeks of primary contests that large majorities of voters and states are
neglected. Voters with little stake in the outcome of presidential primary contests will behave accordingly. In 2000 a mere 17.7 percent of the adult population turned out to vote in all primaries and caucuses, in both parties and all
states *combined*. This is a miserable showing, and it contributes to the polarization that bedevils American politics. Polarized, unfair contests alienate and
discourage the people who gather around the ideological center, permitting
political fringe elements to dominate an unrepresentative share of political
power. The construction of an inclusive, rational, and fair nominating process
could contribute hugely to broadening and elevating the level of participation
in primaries and caucuses.

The first step may be the easiest to describe. The nominating process ought
to be shortened and moved into the four months immediately preceding the
party conventions—instead of dragged out for almost a year and ending
months before the conventions. It's hardly controversial to suggest that the
American public suffers from political campaign fatigue (not to mention the
terrible toll such prolonged campaigns take on staffers, the media, the volun-
teer armies, and the candidates themselves). It is possible to create a system

that begins in March or April and flows directly into August party conventions, culminating in the Labor Day kickoff for the general election. Idealistic as it sounds, these changes would not be difficult to accomplish if the will and the means were present. If the electorate supplies the will, the Constitution can outline the means. The following is proposed in that spirit.

The Regional Lottery Plan

The Congress ought to be constitutionally required to establish four regions of contiguous states (obviously, with contiguity requirements waived for Alaska and Hawaii, and for territories that may one day gain statehood). The regions would likely resemble the natural boundaries many Americans speak of in common parlance—the Northeast, South, Midwest, and West.[14] States in each region would hold their nominating events in successive months, beginning in April and ending in July. The two major-party conventions would follow in August. Already, without any other reforms to the national primary process, this schedule cuts three months off the bloated process that currently prevails in presidential election years.

States would still be free to choose any date they wished within the region's month, and further, they would be free, as they currently are, to choose either the primary or the caucus method of selecting delegates.[15] Separating states into four distinct groups could also help diminish the incentive to front-load. Even if states still vie for the privilege of holding the first primary within their region, just as much, and perhaps more, publicity and attention would likely be paid to states that wait to hold their primaries or caucuses later, perhaps standing alone on a particular day. Such a situation would encourage candidates to spend time and money in the stand-alone state, which, after all, would garner far more headlines than if ten states held primaries on the same day. The scheduling issues, in other words, would take care of themselves. Furthermore, the regional system would allow a candidate to concentrate his or her time in one region for at least a month, offering candidates a better opportunity to learn the problems and peoples of the region and its states. Another advantage that might not occur to the casual observer of politics: The geographic proximity of the campaigning would help cut down on the torturous schedules candidates are forced to keep on the road.

To determine the order of the regions, I suggest establishing a U.S. Election Lottery, to be held on New Year's Day of the presidential election year. A lottery would be fairer than the current system, and it would add a bit of panache to the beginning of the presidential election year. Those giant rotating cauldrons with pop-up ping-pong balls would finally find a more noble purpose than bestowing riches on a stunned lottery winner. For example, four color-coded balls—one for each region—would be loaded into the machine, and by the deft hand of the chairperson of the Federal Election Commission, the regional primary order would be set. Aside from the obvious advantage of making for good television, the drawing would also serve to dismantle part of the modern permanent presidential campaign. Candidates wouldn't be able to campaign on site too far in advance, because no one would know where the political season would begin. Even the richest candidates presumably wouldn't want to waste the money necessary to maintain organizations in all four regions, much less all fifty states.

Even more important, the lottery system would help to equalize the opportunity for every state and region to have a shot at going first, at least over time. This is no small thing. The law of averages may not provide exactly equal distribution year after year, but the system honors the equal-access principle and provides the fairest way to determine the order of primaries. Iowa and New Hampshire would no longer maintain their dominion over the primary process, and other states would have a chance to enjoy the political bounty afforded to those first few contests.

A lottery system would also help curtail the impatient, frantic maneuvering that, today, ensures that the entire competition for the party nominations ends within a few weeks. Holding regional primaries would not only allow candidates to recover from setbacks in one region and to regroup before the next set of contests, but the inevitable power of regional pride and loyalty would likely ensure that the race continued through at least two or three, perhaps even all four, sections of the nation. One can imagine the national news media favoring this plan, because it would permit news outlets to prolong their coverage and spend even more days guessing and revising. Candidates would have the chance to interact with far more people than they do under the current system, which forces candidates to spend half their time in cars, on buses, or flying in planes.

One can imagine the residents of Iowa and New Hampshire politely objecting here. They would claim that when smaller states begin the primary season, candidates have the chance to campaign personally, to get to know individual voters and the problems that affect their lives, and to hone the art of retail politics. And they would have a point. But there is a way to combine the advantages of small-state scrutiny of candidates with the inherent fairness of round-robin regional primaries. The answer lies in another lottery—a second lottery on January 1. The names of all states with four or fewer members in the U.S. House of Representatives (at present, and at least until the 2010 census, twenty states) would be placed in the whirling cauldron of ping-pong balls, and the chairperson of the FEC would select two balls. Those two states (or D.C.) with relatively small populations would lead off the regional contests on or about March 15—at least two full weeks before the initial contests in the first region. These two states would be free to stage a primary or a caucus, and the candidates would be free to participate in none, one, or both. As a practical matter, most candidates would choose both, unless a prominent candidate hailed from one of the leadoff states. Traditionally, a home candidate gets deference and is sometimes unopposed for the state's delegates. Of course, the other party can still have a full-fledged fight in the state's primary or caucus.

All the candidates would usually rush to these leadoff states right after the lottery on January 1, and they would have two and a half months to campaign. But there would be no permanent, four-year campaigns there, and personalized, one-to-one campaigning would be a large part of the effort. In other words, the two states would offer all the advantages of Iowa and New Hampshire, without having always to be Iowa and New Hampshire. In addition, the guarantee of at least two weeks of decompression after the leadoff states make their choices would give voters in the first region a chance to evaluate the results and reevaluate the winners—and possibly to make different choices.

This plan excludes, or ought to exclude, the island territories, which are remote both in location and in significance to the general election in November since they have no electoral votes. The District of Columbia, however, *should* be included, and this would mean twenty-one jurisdictions would have the chance to be selected in the second lottery. Constituting a larger population than Wyoming, and with electoral votes assigned in November, the District's citizens—who currently and shamefully lack full voting representation in either house of Congress—would no doubt relish and deserve this chance, should Lady Luck deliver it.

No plan could completely eliminate the initial rush that begins every presidential nominating season, but the Regional Lottery Plan would achieve several goals that, without constitutional reform, currently seem impossible to implement. The plan would shorten and focus the election campaign, a relief to candidates and voters. All regions and states would have an opportunity to substantially affect the making of presidential nominees. Civic participation would benefit from a rational, conveniently arranged schedule. But all of this positive change can only come about by putting the politics of nominations in its proper place—the United States Constitution.

Notes

1. George Washington, "Farewell Address 1796," available through the Yale Law School's Avalon Project (http://avalon.law.yale.edu/default.asp [November 3, 2008]).

2. Woodrow Wilson, *Constitutional Government in the United States* (Columbia University Press, 1908), pp. 56, 206, 221–22.

3. See Rhodes Cook, *United States Presidential Primary Elections, 1968–1996: A Handbook of Election Statistics* (Washington: CQ Press, 2000), p. 10. Fifteen states and the District of Columbia held presidential primaries in 1968.

4. For an overview of the major questions facing critics of the nominating process, see John Haskell, *Fundamentally Flawed: Understanding and Reforming Presidential Primaries* (Lanham, Md.: Rowman and Littlefield, 1996), pp. 62–78. For an in-depth look at the nominating process, see *Enduring Controversies in Presidential Nominating Politics*, edited by Emmett H. Buell Jr. and William G. Mayer (University of Pittsburgh Press, 2004).

5. This was the so-called Delaware Plan, and it came up in 2000, failing at the convention. Some party officials hoped it might be implemented in time for the 2004 primaries, but it was not. New efforts at reform were considered at the 2008 Republican National Convention, but no changes were enacted once again. See "Nominating Process" in *Presidential Selection: A Guide to Reform* (University of Virginia, Center for Governmental Studies, 2001).

6. A 2005 party commission headed by Representative David Price of North Carolina and approved by the Democratic National Committee added a couple of states to the early process. Iowa still goes first, followed a few days later by caucuses in Nevada, then New Hampshire with the initial primary, followed by the South Carolina primary. New Hampshire continued to fight the plan; moreover, four small states instead of two isn't a dramatic improvement. See Dan Balz, "Balancing Act: Iowa, N.H. vs. Critics: Democrats Weigh Plan to Stretch 2008 Calendar," *Washington Post*, December 28, 2005; David S. Broder, "The Democrats' Dysfunctional Calendar," *Washington Post*, August 31, 2006. For more information, visit the website of the Democratic Commission on Presidential Nomination Timing and Scheduling (www.democrats.org/page/s/nominating [November 3, 2008]).

7. In early 1952, Senator Estes Kefauver of Tennessee defeated President Truman in the New Hampshire primary, after which Truman announced that he wouldn't run again. See Cook, *United States Presidential Primary Elections*, p. 461. Meanwhile, General Dwight Eisenhower managed to defeat the early favorite for the Republican nomination, Senator Robert Taft of Ohio, in a foreshadowing of the convention result. For more on the 1952 New Hampshire primary, visit the New Hampshire Political Library (www.politicallibrary.org/ [November 3, 2008]).

8. LBJ won the primary with just a shade under 50 percent of the vote, with McCarthy at 41 percent. But McCarthy won the lion's share of the delegates at stake in the Granite State, and his psychological victory was huge.

9. In a large field of Democratic candidates, Carter received just 29 percent in Iowa and 28 percent in New Hampshire—remarkably small totals, but more than anyone else—and thus was a president made.

10. Keynote address, National Symposium on Presidential Selection, University of Virginia Center for Politics, April 5, 2001, Charlottesville, Virginia.

11. See Title LXIII of the New Hampshire code, NH ST, Sec. 653:9.

12. See Ben Pershing, "Florida Sen. Nelson Pushes for Electoral Overhaul," *Washington Post*, June 9, 2008. For more information about the legislation, see http:// billnelson.senate.gov/ (November 3, 2008).

13. Congress does not have the power to regulate party primary elections inasmuch as the 14th Amendment applies to protect the voting rights of citizens. "Where a primary election is an integral part of the procedure of choice, the right to vote in that primary election is subject to congressional protection." See Article I of the CRS Annotated Constitution, esp. note 338, citing *United States* v. *Classic*, 313 U.S. 299, 315–21 (1941).

14. These regions have about the same number of states: Northeast (twelve plus D.C.), South (thirteen), Midwest (twelve), West (thirteen).

15. In a few states, such as South Carolina and Virginia, the Democratic and Republican parties can separately choose their preferred method of nomination, without any interference by the state legislature. The legislature does have to pass enabling legislation to hold an election on the dates chosen, which is usually done as a matter of course. Should a party wish to pay for the election by itself, no legislation at all is needed. Given the cost of a statewide election, the parties almost always seek legislative approval. In most states, however, the parties must take their preferred methods and dates to the state legislature and seek its formal assent. On occasion, state legislatures have not given permission, and instead they have chosen another method and date for the nominating contest. Partisanship can come into play; obviously, it helps to be the party in the majority in the state legislature to obtain the most desirable electoral setup.

THOMAS E. MANN

8

Is This Any Way to Pick a President? Lessons from 2008

Shortly after Senator Barack Obama became the presumptive Democratic presidential nominee, four months after Senator John McCain effectively wrapped up the contest to be the Republican Party's standard-bearer, the *New York Times* offered up the conventional wisdom about the process that produced these outcomes: "It takes nothing away from the achievements of Barack Obama and John McCain to take note that the system for choosing the parties' nominees is seriously flawed." Stressing the principle of "one person, one vote," the *Times* editorial argued that "all voters should have an equal opportunity, regardless of who they are or where they live, to affect the outcome. The process should be transparent, the ballot should be secret, and there should be no unnecessary barriers to voting."[1] By these standards, the editorial asserted, the system is in dire need of reform. Caucuses should be abandoned, the schedule of primaries radically restructured, the rules for allocating delegates among the candidates recast to more accurately reflect their percentage of votes in each state, and superdelegates eliminated.

Underlying this diagnosis and prescription were a range of complaints about the 2008 nomination season. The process was said to be too long, extending from early 2007, when virtually all serious candidates felt obliged to commence their campaigns, until June 2008, when the Democrats finally resolved the hotly contested Clinton-Obama race. The schedule of delegate selection events began too early, was too compressed on Super Tuesday (the day on which roughly half of all delegates were chosen), and then too scattered in the final months, with one primary (Pennsylvania's) capturing seven weeks of undivided attention from Clinton and Obama. Two large states (Michigan and Florida) violated both parties' scheduling rules and thereby deprived their voters and the candidates of fully contested primaries and a complete slate of convention delegates. The full delegations were restored at the convention after it became certain that Obama would win the nomination.

Critics argued that the Republican contest was resolved too quickly and serendipitously, with the winner-take-all allocation of delegates in a number of large states producing a winner before party voters had seriously grappled with the choices.

The Democratic Party process, on the other hand, was criticized for fostering party divisiveness by failing to resolve the race in a reasonable period of time. A proportional representation system with byzantine complexity made it difficult for candidates winning a majority of a state's votes to gain a significant delegate advantage. Relatively small numbers of caucus participants reaped a delegate harvest that often dwarfed the gains produced by millions of primary voters. The sui generis Texas "two-step" featured on a single day both a primary and a caucus, which made it possible for Clinton, the winner of the primary, to lose the battle for delegates to Obama. What's more, many citizens and pundits found the prospect of a bloc of party leaders and elected officials ultimately overriding the choice of voters deeply offensive to their democratic values (as well as to their candidate preference).

The 2008 presidential nominating season also witnessed the collapse of the public financing system first put in place in 1976, with all but one serious candidate (John Edwards) opting out, and an explosion of private fundraising that shattered all previous records.

This litany of complaints reinforces and supplements critiques of the presidential nominating process that have been leveled after every election since the advent of the modern selection system in 1972.[2] It discourages the best politicians from running. Candidates are not subject to meaningful peer review. A few small states early in the schedule have disproportionate influence by generating momentum that largely dictates the eventual outcome. An increasingly front-loaded calendar narrows the field too quickly and produces nominees before the vast majority of states and voters have an opportunity to weigh in. The media, instead of political parties, broker the selection of nominees. Horse-race coverage and sound-bite campaigning drown out a serious discussion of the issues. Unrepresentative primary electorates and caucus participants drive each party's nominee and platform to its ideological pole. Money dominates the process. Issue and candidate enthusiasts populate the national party conventions, which no longer play any meaningful role in the nomination of presidential candidates. The nomination process neither tests a candidate's suitability for the White House nor imparts lessons or builds relationships helpful to governing.

A Nominating Process in Flux

The processes by which the two major political parties nominate their candidates for the presidency have long been subject to criticism and change.[3] The early decades of the American republic featured a fitful struggle by emerging parties to replace the nonpartisan elite consensus of the Electoral College with competing nominations by the congressional party caucuses. By 1840, national party conventions had become the dominant means by which parties made their selections, with state parties largely determining the delegate makeup of those conventions. In the early twentieth century, Progressives, in hopes of countering the influence of party bosses, championed the use of primary elections to select delegates. But that plebiscitary system never fully took hold, and conventions retained their role as the setting in which party elites decided who should lead the party in the general election campaign.

The half-century encompassing the 1920s through the 1960s featured a mixed system of presidential selection, with aspiring candidates often testing their popular appeal by competing in selected primaries but investing even more time and energy bidding for the support of party leaders. Increasingly, most of this work was done well before the conventions; the last time a presidential nominating contest extended beyond the first ballot was 1952.[4] The national party conventions became settings for the ratification of decisions made elsewhere and opportunities to present the parties and their candidates to large television audiences. Those decisions continued to be dominated by state and local party officials. Following President Lyndon Johnson's surprising withdrawal from the contest and Senator Robert Kennedy's assassination, Vice President Hubert Humphrey garnered the 1968 Democratic presidential nomination without entering a single primary.

Humphrey's victory proved to be the last of the mixed system of presidential nominations.[5] Facing a deeply divided convention in Chicago, he agreed to support a resolution calling for a reform of the delegate selection process. The McGovern-Fraser Commission (formally, the Commission on Party Structure and Delegate Selection) subsequently produced a report that led to a major rewrite of Democratic Party rules governing selection of delegates to its national party convention. Most important, delegates would have to be selected in a timely fashion (that is, in the year of the presidential election) and in a manner that fairly reflected the candidate preferences of those participating in primary elections or party caucuses.

These new dictates from the Democratic National Committee forced every state Democratic Party organization to amend its delegate selection rules.[6] Many states found it easier to comply with the new rules by switching from traditional party caucuses to primaries. Even those that retained caucuses as mechanisms for the selection of delegates witnessed a shift in initiative and influence from party regulars to candidates and issue activists. Whether state parties turned to candidate primaries or participatory caucuses, they faced new constraints on how delegates were allocated to presidential candidates, demographic targets for the composition of delegates, and a prohibition on ex-officio delegates, the latter part of a larger effort to separate party official-dom from the delegate selection process.[7]

One important consequence, according to Nelson Polsby, was that the national party conventions were transformed from a body of delegates meeting to ratify results of complex negotiations conducted by party leaders to a body dominated by candidate enthusiasts and interest group delegates who ratify choices made in primaries and participatory caucuses.[8] A new plebiscitary system, featuring strong personal campaign organizations, direct popular appeals by the candidates, and a greatly diminished role for party leaders and elected officials, was now in place.

But that system was not static: it was subject to ever-changing rules as Democrats turned to new reform commissions after almost every election to deal with criticisms and controversies that arose in the national convention and (perhaps naïvely) to try to improve their rather dismal electoral performance. That involved moving from winner-take-all primaries to complex formulas for the proportional allocation of delegates; attempting to alter the scheduling of state primaries and caucuses; and seeking ways of reintegrating Democratic Party and elected officials into the national conventions.[9]

Conversely, Republicans largely eschewed the reform impulse that transformed the Democratic presidential nominating process. They continued to allow their state parties almost complete autonomy in setting their delegate selection rules.[10] Most notably, many state Republican parties retained rules allowing the plurality winner of a primary election to garner all of the delegates at stake.[11] Nonetheless, the Republican process was indirectly shaped by two forces largely beyond their control. The first was state laws passed to accommodate the new Democratic Party rules. A number of states set up new presidential primary elections; others shifted the date on which their existing primaries were held. Not surprisingly given their tradition of deference to state autonomy, the Republicans, like the Democrats, came to rely more on primaries for the selection of delegates and saw their calendar of nomination events subject to front-loading as states jostled to time their primaries and caucuses in an effort to play a more influential role in the selection of presidential nominees. More recently, the national Republican

Party felt obliged to pass its own rule punishing states that schedule their primary or caucus before the party's official window for the selection of delegates.[12]

The second factor that shaped Republican as well as Democratic presidential nominating practices was new federal campaign finance law. The 1974 amendments to the Federal Election Campaign Act required candidates to disclose funding sources and set limits on the source and size of contributions to federal candidates; it also established a public funding program that matched small contributions raised by candidates for each party's presidential nomination. These provisions encouraged early entry by candidates into the contest, increasingly nearer to the beginning of the year preceding the presidential election. A failure to adjust the matching amounts and spending limits associated with acceptance of the public subsidy to reflect the realistic costs of campaigning set the stage for the unraveling of public financing starting in the 2000 election.[13]

After many decades of evolution and reform, the presidential nominating system was hardly a system at all. Absent a comprehensive design intended to advance the multiple objectives of candidate selection, party building, and democratic participation, it remained a largely inherited and highly decentralized process in spite of efforts to nationalize and standardize the rules. Differences between the parties and across the states shaped the strategies of the candidates, the relative influence of individual states, the role of party elites, and the opportunities available to voters to participate meaningfully in the choice of nominees. Efforts to refine the new plebiscitary model by reducing the special advantages enjoyed by the Iowa caucuses and New Hampshire primaries and decompressing the front-loaded calendar were largely unsuccessful. In 2008, Iowa and New Hampshire, in response to threats to their standing as first-in-the-nation presidential caucuses and primary, moved up their events to January 3 and 8, respectively, while many other states rescheduled their primaries and caucuses to February 5, the first day of both parties' official window for delegate selection events, producing a Super Tuesday that took on the trappings of a national primary. At the same time, new research suggested that the so-called "invisible primary"—the year before the first formal delegate selection event in Iowa during which candidates launch their campaigns, frame their message and platform, build their organizations, raise money, seek endorsements, and test their popular appeal—was at least as important as it had been in the immediate pre-reform period, and party elites broadly conceived continue to play a highly influential role in the selection of presidential nominees.[14]

The 2008 Nominating Contests

The institutional context of presidential nominations—party rules governing the selection of delegates, the scheduling of primaries and caucuses, and campaign finance law—shape the dynamics and outcomes of each party's contest. As 2008's extraordinary nomination season reminds us, however, these processes do not operate in a vacuum. Both the political environment that defines each party's strategic situation and the field of candidates determine how the rules of the game play out.[15]

The 2008 election cycle was bound to be unusual. It featured open contests for both party nominations—the first time since 1952 with neither a sitting president or vice president on the general election ballot. The outgoing president was leaving office with historically low job approval ratings, and in a time of economic turmoil, an unpopular war, and deep public pessimism about the direction of the country. Republican candidates faced a dispirited party electorate, but one still largely loyal to its president and supportive of his policies. Finding a way to win the nomination without fatally weakening one's appeal among independents and swing partisans in the general election posed a daunting challenge.

Aspirants for the Democratic nomination confronted a party base eager for change (especially with respect to the war in Iraq) and confident that after two surprising and heartbreakingly close electoral losses in 2000 and 2004, their time had finally come. The challenge for each candidate was to distinguish him- or herself as a change agent, an embodiment of the values and interests of the newly ascendant Democratic Party, and a safe bet to lead the party to a victory in November.

Given this political environment, it was no surprise that the Republican field of candidates left many party stalwarts disappointed. The field lacked a natural front-runner, one who appealed to all of the party's major constituencies and was well positioned to be George W. Bush's successor. Starting in 2004, John McCain worked assiduously to fill that role, but his bloody battle with Bush for the 2000 nomination, his prominent embrace of campaign finance reform, his bipartisan leadership on comprehensive immigration reform, and his reputation as a maverick in party circles made him an unlikely consensual choice.

Nor did the other major Republican candidates take comfortably to that role. In spite of Mitt Romney's impressive record of achievement in the private, nonprofit, and public sectors, many Republicans were uncomfortable with his Mormon religious faith, his record as governor of the liberal state of

Massachusetts, and his protean positions on core party issues. Rudy Giuliani's reputation as the tough-minded and successful mayor of New York, enhanced by his favorable national visibility immediately after the September 11 terrorist attacks, seemed unlikely to overcome the skepticism based on his moderate position on social issues, his controversial private life, and his bombastic personal style.

None of the other candidates appeared to have the prominence in party circles or sufficient access to campaign resources to become serious players. Throughout 2007, Republican poll respondents indicated much lower satisfaction with their field of candidates than did their Democratic counterparts with their choices. That dissatisfaction eventually persuaded former senator Fred Thompson to make a late entry into the contest, but his candidacy failed to generate the direction and energy needed to be competitive.

The Democrats, on the other hand, had an abundance of candidate riches. Hillary Clinton quickly assumed the position of front-runner—almost as credible an heir apparent as an incumbent vice president. Early in 2007 Barack Obama established himself as a serious contender by virtue of his fundraising success, timely message, organizational strength, and charisma. John Edwards built from a base of public and activist support generated by his 2004 candidacy. Other experienced Democratic politicians—Joe Biden, Chris Dodd, and Bill Richardson—lent weight to the field if not serious competition to the top tier of candidates.

The front-loaded nomination process did produce some outcomes consistent with well-established patterns.[16] All of the candidates in both parties faced an entry fee in 2007, in the form of early fundraising success that did not depend on a breakthrough showing in Iowa and New Hampshire. Those candidates treated as being in the top tier in both parties were those who had raised large amounts in 2007. The only candidate without a significant early war chest who competed seriously in the caucuses and primaries was Mike Huckabee.

As in previous years, the field narrowed quickly. All eleven Republican candidates except Fred Thompson entered the contest in early 2007. Four withdrew in the second half of 2007 before the first delegate selection event. Three others followed in January 2008. Romney's concession shortly after Super Tuesday on February 5 effectively ended the contest, although Huckabee kept his candidacy active for another month and Ron Paul stuck around until the end of the primary season in June.

The field of ten Democratic candidates also narrowed quickly. One withdrew in late 2006, shortly after announcing his exploratory committee, another in early 2007. The others remained in the field throughout the year of the invisible primary and competed in the Iowa caucuses. But the Iowa results dispatched two and New Hampshire the third of the second-tier candidates; by the end of January, the contest was down to two serious contenders.

Another well-established pattern—an early decision on the nominee made by the handful of states scheduled at the beginning of the process with momentum more important than the accumulation of delegates—was evident in the 2008 Republican contest. Romney was unable to recover from his losses in Iowa and New Hampshire. Giuliani's failure to compete seriously in either Iowa or New Hampshire eroded his early lead in Florida, effectively ending his candidacy before it began. Lacking campaign funds and a national professional campaign organization, Huckabee was unable to extend his astonishing victory in Iowa to South Carolina, whose social conservative bent was fertile territory for him. Fred Thompson's make-or-break focus on South Carolina divided the religious right and extinguished whatever spark of life remained in both candidacies. After putting his candidacy on life support in mid-2007, John McCain exploited the strategic opportunities presented by his adversaries to win plurality victories in New Hampshire and South Carolina, and then a comfortable pre–Super Tuesday victory in Florida. His passage from "near-death" to presumptive Republican nominee was achieved in the month of January, with four states—Iowa, New Hampshire, South Carolina, and Florida—playing the decisive roles. The Super Tuesday results, magnified by the winner-take-all allocation of delegates in many states, affirmed rather than decided who would be the Republican Party presidential nominee.

No such pattern developed on the Democratic side, where the race quickly developed into a very competitive two-person contest that extended over the full five months of primaries and caucuses. The logic of a front-loaded nominating process—with its emphasis on early victories, media attention, and fundraising success and failure—was foiled by the extraordinary resources and resourcefulness of Hillary Clinton and Barack Obama. Both succeeded during 2007 in raising prodigious amounts of money, building impressive national campaign organizations, attracting thousands of volunteers, garnering endorsements from prominent party officials and constituent groups, developing campaign themes and strategies, attracting the lion's share of media coverage, and establishing themselves as the top two Democratic candidates in the national polls. These factors made it very difficult for any of the other candidates to make headway during the invisible primary.

Obama's victory in Iowa established his standing as a candidate with a legitimate shot at winning the nomination and dashed any hopes of John

Edwards making a serious run. Clinton's victory five days later in New Hampshire ensured that Obama would not catapult to the nomination based on momentum generated in the early states. Obama's huge victory in South Carolina denied Clinton any chance to ride her own wave into the Super Tuesday states. At that point it was clear that Clinton and Obama were engaged in a battle for delegates in which all of the institutional features of the system—party rules governing the distribution of delegates among and within states; the allocation of delegates to candidates, and the role of superdelegates; state laws setting the schedule for open and closed primaries; and campaign finance law and practice—would shape the strategies and successes of the two campaigns. Obama's ultimate success is partly attributable to his ability to anticipate well in advance the type of race that would ensue and to structure his campaign to capitalize on the opportunities available to him.

Bad News or Good in 2008?

This essay began with the litany of complaints leveled at the presidential nominating process as it played out in 2008 against the backdrop of criticisms that have surrounded it since the advent of the modern system in the 1972 election. The tenor of much of the commentary was that, whatever the outcome, this was no way to pick a president. Before proceeding to a consideration of that larger question, it is important to balance the ledger by reviewing positive developments associated with this round of presidential selection.

First and most important was the choice of candidates. While none of the candidates naturally appealed to all elements of the Republican Party, John McCain was arguably the strongest general election candidate in the Republican field. Although he led a dispirited party, some of whose loyalists were not thrilled with his nomination, he managed by summer to unify that party while retaining appeal among independents and began to amass the resources needed to compete in November. Given the horrible political environment facing the Republicans, this was no small achievement.

Barack Obama and Hillary Clinton stood out in a strong field of candidates, and either one would have been broadly acceptable within their party and a formidable contender in November; however, who was likely to be the stronger candidate and more effective president was a source of much disagreement during the nomination process. Obama's impressive general election campaign, comfortable victory in November, and impressive transition to governing affirmed the success of the process by producing a strong Democratic nominee.

Second, at a time of deep disenchantment with the state of public life in America, the nominating contests prompted an extraordinary surge in public interest and participation. The emergence of female and African American contenders for the Democratic nomination and a Republican war hero and party maverick energized new voters, created compelling narratives that captured large audiences at home and abroad, and underscored the openness of the presidential selection process to unconventional candidates.

Third, the protracted battle between Clinton and Obama extended to many more states and voters the opportunity to participate meaningfully in the nomination process than has been the norm in recent decades. Democratic primary voters and caucus participants had ample opportunity to see these two candidates tested under stressful circumstances and to deliberate seriously on the choices they confronted. The oversize influence of a handful of early states was matched by a number of those that avoided the rush to the front of the calendar. Moreover, the extended battle between the two candidates, while sometimes bitter and generating hard feelings in both camps, did not damage Democratic unity in the general election.

Fourth, in spite of the collapse of the public funding system and the prodigious amounts of money raised and spent by the candidates, money did not seriously distort or otherwise damage the 2008 nominating process. The large sums were indicative of the extraordinarily high level of public interest in the stakes of the election and the choices offered. Millions of small donors, most contributing via the Internet, provided a substantial percentage of the Obama and Clinton mega-budgets.[17] Yet, money was not the decisive factor in either party's nomination. Obama's 2007 fundraising success was matched by Clinton. Only after his breakthrough victory in Iowa was he able to establish himself as a plausible nominee and to open a fundraising advantage.[18] Even so, Clinton did not fall short because of insufficient funds. She won several primaries in which she was greatly outspent by Obama. Her problems stemmed more from campaign strategy and choices regarding the allocation of her resources.

John McCain won the Republican nomination in spite of his fundraising shortfall. The impressive Romney and Giuliani war chests were insufficient to overcome shortcomings in strategy and performance on the campaign trail. Huckabee's upset victory in Iowa demonstrated that a candidate can overcome long odds with meager resources.[19]

Even the collapse of the public financing system during this nominating season had a silver lining. The extended and highly competitive contest between Clinton and Obama, which mobilized millions of new voters and riveted the attention of publics around the globe, would not have been possible if either had opted into the public matching program and its very low spending limits. And John McCain's late decision to opt out of that program made it possible for him to raise the funds necessary to sustain his general election campaign for the seven months between Super Tuesday and the Republican convention.

Ultimately, the American presidential nominating system managed in 2008 to produce satisfactory results with respect to candidate selection, party unity, and public participation. It facilitated the emergence of unconventional candidates and a surge of public interest and participation, accommodated and fairly resolved an unprecedented level of competition for one party's nomination, and produced candidates broadly acceptable to their parties and qualified to serve in the White House, all without allowing money to damage the process or distort the outcome. This was no mean accomplishment.

Evaluation and Reform

How then should we evaluate the critique of the present system and judge the efficacy of reform proposals to ameliorate the identified problems? The critique is based on both practical considerations and one overarching theoretical argument. The latter is implicit in the *New York Times* editorial cited at the beginning of this chapter. Each party's nomination should be determined through a democratic process in which voters play roughly the same role as in the general election. They should have an equal opportunity to affect the outcome, face no unnecessary barriers to voting, and be able to cast a secret ballot. Their collective decision should translate directly into the selection of delegates in each state. Parties have no legitimate basis for testing the intensity of commitments to candidates, leavening expressions of popular support with judgments by party and elected officials, or adopting rules that depart from proportionality in the allocation of delegates among the candidates.

This perspective on the nominating process is consistent with the sentiments of the McGovern-Fraser Commission, which launched the modern nomination process more than four decades ago. Its pure application, however, has never been achieved; nor can it be without a radical restructuring of law and practice in American politics. Set aside the fact that the Electoral College, with forty-eight states presently awarding all of their votes to the plurality vote winner, obviously limits equal opportunity for voters in the general election.

Consider instead the other features of the present system that work against the "one person, one vote" ideal. Opportunities for voters to participate are affected by state laws and party rules governing registration (twenty-nine provide for registration by party, twenty do not)[20] and access to primary ballots (closed vs. open primaries). Should a uniform national standard defining party registration and the eligible primary electorate be imposed on the states? Is this consistent with the constitutional protections afforded to states in the electoral process and to political parties as private organizations? A sequential process for selecting delegates inevitably makes voters in some states more influential than in others. Is a national primary the only way of leveling the playing field for voters? If so, at what cost? The formal authority for selecting the major party nominees continues to reside in their national party conventions. The delegates to those conventions are selected consistent with rules and processes that vary greatly between parties and across states. Is it desirable and possible to establish delegate selection rules that apply uniformly to both parties and all states? These complications associated with a democratic or plebiscitary perspective on presidential nominations will inform our consideration of three elements of reform: scheduling, delegate selection rules, and campaign finance.

Scheduling

The central feature of the nominating process calendar—front-loading—began decades ago and has become more prominent with each election cycle.[21] States have been motivated to reschedule their primary or caucus earlier in the year in response to the outsized influence of Iowa and New Hampshire and the dominant pattern in both parties of a quick resolution of the contest. Both parties have tried to restrain this rush to the front by setting a time period or window during which all states (except those with special exemptions) must hold their delegate selection events, and by imposing penalties on those that do not comply.

Following recommendations of the Commission on Presidential Nomination Timing and Scheduling, chaired by former U.S. secretary of labor Alexis Herman and Representative David Price, the Democratic National Committee (DNC) adopted rules for the 2008 calendar that added Nevada and South Carolina as states permitted to hold their caucuses or primaries before the delegate selection window. The rationale for this decision was to diversify the demographic makeup and party constituencies of those states with events at the beginning of the calendar and dilute the influence of Iowa and New Hampshire. The DNC rules also awarded bonus delegates to states that avoided the rush to the front of the calendar.[22] Republican rules approved at their 2004 convention exempted only Iowa and New Hampshire from the window commencing on February 5 and imposed a loss of 50 percent of their delegates on states that violated that rule.[23]

What followed is a classic demonstration of the gap between intentions and outcomes, between the stated purpose of rules and their implementation. Republican leaders in Michigan and Florida, with the acquiescence of their Democratic counterparts, rescheduled their primaries for January. South Carolina Republicans did the same.[24] These state parties were willing to accept a loss of delegates to secure a more influential position on the calendar. To protect their "first-in-the-nation" status, Iowa and New Hampshire moved their events even earlier in January, imposing New Year's holiday burdens on candidates and voters alike.[25]

The gamble worked for Republicans, but not for Democrats. McCain secured his nomination by winning the South Carolina and Florida primaries, rendering the loss of delegates irrelevant. But the pledge by Democratic candidates not to campaign in Michigan and Florida marginalized those states in the Democratic contest and produced a major controversy in the struggle between Clinton and Obama. Finally, the incentives approved by the Democrats to avoid further front-loading failed completely, as many states (including several of the largest) moved to the first day of the window and created an almost indigestible Super Tuesday.[26]

The 2008 experience might stimulate some self-correcting movements by individual states. Such changes most importantly would include a later start and a decompression of the schedule, allowing for a more deliberative process. A shift by Michigan and Florida Democrats back to their original, post–Super Tuesday dates would allow Iowa and New Hampshire to move later in January, even with the addition of Nevada and South Carolina. Other states might be tempted to move out of their Super Tuesday time slots to later parts of the calendar that are less congested.

The alternative for both parties is to attempt to restructure the calendar into four or five clusters of states based on region, size, or random selection.[27] Some of the reform plans in this vein retain a special place for Iowa and New Hampshire, while others do not. Most would rotate the regions or other groupings of states each election to prevent any from having a permanent advantage. Some achieve their objective by changing national party rules, others through federal legislation. All would need states to adopt laws scheduling primaries consistent with the new calendar for one or both parties.

The rationale for all of these plans is to reverse the front-loading of the calendar, to allow for a less compressed and more deliberative process, to avoid the equivalent of a national primary on the first day of the window, and to

prevent the same early states from dominating the selection of nominees election after election. The obstacles to their adoption and successful implementation are enormous, and it is not at all clear that any of the plans would
realize their intended objectives. As we saw in the 2008 cycle, the strategic
position of the parties and the particular field of candidates substantially
shapes how the calendar and rules play out. Moreover, the invisible primary,
and the dominant role of party elites in it, is likely to trump the intended
effects of the new calendar in most election cycles.

Both parties took steps at their 2008 national conventions that make it
possible to alter the schedule of events in the 2012 nominating cycle. Democrats approved a resolution establishing a Democratic Change Commission
whose mandate includes the timing of primaries and caucuses. The resolution
charged the commission with ensuring that the window for delegate selection
events commence no earlier than the first Tuesday in March (a month later
than the 2008 calendar allowed) and that approved pre-window states hold
their primary or caucus during the month of February. It also instructed the
commission to identify ways of reducing the front-loading of events within
the window. Recommendations from the commission are to be presented to
the Democratic National Committee, which has the authority to approve the
delegate selection rules for the next election.[28]

Republicans, unlike Democrats, traditionally require that any change in
party rules governing the presidential nominating process be adopted at the
prior convention. While rejecting an ambitious plan to restructure the primary schedule, the 2008 Republican National Convention did take the
unprecedented step of establishing a Temporary Delegate Selection Committee to recommend changes in the schedule for the 2012 nominating cycle.
Any changes in the rules governing the schedule could be adopted with a
two-thirds vote of the Republican National Committee at its 2010 summer
meeting.[29]

Delegate Selection Rules

Critics of the current delegate selection rules have directed much of their fire
at caucuses, automatic delegates, and delegate allocation rules that depart
from proportional representation.

CAUCUSES VS. PRIMARIES. Should state parties retain the option of selecting their delegates to the national party conventions in party caucuses rather
than primary elections? Although rules and procedures vary among caucus
states, critics correctly note that it is much more difficult to participate in a
caucus than to vote in a primary. Most caucuses are held in the evening over

several hours, in fewer and less familiar locations than general election voting precincts, with participants often required to stay much longer than it would take to cast a ballot; and to indicate their candidate choice publicly. There are no opportunities for military personnel and others away from their home election districts to participate by absentee ballot. Not surprisingly, rates of participation in caucuses are a small fraction of turnout in primaries. Obama's success in winning almost all caucus contests and amassing a considerable delegate lead based on that success was considered by some critics to be an artifact of a nondemocratic process.

Of course, Obama competed under the rules as they existed; Clinton could have contested him in caucus states by investing more time and resources in them (although the demographic profile of her supporters, especially lower-income and older voters, put her at somewhat of a disadvantage). Caucuses test candidates' strategic acuity, organizational strength, and intensity of support, qualities not irrelevant to performance in the general election and in the White House. This is one reason many reformers were disconcerted when a number of states switched from caucuses to primaries in 1972 to comply more easily with the McGovern-Fraser guidelines for delegate selection.[30]

Given the many other non-plebiscitary features of the nominating system and the long tradition in a number of states for caucuses, it is hard to see how states should and could be denied this option.

AUTOMATIC DELEGATES. As recounted by William Mayer in chapter 5, the McGovern-Fraser rules banning automatic or ex-officio delegates led to a dramatic decline in the number of major Democratic elected and party officials at the national party conventions. (Mayer also explains why a comparable decline did not occur at Republican conventions.) The Democratic Party responded in the early 1980s by instituting a new class of ex-officio delegates to increase their numbers at the convention. These delegates, who were quickly given the moniker "superdelegates," were free agents, appointed without regard to their support for a particular presidential candidate.[31] By the 2008 election cycle, they constituted about 20 percent of the delegates to the Democratic National Convention.[32]

Their major purpose was to be a steadying influence at the convention, acting in various ways to look out for the interests of the party rather than the interests of candidates or issue advocacy groups. They played a modest role in 1984, by pushing Walter Mondale into the majority before the convention, ensuring a first-ballot nomination and a somewhat less divisive convention. But Mondale already had a substantial lead over Gary Hart among pledged

delegates, so the superdelegate vote in no way reversed the expressed preference of primary voters and caucus participants.[33] Until 2008, subsequent
nomination contests produced early victors, with no consequential role for
superdelegates in the choice of nominee.

The hotly contested Clinton-Obama race elevated the visibility of superdelegates and aroused fears that they would "steal" the nomination from the
hands of rank-and-file Democrats. In the end, superdelegates played their
intended role. Over the course of the primary season, they shifted their support from Clinton to Obama and once again ratified the choice produced by
the primaries and caucuses. Importantly, their support for Obama produced
a margin of victory that exceeded the number of disputed delegates from
Michigan and Florida, reducing the incentive for Clinton to take her fight to
the convention and beginning the process of reconciliation shortly after the
end of the primary season.

The 2008 experience reinforces the rationale for including ex-officio delegates in the Democratic presidential nominating process. I see no compelling
reason or incentive for Democrats to reverse course on this provision of their
rules, although the Democratic Change Commission was instructed to recommend revisions in the delegate selection rules "to provide for a significant
reduction of the number of unpledged party leader and elected official
(PLEO) delegates in order to enlarge the role and influence of primary and
caucus voters in the presidential nominating process."[34]

ALLOCATION OF DELEGATES. The two parties diverge dramatically in their
rules governing the allocation of delegates to candidates based on the results
of primaries and caucuses. The national Republican Party rules give states
wide discretion to allocate delegates in whatever fashion they choose. Some
states award all of their delegates to the winner of the statewide vote; others have a system of winner-take-all by congressional district; still others
have adopted some form of proportional allocation pegged to the congressional district or state vote, or both. The national Democratic Party rules,
in contrast, require proportionality in the awarding of delegates to candidates. Their directives to state parties are detailed and constraining, with no
discretion on the percentage of delegates awarded based on the congressional district and statewide vote, or on how proportionality is defined
within congressional districts.

Republican rules are criticized on democratic grounds for not reflecting the
popular support for all of the candidates in the selection of delegates, but
admired politically for their ability to produce an early winner. Democratic
rules satisfy the democratic test of proportionality, but are criticized for per-

verse incentives to candidates presented by some of the detailed rules and the difficulty of translating narrow but politically significant popular vote victories into delegate harvests.

The democratic critique is unlikely to persuade the Republican Party to abandon its traditional embrace of a decentralized system centered on state autonomy or to take umbrage at departures from proportional representation. Nor can Democrats be expected to move back toward anything approaching winner-take-all rules. They might be persuaded to adjust their rules to make it a bit easier for winners of the popular vote to translate their victories more predictably into delegate victories.

Campaign Finance

The immediate and central campaign finance reform question highlighted by 2008 is whether and how to revive the presidential public financing program. For purposes of this volume and chapter, the public match in the nominating phase (not the public grant for the general election campaign) merits our attention. As presently structured, this program makes no sense whatsoever for major candidates and creates debilitating disincentives for minor ones as well. Its very low spending limits relative to what serious candidates have raised and spent in recent election cycles, together with its separate state spending limits,[35] have understandably led to its collapse.

It is possible to update the program to increase its attractiveness by enriching the public match, eliminating state spending limits, and doubling or tripling the cap on national spending to $100 or $150 million. This might not be sufficient to entice well-known candidates to accept public funding, but it would hold out a lifeline to candidates without the celebrity status or connections to large donors to compete for the nomination. The entry fee for those aspiring to their party's nomination remains very high. A robust public financing system would help diversify the field of candidates and help extend competition for the nomination beyond the initial delegate selection events.

Consideration might also be given to decoupling the public matching funds from spending limits. The reality of long, expensive pre-convention general election campaigns requires those who win their party's nomination to raise and spend large amounts of money after becoming the presumptive nominees. The rise of Internet-based small donors and increasingly productive fundraising bundlers make that possible.[36] Perhaps public funding should be reconceived as seed money to increase the pool of qualified candidates, not as a means of limiting spending.

Conclusion

If we had an opportunity to design from scratch a way to pick a president, it is inconceivable that we would arrive at our present system. It is an inherited system with evident archeological strata, the accumulation of decisions made in past decades—even centuries—reflecting conflicting interests and ambitions. In spite of efforts to nationalize and democratize the process, it remains highly decentralized and resistant to those seeking uniformity.

At the same time, our presidential nominating system is open and adaptable, responsive to each election cycle's strategic political environment and field of candidates. It is also a system whose formal shortcomings can be overcome by informal processes, including the invisible primary, during which party elites work to put their own imprint on the choice of a nominee.

So yes, this is a way to pick a president, though not an optimal one and certainly not a pretty one. It deserves the regular critiques it receives and the constant efforts to improve it. But it should not be a source of despair.

Such despair often leads to appealing ideas that promise the transformation of a broken system but that risk doing substantially more harm than good. For the reasons set out earlier in this chapter, I believe that any serious effort to convert both parties' presidential nominating processes into a purely plebiscitary one is a fool's errand. Party nominations are not general elections and should not be structured by the same set of values, interests, and design principles that apply to the latter. Superdelegates and party caucuses play legitimate roles in the process; there is no compelling reason to abandon them. National parties ought to retain broad authority over how they organize their affairs and choose their nominees, including the degree of autonomy they provide to their state parties. When federal laws are passed to override party practices (such as the limitation on the source and size of campaign contributions to parties), they should entail limited means for achieving compelling objectives.

This leaves ample scope for those working to improve aspects of the presidential selection system. Based on the evidence and arguments in this chapter, I would identify three priorities. First, the calendar of primaries and caucuses should continue to have a small number of states begin the process on separate dates, but they should commence later than they did in 2008; the rest of the calendar should be decompressed. Scheduling almost half of the states on a single day at the beginning of the delegate selection window makes it very difficult for most candidates to compete, for meaningful campaigns to be waged, and for voters to become informed about their choices. Decompression might be attempted incrementally, with additional incentives to states to move away from Super Tuesday and reschedule their primaries or caucuses later in the window. Alternatively, the parties might reach for a more ambitious plan to cluster the states on four or five dates over a three- or four-month period to encourage a more measured and deliberative process. In practical terms, such a plan probably requires informal agreement between the parties on a new calendar.

Second, the parties could separately take steps to clean up some of their rules and procedures that sow confusion among voters and present perverse incentives to candidates. For Democrats, that would include persuading Texas to choose a primary or caucuses instead of both, and permitting less rigid applications of their proportionality requirement to make it possible for vote winners to realize genuine delegate victories. Republicans might consider moving slightly in the opposite direction, by encouraging a shift in some states away from statewide winner-take-all allocation rules. Both parties ought to consider reviewing procedures used by caucus states and encouraging small steps that would ease the burden on participants.

Third, Congress should modernize the public matching funds program for candidates seeking their party nomination by reconceptualizing it as publicly subsidized seed money for presidential candidates. This would entail dropping the link to state and national spending limits, increasing the size of the public match for small donations, and setting a cap on the amount of public funds any one candidate can draw from the public till.

If adopted, these recommendations would not transform the presidential nominating system; but, as I have argued, transformation is neither necessary nor desirable. They would, however, be consistent with our long history of self-criticism and reform, and make modest improvements in the way we pick our president.

Notes

1. Editorial, "Primary Reforms," *New York Times,* June 8, 2008.

2. See, for example, David E. Price, *Bringing Back the Parties* (Washington: CQ Press, 1984).

3. This history is nicely recounted by James W. Ceaser in *Presidential Selection: Theory and Development* (Princeton University Press, 1979).

4. Chuck Plunkett, "Democrats Fear Brokered Convention," *Denver Post,* March 9, 2008.

5. Nelson W. Polsby, *The Consequences of Party Reform* (Oxford University Press, 1983).

6. Byron Shafer, *Quiet Revolution: The Struggle for the Democratic Party and the Shaping of Post-Reform Politics* (New York: Russell Sage Foundation, 1983).

7. Ibid.

8. Polsby, *Consequences of Party Reform.*

9. For information on the evolution of delegate allocation within states, see James I. Lengle and Byron Shafer, "Primary Rules, Political Power, and Social Change," *American Political Science Review* 70, no. 1 (March 1976): 25–40; Gerald M. Pomper, "New Rules and New Games in Presidential Nominations," *Journal of Politics* (August 1979): 785–87; Anthony Corrado and Thomas Devine, "Party Rules Reform and Candidate Nomination Strategies: Consequences for the 1990s" (http://devinemulvey.com/media/pdf/party_rules_reform_91.pdf [November 3, 2008]), p. 1; John G. Geer, "Rules Governing Presidential Primaries," *Journal of Politics* 48, no. 4 (November 1986): 1006–25. For information about the evolution of the primary calendar between 1972 and 1988, see William G. Mayer and Andrew E. Busch, *The Front-Loading Problem in Presidential Nominations*, (Washington: Brookings, 2004), pp. 141–44, and Corrado and Devine, "Party Rules Reform," pp. 5–6; for 1992, see Democratic National Committee, *Delegate Selection Rules for the 1992 Democratic National Convention* (Washington: Democratic National Committee, 1990); for 1996, see Michael L. Goldstein, *Guide to the 1996 Presidential Election* (Washington: CQ Press, 1995), p. 24; for 2000, see Terry Michael, *The Democratic Party's Presidential Nominating Process*, 4th ed., (Washington: Washington Center for Politics and Journalism, 2000), p. 3 (http://terrymichael.net/PDF%20Files/DNC_PrezNomProcess.pdf [November 3, 2008]); for 2004, see William G. Mayer, *The Making of the Presidential Candidates 2004* (Lanham, Md.: Rowman and Littlefield, 2003), p. 9, and Rhodes Cook, *The Presidential Nominating Process: A Place for Us?* (Lanham, Md.: Rowman and Littlefield, 2004), p. 147. For information on reintegrating Democratic party and elected officials into the national conventions, see Thomas E. Mann, "Elected Officials and the Politics of Presidential Selection," in *The American Elections of 1984*, edited by Austin Ranney (Duke University Press, 1985), pp. 100–28; Michael L. Goldstein, *Guide to the 1988 Presidential Election* (Washington: CQ Press, 1988), p. 16; Ronald D. Elving, "Insiders Seek Soul Possession: Democrats Struggle to Define Their Destiny," *CQ Weekly*, July 16, 1988, pp. 1946–48; Corrado and Devine, "Party Rules Reform," pp. 4–7; "Democratic Rules: A Recent History," *CQ Weekly*, March 17, 1990, p. 848; Goldstein, *Guide to the 1996 Presidential Election*, pp. 24–25; Michael, *The Democratic Party's Presidential Nominating Process*, pp. 9–15; and David Nather, "Leaping Voters in a Single Bound," *CQ Weekly*, February 25, 2008, pp. 482–84.

10. Robert J. Huckshorn and John F. Bibby, "National Party Rules and Delegate Selection in the Republican Party," *PS: Political Science and Politics* 16, no. 4 (Autumn 1983): 656–66.

11. See "The Rules of the Republican Party as Adopted by the 2004 Republican National Convention, August 30, 2004" (www.gop.com/About/AboutRead.aspx?Guid=a4cc4fcb-6043-4af2-860a-41ae912a2c42 [November 3, 2008]).

12. Michael L. Goldstein, *Guide to the 2004 Presidential Election* (Washington: CQ Press, 2003), p. 32.

13. David D. Kirkpatrick, "Death Knell May Be Near for Public Election Funds," *New York Times*, January 23, 2007.

14. Marty Cohen, David Karol, Hans Noel, and John Zaller, *The Party Decides: Presidential Nominations Before and After Reform* (University of Chicago Press, 2008).

15. John H. Aldrich, *Before the Convention: Strategies and Choices in Presidential Nomination Campaigns* (University of Chicago Press, 1980).

16. Mayer and Busch, *The Front-Loading Problem in Presidential Nominations*.

17. See "April Presidential Reports: Small Donations Continue to Fuel Democrats; McCain Has His Best Month; Clinton's Debts Rise to $19.5 Million," Campaign Finance Institute, May 22, 2008 (www.cfinst.org/pr/prRelease.aspx?ReleaseID=191 [November 3, 2008]).

18. See "Newly Released 2007 Reports Give Clues to Candidates' Financial Strengths and Vulnerabilities Going into Super Tuesday," Campaign Finance Institute, February 2, 2008 (www.cfinst.org/pr/prRelease.aspx?ReleaseID=177 [November 3, 2008].

19. Matthew Mosk and Sarah Cohen, "With Crucial Loan, McCain Put His Bid Back in the Black," *Washington Post*, February 1, 2008.

20. Ann Fisher, "Crossover Voters Not at Fault; Fix Rules," *Columbus Dispatch*, March 24, 2008.

21. Mayer and Busch, *The Front-Loading Problem in Presidential Nominations*.

22. Dan Balz, "Democratic Unit Votes to Add Early '08 Contests; Iowa Caucuses and New Hampshire Presidential Primary Remain First in the Nation," *Washington Post*, December 11, 2005; editorial, "Democrats Add January Voting in 2 More States," *Washington Post*, August 20, 2006.

23. See Rules 15 and 16, Republican National Committee, "The Rules of the Republican Party as Adopted by the 2004 Republican National Convention, August 30, 2004" (www.gop.com/About/AboutRead.aspx?Guid=a4cc4fcb-6043-4af2-860a-41ae912a2c42 [November 3, 2008]).

24. Katharine Q. Seelye, "Michigan Joins the Race for a 'Me First' Primary," *New York Times*, August 22, 2007.

25. Julie Bosman, "New Hampshire Selects Jan. 8 for Its Primary," *New York Times*, November 22, 2007.

26. Adam Nagourney, "Big States' Push for Earlier Vote Scrambles Race," *New York Times*, January 25, 2007.

27. National Association of Secretaries of State, "Fact Sheet: Alternative Presidential Nominating Proposals for 2012 and Beyond."

28. Lauren R. Dorgan, "Change in Air for Democrats' 2012 Primaries; State Party Chairman Expects N.H. Leadoff," *Concord Monitor*, August 28, 2008.

29. David Yepsen, "Iowa Caucuses Still in First Place, for Now," *Des Moines Register*, September 4, 2008; Marc Ambinder, "RNC's Calendar Fight Could Be Chaotic,"

(http://marcambinder.theatlantic.com/archives/2008/09/rncs_calendar_could_be_chaotic.php) [September 2, 2008].

30. Shafer, *Quiet Revolution*.

31. Mann, "Elected Officials," p. 105.

32. "Primary Reforms," *New York Times*.

33. Mann, "Elected Officials," pp. 105–11.

34. "A Resolution Establishing the Democratic Change Commission," Rules Committee of the Democratic National Convention, August 21, 2008.

35. See Federal Election Commission, "Public Funding of Presidential Elections," February 2008 (www.fec.gov/pages/brochures/pubfund.shtml [November 3, 2008]).

36. See "Obama's Small Contributions Surged in June, but McCain's Party-Based Strategy Gave the GOP Side a Combined Cash Advantage on June 30," Campaign Finance Institute, July 22, 2008 (www.cfinst.org/pr/prRelease.aspx?ReleaseID=201 [November 3, 2008]).

DANIEL H. LOWENSTEIN

9

Presidential Nomination Reform:
Legal Restraints and Procedural Possibilities

Discontent with the presidential nominating process has been a constant in American politics for at least the past five decades. From the 1960s
through the 1980s, the leading causes of controversy included the limited
ability of ordinary voters to directly influence the selection of major party candidates and the demographic representativeness of delegates to the national
nominating conventions. Beginning in the 1980s and continuing through the
period leading up to the 2008 nominations, the greatest cause for concern has
been the timing of "nominating events"—a term I shall use to refer collectively
to presidential primaries and caucuses.

This chapter concerns itself primarily not with the substantive merits of the
various proposals that have been adopted or proposed to reform presidential
nominations, but with the processes by which reforms may be adopted and
the legal constraints to which they may be subject. The politics and law of
presidential nomination reform are complicated by the multiple entities that
play a direct and major part in determining the nomination process. The
actual nominations take place at the Democratic and Republican National
Conventions in each presidential election year. For more than a century, from
the 1830s when national nominating conventions began,[1] through the 1950s,
selection of delegates was mostly controlled by state party organizations,
though beginning early in the twentieth century delegates in a minority of the
states were elected in direct primaries.[2] Since the national parties—especially
the Democrats—sought to regulate delegate selection following the troubled
Democratic National Convention in 1968, nomination procedures have been
determined by cooperation, infighting, and bargaining between the state parties, the state legislatures, and the national parties.[3]

In recent years, as the timing of nominating events has attracted greater attention, the pursuit of national legislation has increased concomitantly. The possibility of congressional intervention raises a new set of legal and political questions that are addressed in this chapter. Early on, reformers complained that the nominating process was too long and drawn out,[4] but more recently "front-loading" became the primary cause of concern, as states moved their nominating events earlier and earlier.[5] This problem appeared to reach an alarming climax in the period leading up to 2008.[6] The Senate Rules Committee conducted hearings in September 2007 on a bill to require states to hold regionally oriented nominating events on specified dates.[7] Other proposals have abounded.

Some observers may have believed that in 2008 the compression of nominating events would create a sufficiently negative reaction in the public to make congressional action against front-loading a political possibility. To almost everyone's surprise, however, the nominating contests did not end in a relative flash. Even on the Republican side, although John McCain had pretty clearly emerged as the nominee following the February 5 Super Tuesday—by historical standards a very early finish—the Republican contest had gone through enough twists and turns, many of them surprising and dramatic, that the public's impression of compression, if any, was mitigated. In any event, given the current Democratic control of the government, the Democratic contest is more likely to affect the prospects for legislation in the immediate future. By the time the close contest between Barack Obama and Hillary Clinton was resolved, most Democrats were bemoaning the length rather than the brevity of the primary season. No one can doubt that Iowa, New Hampshire, other early states such as South Carolina, and the states that voted on February 5 all had considerable influence on both contests. Nevertheless, on the Democratic side, later states such as Maryland, Virginia, and the other states that gave Obama a string of victories and a slender but decisive stable lead that Clinton was unable to overcome, and even later states such as Ohio and Pennsylvania that permitted her to come close, were also influential.

Given these events, the pressure for legislative action to mitigate or prevent front-loading will probably soften, at least to some degree. But 2008 did not eliminate the causes of front-loading and the debate will no doubt continue. This chapter reviews the legal question of whether Congress may, under the Constitution, control when nominating events take place in the states. The question is complex, in part for the very reason that Congress has declined recently to intervene in presidential nominations, meaning that there is a paucity of precedents defining the limits of Congress's power. I conclude, as the majority of scholars have done, that while there is no certain answer, congressional action probably would be constitutional. However, I give reasons for moderate skepticism over whether far-reaching congressional regulation is likely to be beneficial. A simple ban of nominating events before a specified date, say the beginning of March, could do little harm and might be of some benefit. Beyond that, if Congress finds it necessary to intervene at all, it ought to consider facilitating solutions devised by the national parties rather than imposing its own solutions.

Congress could seek to regulate other aspects of the presidential nominating process besides the timing of nominating events. For example, Congress could seek to control the allocation of delegates to the conventions or control the form of the ballot used in presidential primaries.[8] Much of the following analysis would be applicable to these and other forms of regulation, though each would have to be evaluated on its own merits. However, experience shows that Congress is not easily induced to intervene in the presidential nomination process. That could change, but for the foreseeable future it appears that if Congress intervenes at all it will be on the subject of timing.

Constitutional Limits on Congressional Power

There are two distinct constitutional questions raised by proposals for Congress to regulate the timing of presidential nominating events in the states. Because the powers of the federal government are limited to those delegated to it in the Constitution and do not include the residual powers enjoyed by the states and other sovereigns, any congressional intervention in the presidential nominating process must be the exercise of a delegated power. By its terms, the Constitution appears to give Congress considerable power to oversee congressional elections but very limited powers over presidential elections. Thus the first question is whether the Constitution affirmatively empowers Congress to regulate presidential nominating procedures, such as by controlling the timing of nominating events.

Once it is established that a power is delegated to the federal government by the Constitution, that power must still be exercised in a manner consistent with limitations placed on Congress's power, such as the prohibition in the 5th Amendment against taking property without due process of law. The particular limit that is most relevant to governmental intervention into the presidential nominating process is the 1st Amendment protection of freedom of association. True, if you check your pocket copy of the Constitution, you will not find any mention of freedom of association in the 1st Amendment, but the

Supreme Court has long maintained that such freedom is implied by the other freedoms that are expressly protected.[9] Thus the second question is whether a congressional exercise of power to regulate presidential nominations, assuming such a power exists, violates the parties' freedom of association.

Congress's Affirmative Power

The Constitution expressly gives Congress only one discretionary power in connection with presidential elections, the power to designate two dates. In the words of Article II, section 1: "The Congress may determine the Time of chusing the Electors, and the Day on which they shall give their Votes; which Day shall be the same throughout the United States."[10]

The Constitution does not by its terms give Congress power to regulate the timing of presidential nominating events or, indeed, to regulate the presidential nomination process in any way.[11] However, powers delegated to Congress may be implied by the Constitution. Indeed, the Constitution expressly calls for recognition of implied powers in Article I, section 8: "The Congress shall have Power . . . To make all Laws which shall be necessary and proper for carrying into Execution the foregoing Powers, and all other Powers vested by this Constitution in the Government of the United States, or in any Department or Office thereof." This "Necessary and Proper Clause" has long been interpreted to permit Congress broad latitude to legislate even on matters that are distantly and indirectly related to its enumerated powers.[12] The clause can be and has been invoked in defense of proposed congressional regulation of presidential nominating events.[13]

If Congress limits itself to requiring that presidential nominating events occur not before a specified date, or that they occur during a specified time period, the case that its action is authorized by the Necessary and Proper Clause would be a persuasive one. Congress is delegated the express power to set the date for choosing presidential electors. In a sequential electoral system, consisting of nominating events followed by the party national conventions followed by the national election, it is prudent to ensure that the first of these steps is neither too distant in time from the last nor too close. Congress's determination that nominating events should take place within a specified time period would be a means of ensuring that its expressly delegated power to set the date of the national election could be exercised effectively.

By and large, however, those defending congressional power to regulate the nominating process have relied less on the Necessary and Proper Clause and more on structural interpretation of the Constitution. The premise of structural interpretation is that the Constitution in its entirety creates a government of a certain nature, from which certain powers or limits on power can be derived.[14] There are several reasons why lawyers and scholars have turned to structural arguments in support of Congress's implied power to regulate the presidential nominating process.

First, although the Necessary and Proper Clause would work well to support a simple requirement that nominating events occur within a specified time period, it is less clear that further regulation of the dates on which particular states should hold their nominating events—for example, by region—are related to Congress's express power to set the date for the national election. The Necessary and Proper Clause would provide even less support for regulation of the nominating process beyond the timing of nominating events. Second, the structural argument is plausible when applied to congressional regulation of presidential nominations. The president is the head of one of the three branches of the federal government and the single most powerful official in the United States. It seems a matter of common sense that it should be within Congress's power to ensure that the presidential selection process is sound. As we shall see, there is a potent counterargument, but not one that will detract from this commonsense plausibility. Third, the structural argument appears to be well supported by precedent.

The leading case is *Burroughs v. United States*.[15] In *Burroughs*, the defendants challenged the constitutionality of campaign finance disclosure provisions of the Corrupt Practices Act, which applied to committees seeking to influence the election of presidential electors in more than one state. The defendants' constitutional argument was that Congress's power over presidential elections, under the provisions we have reviewed, was limited to setting the date for Election Day. The key passage from the Court's opinion is worth quoting at some length:

> The congressional act under review seeks to preserve the purity of presidential and vice presidential elections. Neither in purpose nor in effect does it interfere with the power of a state to appoint electors or the manner in which their appointment shall be made. It deals with political committees organized for the purpose of influencing elections in two or more states, and with branches or subsidiaries of national committees, and excludes from its operation state or local committees. Its operation, therefore, is confined to situations which, if not beyond the power of the state to deal with at all, are beyond its power to deal with adequately. It in no sense invades any exclusive state power.

... The President is vested with the executive power of the nation. The importance of his election and the vital character of its relationship to and effect upon the welfare and safety of the whole people cannot be too strongly stated. To say that Congress is without power to pass appropriate legislation to safeguard such an election from the improper use of money to influence the result is to deny to the nation in a vital particular the power of self protection. Congress, undoubtedly, possesses that power, as it possesses every other power essential to preserve the departments and institutions of the general government from impairment or destruction, whether threatened by force or by corruption.

One obvious objection to applying *Burroughs* to congressional regulation of presidential nominations is that the *Burroughs* defendants were prosecuted for campaign disclosure requirements in the general election, not in primaries. However broad Congress's implied powers may be in connection with the actual selection of presidential electors, does it apply to party nominations, which are nowhere mentioned in the Constitution? That question appears to have been answered in the affirmative in *United States* v. *Classic.*[16] In that celebrated case, defendants were charged with federal offenses for falsely counting ballots cast in a congressional primary election in Louisiana. The Court rejected their defense that Congress's power to regulate congressional elections—which, as we shall see, is broader than its power to regulate presidential elections—does not extend to primaries, which were not contemplated when the Constitution was adopted. The primary, said the Court, is "an integral part of the procedure for the popular choice of Congressman."[17] That primaries were unknown to the framers of the Constitution was not dispositive, because "in setting up an enduring framework of government they undertook to carry out for the indefinite future and in all the vicissitudes of the changing affairs of men, those fundamental purposes which the instrument itself discloses."[18] The result in *Classic* was surely influenced in part by the single-party dominance that made the Democratic primary dispositive in Louisiana elections in 1941. Nevertheless, the statement that the primary is "an integral part" of the overall election process is equally true of the much more competitive presidential elections of that time and ours. *Classic* makes it difficult to argue against the application of *Burroughs* to presidential nominations simply on the premise that Congress's powers to regulate elections do not extend to primaries. But it leaves open the more difficult question whether the structural principles of *Burroughs* extend to congressional regulation of the timing of presidential nominating events.

The greatest obstacle to a structural argument for broad congressional power to control presidential nominations is the contrast in the Constitution between the power given to Congress over presidential and congressional elections. As we have seen, the only powers expressly delegated for presidential elections are to set the times for the appointment of electors and for the electors to cast their votes for president and vice president. In contrast, Article I, section 4, of the Constitution gives Congress final control of congressional elections: "The Times, Places and Manner of holding Elections for Senators and Representatives, shall be prescribed in each State by the Legislature thereof; but the Congress may at any time by Law make or alter such Regulations, except as to the Places of chusing Senators."

Scholars who argue for congressional power to regulate at least the timing of presidential nominating events usually concede the negative implication of the express grant of power to Congress to "make or alter" regulations affecting the "Manner" of conducting congressional elections in conjunction with the very limited grant of power over presidential elections. The question is whether *Burroughs* and *Classic* nullify such textual considerations. William Mayer and Andrew Busch, whose book *The Front-Loading Problem in Presidential Elections* qualifies them as the leading students of front-loading, are also the leading skeptics of congressional power to regulate.[19] Mayer and Busch read *Burroughs* narrowly to give Congress only the ability to protect the "purity" of presidential elections against "force or corruption."

Given the emphasis in the passage from *Burroughs* quoted above on the importance to the nation of the office of president, it may be somewhat arbitrary to suppose that Congress can protect against force and corruption, but not against other problems that might seriously impair presidential elections. This is especially so given the Court's observation that the campaign disclosure requirements of the Corrupt Practices Act were directed only to interstate activities "beyond [an individual state's] power to deal with adequately." A similar problem of coordination makes it difficult for states to solve the problem of front-loading, which arises not because of the action of any one state but because of the aggregate effect of states seeking to avoid a competitive disadvantage in influence over the nominations.

The reasoning of *Burroughs* therefore seems fairly applicable to congressional efforts to control problems in addition to force and corruption. Nevertheless, the *Burroughs* structural interpretation of the Constitution does not necessarily solve the textual problem for supporters of congressional intervention against front-loading. As *Burroughs* noted, "Neither in purpose nor in effect does [the Corrupt Practices Act] interfere with the power of a state to appoint electors or the manner in which their appointment shall be made." The use of the word "manner" is probably no accident, as it is the "Manner" of holding elections that Congress is authorized to regulate in congressional but not presidential elections. The Corrupt Practices Act did not regulate the administration of the presidential election, but only the activities of individuals and committees seeking to affect the outcome of the election. The structure of the original Constitution, giving Congress authority over the "Manner" of holding congressional but not presidential elections, suggests an intention to leave the states free from federal control over the latter, except as to the date of selecting the electors. In *Burroughs*, the Court pointed out that when Congress regulated campaign committees, it was leaving the states alone to administer the election in whatever "Manner" they wished.

In *Oregon* v. *Mitchell*, the Supreme Court upheld Congress's ability to lower the voting age to 18 for federal elections but struck down its attempt to do the same for state elections.[20] Four justices would have upheld the reduction of the voting age for all elections and four would have struck it down for all elections. Because Justice Black was the only justice who found the reduction valid for federal but not state elections, he held the decisive vote on the Supreme Court. In his opinion, he wrote:

> I would hold, as have a long line of decisions in this Court, that Congress has ultimate supervisory power over congressional elections. Similarly, it is the prerogative of Congress to oversee the conduct of presidential and vice-presidential elections and to set the qualifications for voters for electors for those offices. It cannot be seriously contended that Congress has less power over the conduct of presidential elections than it has over congressional elections.

The only explanation he gave for the latter conclusion—other than a reference to *Burroughs*, which for the reasons given in the previous paragraph may not be sufficient—was in a footnote:

> Inherent in the very concept of a supreme national government with national officers is a residual power in Congress to insure that those officers represent their national constituency as responsively as possible. This power arises from the nature of our constitutional system of government and from the Necessary and Proper Clause.[21]

Although Justice Black's vote was decisive in *Oregon* v. *Mitchell*, he wrote only for himself. Therefore his stated rationale for his decision does not have binding force. Nor is his structural argument persuasive, for two reasons. One is that it does not account for the constitutional text's sharply different authority given to Congress in presidential and congressional elections. Furthermore, like most of the scholars who have argued for congressional authority to regulate presidential nominations, he does not acknowledge the decentralized system that the framers of the Constitution seem to have had in mind for presidential elections. It was the *design* of the original Constitution that the selection of electors in each state and the electors' deliberations over potential presidents should occur independently of other states. In the words of one historian:

> Article II, section I sought to maximize participation in presidential elections by rejecting the establishment of a single electoral college located at the nation's capitol. Electors chosen for the specific purpose of electing a President, holding no federal office[,] having no legislative business, congregating in their own states, having little time to consult electors in other states, being required to vote on the same day and for two persons for President, and being disbanded promptly afterwards, would be insulated from corruption.[22]

If the original Constitution had never been amended, then Justice Black's reasoning and that of many contemporary scholars would stand on a weak historical foundation. However commonsensical we may find Justice Black's assertion that there should be a residual power in Congress to ensure that the president and other federal elected officials "represent their national constituency as responsively as possible," the framers acted on the belief that the best way to ensure the integrity of the process was to decentralize it in the states. That historical understanding explains well the different delegations to Congress of power over presidential and congressional elections.

In my judgment, what redeems the structural argument for congressional authority, at least over the timing of presidential nominating events, is the 12th Amendment. Under the original Constitution, each elector cast electoral votes for two people. If the top vote-getter's total equaled a majority of the number of electors casting votes, then he was elected president and the next highest vote-getter was vice president. This system reflected the understanding of the framers described above, that the system would be decentralized and uncoordinated. By 1800, however, national politics had crystallized into a competition between Jefferson's Democratic-Republican Party and Adams's Federalist Party. Jefferson won the 1800 election, and his electors all dutifully cast electoral votes for Jefferson and for his running mate, Aaron Burr. The result was that Jefferson and Burr received the same number of electoral votes, throwing the presidential election into the House of Representatives. With the help of the Federalists, Burr tried to capture the presidency for himself. This effort failed in the end, but not before causing what appeared to be a constitutional crisis. In response, and before the next election, Congress proposed and the states ratified the 12th Amendment, which called for each elector to cast separate votes for a presidential and a vice presidential candidate.

The importance of the 12th Amendment for understanding the Constitution's treatment of presidential elections has been underappreciated. Although by its terms it merely introduced a seemingly modest and mechanical change in the process of choosing a president, it was based on an entirely different conception of how presidents actually were being elected than had been foreseen by the framers. The incident that gave rise to the 12th Amendment resulted from a national party system in which electors were selected in each state for the specific purpose of voting for one of the parties' candidates. The expectation of a decentralized process had been displaced by the reality of a party-based, nationally coordinated process. A proper structural interpretation of the Constitution should take into account its amendments, not simply the original Constitution. As amended, the Constitution contemplates at least the possibility that presidential electors will be pledged to support candidates nominated by national parties. For a Constitution with that contemplation, unlike the original Constitution, Justice Black's assertion that there must be a residual power in Congress to maintain the proper working of the nomination system is sound.

It appears, then, that although the reasoning of some of the scholars who have found an implied power in Congress to regulate at least the timing of presidential nominating events may have been incomplete, their conclusion is probably correct.

Parties' Freedom of Association

Assuming that regulation of at least the timing of nominating events is within the delegated powers of Congress, there remains the question whether a given regulation would be void as a violation of rights guaranteed by the Constitution. To resolve that question, it is crucial to ask who would object to whatever regulation Congress might adopt. In the case of congressional regulation of the timing of nominating events, there are three major types of entities that might object: state governments, state parties, and national parties.

State governments are not protected by the Bill of Rights. If, as we are now hypothesizing, an action comes within Congress's delegated powers, the states have no ground on which to challenge it. In contrast, parties may claim the protection of the Bill of Rights. As we shall see, under certain circumstances the chances of a national party's succeeding in a challenge to congressional regulation of the timing of nominating events would be better than the chances of a state party. That is a matter of considerable practical importance, because the likelihood of Congress's regulating the timing of nominating events over the strenuous objection of the national parties is much less than the likelihood of its doing so over the strenuous objection of one or more state parties. Indeed, strenuous objection by some state parties to any imaginable timing requirements set by Congress, with the possible exception of the proscription of nominating events before a specified date, is nearly inevitable. For example, any such regulation that Congress adopted would have to either recognize the customary priority that has been given to New Hampshire and, more recently, Iowa, or not do so. In the former event, some other state parties—those of Michigan, for example, which held its 2008 primaries earlier than allowed by either national party, largely to protest the Iowa and New Hampshire priority—would almost surely object. In the latter event, the state parties in Iowa and New Hampshire would object.

To understand why a challenge by the national parties to congressional regulation could have a better chance of succeeding than a challenge by state parties, we must review the relation between parties, nominations, and the Constitution. Elsewhere, I have suggested that the history of party regulation can usefully be divided into three broad periods.[23]

The first period, extending into the 1880s, was one of benign neglect. Parties were regarded as private associations and were left by the state and federal governments to their own devices. The second period, extending through the 1960s, was one of increased regulation of parties. The introduction of the secret ballot made a degree of regulation almost inevitable. The secret ballot had to be provided by the state at the polling place, meaning the state had to develop criteria for listing parties and their candidates on the ballots. Another major cause for increased regulation was the suspicion and even hostility often expressed toward parties by political movements such as the Mugwumps, the Populists, and the Progressives. The most important form of regulation of parties around the turn of the twentieth century and later was the requirement for nominations by direct primaries.

Though this early regulation of parties was sometimes challenged on constitutional grounds, the regulations were almost invariably upheld by judges who often shared the antiparty outlook of the Progressives.[24] Later, the judiciary used the Constitution affirmatively to further regulate the parties. Most important were the *White Primary Cases*, in which the Supreme Court prohibited the exclusion of African Americans from the Democratic primaries in Texas.[25]

It is the third period, in which parties began to receive judicial protection from regulation, that is most important for our present purpose. This period can itself be divided into two sets of Supreme Court cases. The first began in the 1970s with a series of controversies in which state parties, state legislatures, state courts, and the national parties contested the procedures for delegate selection.[26] Generally speaking, though with some nuances we shall have to consider, the Court resolved these controversies in favor of the national parties. There were two major constitutional elements in these cases. One was a fairly conventional application of the 1st Amendment right of freedom of association, first recognized by the Court in *NAACP* v. *Alabama.*[27] The other was an analogue of federalism. Just as the national government in our federal system is given various powers because of the need for a unified national policy, so the national parties require a degree of autonomy from state governments and state parties if they are to carry out a nationally coherent presidential nominating process. Because both of these elements were present in the first set of Supreme Court decisions, it was difficult to be sure whether either element, taken in isolation, was either necessary or sufficient for a decision in favor of the national party.

The last and most important case of that type, *Democratic Party of United States* v. *Wisconsin ex rel. La Follette*, was decided in 1981.[28] The later set of cases began with *Tashjian* v. *Republican Party of Connecticut.*[29] Most of the later set were controversies over who could vote in party primaries. In all the cases, state parties invoked their freedom of association under the 1st Amendment to challenge state regulations. Both sets of cases have been given extensive analysis elsewhere that will not be repeated here.[30] But a review of the highlights and of certain points is necessary for understanding the constitutional questions raised by congressional regulation of presidential nominations.

The first set of cases began with controversies over the seating of delegates from Illinois and California in the Democrats' 1972 convention. In *Brown* v. *O'Brien* the Supreme Court overturned a ruling of a lower court, adjudicating which delegations from these states should be seated.[31] Giving as its reason the shortage of time and the fact that the rejected delegations could appeal to the convention itself for relief, the Court also expressed "grave doubts" about judicial intervention because of possible infringement of "vital rights of association." In Illinois, a state court had ordered one of the contesting groups of delegates, known as the Cousins group, not to accept delegate seats. The convention seated them anyway and a state court held the Cousins delegates in contempt for violating the pre-convention order. In *Cousins* v. *Wigoda* the Supreme Court overruled the contempt finding on the ground that a state court could not control the actions of the national convention.[32]

La Follette arose out of the Democratic National Committee's effort to require closed primaries for the 1980 convention.[33] The Democratic National Committee was trying to enforce a policy that the Democratic candidate should be chosen only by Democrats. But Wisconsin had been using open primaries since 1903 and was unwilling to switch.[34] The state party induced a state court to order the Democrats to seat the delegation chosen in the Wisconsin open primary. The Democrats did so, in violation of their rules, despite the fact that the Supreme Court stayed the Wisconsin court order before the convention. In *La Follette*, decided the following year, the Supreme Court overruled the Wisconsin court.

The Supreme Court did not say that the national party could prevent the state and the state parties from conducting an open primary. Justice Stewart, writing for the Court, claimed that Wisconsin's interest in conducting its primaries as it wished and the national party's interest in controlling how the delegates to its convention were selected were compatible: "The National Party rules do not forbid Wisconsin to conduct an open primary. But if Wisconsin does open its primary, it cannot require that Wisconsin delegates to the National Party Convention vote there in accordance with the primary results, if to do so would violate Party rules."[35]

Justice Powell made the point in dissent that the purpose of holding a primary is to determine how much support the competing presidential candidates will receive from the state's delegation to the national convention. What good does it do to tell the state that it is perfectly free to run its primary any way it chooses, but that the primary will count only if it is run the way the national party orders?

However telling Justice Powell's logic may have seemed, he overlooked the politics of the situation. As events showed, Justice Stewart was right that his ruling preserved both the state's and the national party's interests. True, his ruling gave the national party the last word. But that last word must be exercised, in the end, in the highly public setting of the national convention. As we have seen, the Democrats seated the Wisconsin delegation, chosen in an open primary, despite the fact that by the time of the convention they were under no legal compulsion to do so. In 1984, Wisconsin used caucuses to select delegates, as the national party took a more firm position against the open primary. But by 1988 the national party had given in, modifying its rules to allow Wisconsin to use an open primary.[36] The political balance that exists between the states and the national party, despite the national party's "last word" thanks to *La Follette*, became apparent again in 2008, when the Democrats lacked the political will to entirely deny seating to the delegations from Michigan and Florida, despite the fact that their rules called for exclusion by reason of the two states' conducting their presidential primaries earlier than was permitted.

The Supreme Court's opinions in *O'Brien, Cousins,* and *La Follette* all contained language supportive of the national parties' associational rights guarding the national conventions from interference by state legislatures and state courts. However, these cases were also noteworthy on other grounds.[37] One was the degree to which the Court recognized the coordinating function of the national parties in presidential nominations. The clearest statement of this point was in *Cousins,* in response to the contention by Illinois that its control of the Democratic primary was in furtherance of the right of its citizens to vote:

> Respondents overlook the significant fact that the suffrage was exercised at the primary election to elect delegates to a National Party Convention. . . . Delegates perform a task of supreme importance to every citizen of the Nation regardless of their State of residence. The vital business of the Convention is the nomination of the Party's candidates for the offices of President and Vice President of the United States. . . . The States themselves have no constitutionally mandated role in the great task of the selection of Presidential and Vice-Presidential candidates. If the qualifications and eligibility of delegates to National Political Party Conventions were left to state law each of the fifty states could establish the qualifications of its delegates to the various party conventions without regard to party policy, an obviously intolerable result. Such a regime could seriously undercut or indeed destroy the effectiveness of the National Party Convention as a concerted enterprise engaged in the vital process of choosing Presidential and Vice-Presidential candidates—a process which usually involves coalitions cutting across state lines. The Convention serves the pervasive national interest in the selection of candidates for national office, and this national interest is greater than any interest of an individual State.[38]

Tashjian v. *Republican Party of Connecticut* (1986) resolved whatever doubt may have been left by the delegate selection cases whether the associational rights of parties are strong enough to protect the parties' right to determine who can vote in their primaries, in the absence of national coordinating concerns.[39] Connecticut statutes called for closed primaries. Connecticut Republicans decided that they wanted to open their statewide primaries to independent voters as well as Republicans, while keeping state legislative and other local primaries entirely closed. The Democrats, who controlled the state legislature, refused to enact the proposed change into law for the Republican primaries. After the Republicans won control of the legislature they tried again, but were foiled when their bill was vetoed by a Democratic governor. When they then sought relief from the federal judiciary, the Supreme Court ruled that they had an associational right to allow independents to vote in their primaries. Justice Marshall, writing for the majority, made it clear that the Court was not favoring open over closed primaries. That was a question for the parties, not for the courts. The key point was that the nomination of candidates was central to the party's mission, meaning the party had the right to determine which voters should participate in that function.

Tashjian's holding was reaffirmed in *California Democratic Party* v. *Jones.*[40] In a sense, *Jones* was the reverse of *Tashjian*, because the party was seeking a more closed primary than was provided for in state law. Although California had long held closed primaries, an initiative put into place a "blanket primary." In an ordinary open primary, a voter requests the ballot of whichever party he chooses, regardless of his own party affiliation. In a blanket primary there is one ballot, containing the candidates for nomination of each party. A voter can vote for one candidate for each office. For example, a voter could vote for a Republican for governor, a Democrat for attorney general, and a Libertarian for secretary of state. But as was described above, the reasoning of *Tashjian* did not turn on whether the party wanted a more closed or a more open primary than the state, but on the party's right to determine which voters could participate in its primaries. Therefore the blanket primary was struck down, at the behest of both major parties and some of the minor parties in California.

In 1989 the Court had extended *Tashjian* beyond the question of who can vote in the party's primaries. *Eu* v. *San Francisco County Democratic Central Committee* gave parties the right to determine their own governance procedures and to endorse candidates in their primaries, notwithstanding state statutes to the contrary.[41] Nevertheless, the associational rights of parties are not without limits. A dictum in *Jones* said that although the state cannot control who votes in primaries over the party's objection, it can require that candidates be nominated in primaries rather than by other methods. In *Clingman* v. *Beaver*, Oklahoma's laws called for "semi-closed" primaries, in which a party could choose to allow independent voters to vote in its primaries, but not voters registered in another party.[42] The Libertarian Party sought to open its primaries to all voters, including those registered as Democrats, as Republicans, or as members of other parties. The Supreme Court rejected the Libertarians' claim that it had an associational right to invite members of other parties to vote in its primaries.

We are now in a position to evaluate constitutional claims that might be brought against congressional determination of the dates on which presidential primaries can be or must be conducted in particular states. Let us suppose that Congress has passed a law calling for four or five regional primaries to be held a few weeks apart, with the ordering of the regions either to be chosen before each election year by lot or to rotate from one election to the next. Numerous other plans have been suggested, each of which has its pros and cons, but for our purposes there probably is little difference between them.[43] Let us then imagine that the Democratic or Republican Party (or both parties), in one of the states, claims that its associational rights are violated because it wishes to hold its presidential primary earlier than the system enacted by Congress permits.[44]

These state party plaintiffs could and would rely on *Tashjian* and its progeny, but their claims would be significantly weaker than those of the successful plaintiffs in those cases. *Tashjian* and *Jones* turned on the question of who could participate in the selection of the party's candidates, a question that lies at the heart of the party as an association. *Eu* shows that who is permitted to vote is not the only aspect of party primaries that is protected by the 1st Amendment. But the restriction on the party in *Eu* was a restriction on endorsing candidates in primaries. An endorsement of a candidate is a prototypical speech activity protected by the 1st Amendment.[45] In our hypothetical case, the restriction is not as closely related to the 1st Amendment. The party's interest in controlling all aspects of its nomination process, including timing, probably will receive less weight than the interests at stake in *Tashjian*, *Eu*, and *Jones*. In those cases, but not in our hypothetical case of timing, speech or the direct associational question of who could participate in the nomination process was at stake.

This conclusion is especially strong when the question of federalism is considered. In *Cousins* and *La Follette*, the national party plaintiffs benefited from the Court's recognition of the need for coordination in a coherent nomination process. In our hypothetical case, that need would work in favor of Congress and against state parties. Furthermore, just as the question of timing is less closely related to associational rights than the question of who can participate, so is the timing of a state's primary more obviously and directly related to the need for coordination than who is allowed to vote.

Now let us suppose that the congressional scheme of regional primaries is challenged by one or both national parties. As was mentioned at the beginning of this section, it is less likely that legislation affecting presidential nominations would be passed over the objection of either of the national parties than over the objection of some state parties. For the party in power to pass such a law over the objection of the opposing party would undoubtedly require not only unified control of the government by one party, but also a filibuster-proof Senate or something close to it. Legislation opposed by both parties is even more unlikely. True, Democrats and Republicans in Congress do not always have the same outlook as the Democratic and Republican National Committees. But the perceived electoral pressure on Congress would probably have to be intense to induce legislation of the sort we are hypothesizing under any circumstances, and it would have to be extremely intense to induce legislation opposed by both national parties. In short, the constitutional issue we are about to consider is one that theoretically could arise, but is quite unlikely.

Let us nevertheless suppose, however improbably, that a system of regional primaries enacted by Congress is challenged by one or both national parties as a denial of freedom of association. In *O'Brien, Cousins,* and *La Follette,* the need for coordination was on the side of the national parties and against the states. In the hypothetical litigation considered above, in which state parties challenged Congress's regional scheme, coordination was on the side of Congress. But if the national parties challenged a regional system adopted by Congress, it would be a contest between national forces on both sides, each capable of coordinating the nomination system as a whole.

The case, then, would be more like the cases of a state party objecting to state regulation, because the element of coordination would be a wash and the outcome would turn solely on the parties' freedom of association. Because there is no precedent for a federal statute regulating presidential nominations being challenged by a national party, no one can say with complete confidence how the case ought to be decided. Although the state parties have been successful in several of the cases challenging state regulations—*Tashjian, Eu,* and *Jones*—there are three reasons to believe the hypothesized national legislation is constitutional.

First, as we have already seen, regulation of the timing of primaries does not infringe on 1st Amendment rights to the same degree as regulation over who can vote in primaries or endorsements of candidates. If Congress were to require all presidential nominating events to be closed—or, alternatively, to be open—a party objecting to the requirement would have a stronger 1st

Amendment claim than the party objecting to a congressionally enacted scheme of regional primaries.

Second, logic may dictate that whatever the force and whatever the limits of the right of free association protected by the 1st Amendment, that right ought to be the same against either state or federal infringement. In practice, however, the Supreme Court sometimes is more reluctant to overturn federal than state legislation.

Third, though both Congress and the national parties can consider the nomination process as a whole, the national parties have found it difficult to enforce their rules against the states and state parties.[46] The longer this continues to be the case, the more plausible it will be to conclude that though both Congress and the national parties can take the national view, only Congress is capable, as a practical matter, of providing the necessary coordination of presidential nominations, at least so far as the timing of nominating events is concerned.

To summarize, if Congress were to coordinate presidential nominations by imposing some system such as regional primaries, it likely would be challenged by state parties, but the challenge would likely fail. If the system were challenged by either or both of the national parties, the outcome would be less certain, but it is still unlikely that the congressionally enacted scheme would be unconstitutional. It is even less likely, however, that Congress will pass a scheme objectionable to either, or especially both, national parties.

A Constructive Role for Congress?

I therefore conclude that if Congress acts to remedy front-loading, it will probably do so constitutionally. Whether Congress ought to act is a different question. My assignment in this chapter, to survey legal and procedural questions relating to presidential nominations, has given me the luxury of avoiding hard questions about whether the increasing trend, now persistent over decades, toward front-loading is harmful; if so, in what ways; and what, if anything, should be done about it. Mayer and Busch conclude that front-loading is harmful for several reasons; that all of the proposed solutions, especially those that confront front-loading directly, are seriously flawed; and that an important drawback of any direct solution imposed by Congress is that it would be a rigid system whose consequences would be hard to predict.[47]

The one insight I should like to add to Mayer and Busch's thoughtful discussion is that debates over presidential nominations, like many other debates in election law, are particularly subject to the phenomenon that the grass appears greener on the other side of the fence. When presidential nominations were settled in back rooms by state party leaders, it seemed that the grass would be greener if we had more direct popular participation. When we had lots of popular participation it seemed, even to some of the keenest political analysts, that the grass would be greener if we handed more of the decision back to the political pros.[48] When contested primaries lasted from February to June, we thought that a quicker process would be more verdant, but when we were besieged by front-loading we tried to think of ways to spread out the process—until, that is, the Obama-Clinton contest made Democrats, at least, think that quicker might be better after all. If we take the long view, it is difficult to find that the quality of the presidents we have produced has been systematically influenced by the portion of the meadow we have occupied at any given time.

There are good reasons, then, for agnosticism on the substantive question of whether the schedule of nominating events ought to be reformed—with one small exception. As has already been intimated, little harm could be done and some good perhaps accomplished by starting the nominating events later in the presidential election year. In 2008 the Iowa caucuses were held on January 3. The point is not, as some may suppose, that moving the starting date later would shorten the period of presidential campaigning. Nowadays, the beginning date of most presidential campaigns is set more by the date of the preceding presidential election or the preceding off-year congressional election than by the beginning and end points of the presidential nominating events.

Nevertheless, a very early starting date, such as we experienced in 2008, can have some modestly harmful effects. Although the Democratic contest lingered until June, in a more typical election both major-party candidates would have been identified by February, which would mean a lengthening of the period between the end of the nominating contests and the national conventions. It is hard to see any benefit from that. Perhaps the most harm caused by the early starting date in 2008 was not to the electoral process itself, but was simply the inappropriate intrusion of politics into the Christmas and New Year's season. A starting date in, say, mid-February or early March would be an improvement and could be imposed by Congress.

Beyond the starting date, there are two structural influences on the process that might be addressed, consistent with agnosticism on whether reform is desirable. First, the tendency for the first few states that hold nominating events to wield disproportionate influence has created an incentive for states to race to the start. This situation may be conceived as a tragedy of the commons or as a multiplayer prisoner's dilemma. It is consistent with agnosticism to recognize that leaving each state to set the date for its own nominating event creates an incentive structure that leads to front-loading even if there are no actors in the system who favor front-loading.

Second, the national parties face two structural difficulties in their efforts to override the front-loading that occurs as a by-product of that incentive structure. First, as we have seen, it is hard for them to enforce their rules against state parties. Second, although occasionally the Republicans and Democrats hold their nominating events in a given state on different dates, it is cumbersome and costly to the state for them to do so. Therefore, the best way for each national party to coordinate its own nomination process would be for the two national parties to do so jointly. But this is difficult for various reasons, not all of which are obvious. For example, the Republican National Convention adopts rules for the next convention, while the Democratic National Committee adopts its party's rules during the year or so following its party's convention.

Without taking a position on what coordination system, if any, is best, Congress could adopt modest measures to assist the national parties in overcoming the structural problems that prevent them from coordinating nominating events in the states. To help the national parties enforce their rules, Congress could condition aid to the states—either new aid to help finance the primaries, or existing aid such as that under the Help America Vote Act—on compliance with national party rules that meet certain requirements, including that the rules of the two national parties be compatible with each other.

To assist the parties in exploring the possibility of a joint plan, Congress could set up and finance a structure within which the parties could conduct joint deliberations and negotiations. To overcome the problem resulting from the parties' adopting their rules at different times, the process should be pointed toward the second presidential election after the period within which the process takes place. For example, if Congress and the parties created such a process starting in 2009, it would be working on a system for 2016, not 2012. Such a system, if agreed on, could be adopted by the Republicans at their 2012 convention and by the Democratic National Committee thereafter. Congress could provide various benefits to the parties if they participated in an agreed-upon system, such as more funding for the national conventions.

The purpose of such measures would not necessarily be to induce the parties to agree on a coordinated system that would be effectively enforced against the states by Congress. It may be that such a system would not be beneficial or that one or both of the parties would have no interest in creating such a system, regardless of structural obstacles that presently prevent them from doing so. In the spirit of agnosticism, the point would be simply to eliminate the structural obstacles, without which the parties conceivably would come to some agreement.

Conclusion

Congress has not intruded into presidential nominations except in peripheral ways, such as the regulation of campaign finance. In the absence of direct precedent, it is difficult to be confident of the constitutional limits on the power of Congress to intervene. For the reasons set forth above, it is likely that Congress has the power under the Constitution to adopt any form of regulation it is at all likely to adopt in the foreseeable future.

Despite Congress's probable power to regulate under the Constitution, there is little reason to believe Congress is capable of coming up with a particularly beneficial system, and any system it imposed on the nation would have unpredictable consequences that would be difficult to remedy. Short of major substantive regulation, Congress might constructively prohibit states from holding nominating events until some time in February or early March of a presidential election year. Beyond that, Congress could adopt modest steps to assist the national parties in enforcing their rules against the states and to create a structure within which the parties could explore possibilities for an agreed system of nominating events. Although there is no particular reason to believe such an agreement would emerge, Congress could give whatever possibility exists a fair chance by removing structural obstacles that presently bar the way.

Notes

1. Richard McCormick, *The Presidential Game: The Origins of American Presidential Politics* (Oxford University Press, 1982).

2. Gerald Pomper, *Nominating the President: The Politics of Convention Choice* (Northwestern University Press, 1963).

3. Byron Shafer, *Quiet Revolution: The Struggle for the Democratic Party and the Shaping of Post-Reform Politics* (New York: Russell Sage Foundation, 1983).

4. Morris K. Udall, "A Proposal for Presidential Primary Reform," *N.Y.U. Review of Law and Social Change* 10 (1980–81): 19–35.

5. William G. Mayer and Andrew E. Busch, *The Front-Loading Problem in Presidential Nominations* (Washington: Brookings, 2004).

6. See "Ugly Infighting Yields a Breakneck Primary Schedule," 2008 (www.usnews.com/articles/news/politics/2007/11/06/ugly-infighting-yields-a-breakneck-primary-schedule.html [November 4, 2008]).

7. See Senate Committee on Rules and Administration Hearing on S.1905, "The Regional Primary and Caucus Act of 2007," 2007 (http://rules.senate.gov/hearings/2007/091907TranscriptCorrected.pdf [November 4, 2008]).

8. See Richard Hasen, "'Too Plain for Argument?' The Uncertain Congressional Power to Require Parties to Choose Nominees through Direct and Equal Primaries," *Northwestern University Law Review* 102 (2008): 2009–19; Dan T. Coenen and Edward J. Larson, "Congressional Power over Presidential Elections: Lessons from the Past and Reforms for the Future," *William and Mary Law Review* 43 (2002): 851–926.

9. Laurence H. Tribe, *American Constitutional Law*, 2nd ed. (Mineola, N.Y.: Foundation Press, 1988).

10. Article II, section 1, also gave the component parts of Congress certain additional duties and powers. These provisions were superseded by the 12th Amendment, which provides that after the certified electoral votes have been sent to the government of the United States, "The President of the Senate shall, in the presence of the Senate and House of Representatives, open all the certificates and the votes shall be counted." The 12th Amendment further provides that if there is less than a majority in the Electoral College, the House selects the president from the three top electoral vote-getters and the Senate selects the vice president from the top two.

11. The statement in the text is overly broad in a respect that does not affect the subject of this essay. Various amendments to the Constitution give Congress authority to enforce those amendments. Congress can regulate presidential nominating events, as it can regulate anything else, in the course of enforcing those amendments. For example, Congress can legislate to prevent the denial of voting rights in primaries on grounds of race, pursuant to its power to enforce the Equal Protection Clause of the 14th Amendment and the 15th Amendment. (See *Smith* v. *Allwright*, 321 U.S. 641, 1944.) However, no one has suggested that any of the amendments expressly enforceable by Congress controls the timing of presidential nominating events.

12. The seminal case is *McCulloch* v. *Maryland*, 17 U.S. 316 (1819).

13. See Hasen, "Too Plain for Argument?" p. 2017.

14. Charles Lund Black, *Structure and Relationship in Constitutional Law* (Louisiana State University Press, 1969).

15. *Burroughs* v. *United States*, 290 U.S. 534 (1934).

16. *United States* v. *Classic*, 313 U.S. 299 (1941).

17. 313 U.S. at 314.

18. 313 U.S. at 316.

19. William G. Mayer and Andrew E. Busch, "Can the Federal Government Reform the Presidential Nomination Process?" *Election Law Journal* 3 (2004): 613–25; William G. Mayer and Andrew E. Busch, *The Front-Loading Problem in Presidential Nominations* (Washington: Brookings, 2004).

20. *Oregon* v. *Mitchell* 400 U.S. 112 (1970). Soon after, the 26th Amendment lowered the voting age to 18 for all elections.

21. 400 U.S. at 124 n. 7.

22. Tadahisa Kuroda, *The Origins of the Twelfth Amendment: The Electoral College in the Early Republic, 1787–1804* (Westport, Conn.: Greenwood Press, 1994), p. 23.

23. Daniel H. Lowenstein, "Political Parties and Elections," in *The Oxford International Encyclopedia of Legal History*, edited by Stanley N. Katz (Oxford University Press, forthcoming).

24. Adam Winkler, "Voters' Rights and Parties' Wrongs: Early Political Party Regulation in the State Courts, 1886–1915," *Columbia Law Review* 100 (2000): 873–99.

25. The key decision was *Smith* v. *Allwright* (1944). For a detailed history of the *White Primary Cases*, see Steven F. Lawson, *Black Ballots: Voting Rights in the South* (Columbia University Press, 1976).

26. Actually, in all the cases to reach the Supreme Court in the 1970s the party in question was the Democratic Party. This was not a coincidence. During that period, it was the Democratic Party that was fighting most of the battles over the presidential nomination process.

27. *NAACP* v. *Alabama*, 357 U.S. 449 (1958).

28. *Democratic Party of United States* v. *Wisconsin ex rel. La Follette*, 450 U.S. 107 (1981).

29. *Tashjian* v. *Republican Party of Connecticut*, 479 U.S. 208 (1986).

30. Elizabeth Garrett, "Is the Party Over? Courts and the Political Process," *Supreme Court Review* (2002): 95–152, Daniel Hays Lowenstein, "Associational Rights of Major Political Parties: A Skeptical Inquiry," *Texas Law Review* 71 (1993): 1741–92; Daniel H. Lowenstein, "Legal Regulation and Protection of American Parties," in *Handbook of Party Politics*, edited by Richard S. Katz and William J. Crotty (London: Sage, 2006); Lowenstein, "Political Parties and Elections"; Nathaniel Persily, "Toward a Functional Defense of Political Party Autonomy," *New York University Law Review* 76 (2001): 750–824.

31. *Brown* v. *O'Brien* 409 U.S. 1 (1972).

32. *Cousins* v. *Wigoda* 419 U.S. 477 (1975).

33. A "closed primary" is one in which only members of the party can vote, in contrast to an "open primary," in which all voters can select the party whose primary they wish to vote in, regardless of their party affiliation.

34. Gary D. Wekkin, *Democrat versus Democrat: The National Party's Campaign to Close the Wisconsin Primary* (University of Missouri Press, 1984).

35. *Democratic Party of United States* v. *Wisconsin ex rel. La Follette*, 450 U.S. 107, 126 (1981).

36. Leon D. Epstein, *Political Parties in the American Mold* (University of Wisconsin Press, 1986), p. 400, n. 81.

37. Lowenstein, "Associational Rights of Major Political Parties," pp. 1771–77.

38. 419 U.S. at 489–90 (1975). (Internal quotation marks and citations omitted.)

39. *Tashjian* v. *Republican Party of Connecticut*, 479 U.S. 208 (1986).

40. *California Democratic Party* v. *Jones*, 530 U.S. 567 (2000). The doctrine was further refined in *Washington State Grange* v. *Washington State Republican Party*, 128 S.Ct. 1184 (2008), but not in a manner likely to influence the constitutional questions we are concerned with here.

41. *Eu* v. *San Francisco County Democratic Central Committee*, 489 U.S. 214 (1989).

42. *Clingman* v. *Beaver*, 544 U.S. 581 (2005).

43. For an overview of the types of plans that have been proposed, see Mayer and Busch, *The Front-Loading Problem in Presidential Nominations*, chap. 5.

44. To simplify, we shall assume that the state party has state law on its side. We also assume that the federal legislation permits the state to hold its presidential primary later than the prescribed date, but not earlier. Most of the proposals for federal legislation seem to include that feature. If the federal statute required a state to hold its primary on a specific day, the case for the state party challenging the law would be slightly stronger, but probably not enough to be decisive.

45. One point elided in *Eu* was that the purpose of the primary is to determine who the party's choice will be. Therefore, a pre-primary decision to endorse must be made by some instrumentality that is a part of the party, such as the state committee or the state convention. It is easy to see why the Court would have held that these entities should have the constitutional right to endorse candidates in primaries, but less easy to see why they should have the right to endorse in the name of the party. For criticism of *Eu* along these lines, see Lowenstein, "Associational Rights of Major Political Parties."

46. Leonard P. Stark, "The Presidential Primary and Caucus Schedule: A Role for Federal Regulation?" *Yale Law and Policy Review* 15 (1996): 331–97.

47. Mayer and Busch, *The Front-Loading Problem in Presidential Nominations*.

48. Nelson W. Polsby, *Consequences of Party Reform* (Oxford University Press, 1983).

Contributors

JAMES L. GIBSON
Washington University

KATHLEEN HALL JAMIESON
University of Pennsylvania

BRUCE W. HARDY
University of Pennsylvania

DANIEL H. LOWENSTEIN
University of California–Los Angeles

THOMAS E. MANN
Brookings Institution

WILLIAM G. MAYER
Northeastern University

THOMAS E. PATTERSON
Harvard University

LARRY J. SABATO
University of Virginia

STEVEN S. SMITH
Washington University

MELANIE J. SPRINGER
Washington University

GERALD C. WRIGHT
Indiana University

Index

American Plan. See California Plan
Arizona, 51, 53

Battaglia, Basil, 114
Brown v. *O'Brien,* 184–85
Burroughs v. *United States,* 177–78
Busch, Andrew, 179
Bush, George W., 66

California, 51–53, 187
California Democratic Party v. *Jones,* 187
California Plan, 16–17, 114–15
Carter, Jimmy, 6, 90–91, 98, 143
Caucuses: advocates for, *x,* 37, 165; criticisms of, 37–38, 164–65; demands on participants as determinant of participation, 33–34, 37; historical evolution of nomination process, 46; ideological representativeness of participants, 37–38; sequencing effects on turnout, 55; start of electoral calendar, *vii;* state variation, 111; turnout in 2008 election, 54–55; turnout in primaries and, 46, 47; voter political ideologies in 2008 elections, 24–25, 34–36, 38. *See also* Primaries

Celebrity and group endorsements, 64
Clingman v. *Beaver,* 187–88
Clinton, Bill, 101
Clinton, Hillary, 53, 65. *See also* Democratic 2008 nomination process
Congressional role in nomination process reform, 190–93; constitutional authority, *xiv,* 20, 174–82, 193, 194nn 10–11; disadvantages, 19; proposals for primary reforms, 115–16, 134n17, 144; prospects, 144, 174; as violation of constitutionally guaranteed rights, 182–90
Connecticut, 186–87
Constitution: absence of nomination process rules, 136–37; Congressional authority to reform nomination process, *xiv,* 20, 174–82, 193; Congress's regulation of nomination process as challenge to rights of political parties, 182–90; freedom of association, 175–76, 184, 189–90; implied powers concept, 176; Necessary and Proper Clause, 176, 177; structural interpretation, 176–80; Twelfth Amendment, 181–82